THERE'S AN AWFUL LOT OF BUBBLY IN BRAZIL

THE LIFE AND TIMES OF A BON VIVEUR

THERE'S AN AWFUL LOT OF BUBBLY IN BRAZIL

THE LIFE AND TIMES OF A BON VIVEUR

ALAN BRAZIL WITH MIKE PARRY

A *RACING POST* COMPANY

DEDICATION

To my wife Jill and daughters Michelle, Lucy and Steffie

This paperback edition published in 2007 by Highdown
an imprint of Raceform Ltd
Compton, Newbury, Berkshire, RG20 6NL

First published in 2006

A catalogue record for this book is available from the British Library.

ISBN 978-1-905156-36-8

Cover designed by Adrian Morrish
Interiors designed by Fiona Pike

Printed by Creative Print & Design, Wales

CONTENTS

CHAPTER ONE

THE CHELTENHAM SACK RACE

'Al, it's Mike,' he said. 'It's not good news.'

'Go on.'

'I've been conducting an inquest into what happened at Cheltenham.'

'And?'

'I am afraid that I've got to tell you that you are sacked. I am cancelling your contract.'

IT WAS the most beautiful evening you could imagine in the ski resort of Meribel. The sky was inky black, the snow was as white as a tin of Dulux paint, and the stars sparkled over the mountains that loomed up all around me.

It was below zero and the freezing wind was lashing my face and making my eyes weep as I raced down the slopes. I didn't have any ski poles. I was traversing my way across the snow with a score of friends and we were holding flares above our heads, burning back at the intense cold. To the crowds of beautiful people sitting on the balconies and terraces of their million-pound apartments below us it would have looked like a firey snake was on its way to gobble them up. I had watched a similar spectacle many times involving my two older daughters, both international skiers, who were with me now.

Confidently, I turned my hips left and right as though I was back on a football pitch in front of 50,000 people, making mincemeat out of clod-hopping defenders. And then, in an instant, a bolt of terror shot through me as I realised I had come off line, and suddenly I was heading at full speed into a ski-lift pylon just a few yards away.

This is it, I thought. I'm going to die. In a split-second I remembered a story we had been covering on my radio station, talkSPORT, earlier, about a member of the dynastic American family, the Kennedys, who had killed himself when he hit a tree in Aspen. He wasn't carrying any poles either.

In the same instant I was sprawled all over the snow. The flare was 30 yards away and my skis had cartwheeled through the night. I felt a tremendous pain in my chest. I couldn't breathe. I didn't know whether I had caved in my ribs or I was suffering a heart attack. I reached up to feel my face and panicked as I thought I could feel blood and my own brains bursting out of my head. But when I looked at my hand it was mud and gravel that my ski must have scooped out of the ground at the base of the pylon stanchion. Protective netting had wrapped itself around my neck, which was why I couldn't breathe.

Members of our group had stopped in alarm and were now trying to make their way back up the slope towards me. At least one of my daughters was screaming, 'Daddy, Daddy, what have you done?'

I tore the netting from my neck and, thankfully, as I started breathing again, my chest started moving up and down. The leader of our party was back with me and he frantically tore at my ski suit to try to discover the extent of the damage. The freezing night air that attacked my chest and stomach acted like a stimulant and immediately brought me out of my stupor.

Amazingly, I had hardly hurt myself at all. I didn't realise it at the time, but the stanchions are covered in the same sort of polystyrene padding you see on rugby posts at Twickenham. My eighteen-stone bulk had bounced off the ski-lift support, and, apart from a developing bruise on my sternum and a whiplash injury to my neck, I had escaped. Not for the first time in my life my guardian angel had been looking down on me.

As my weeping daughters picked me up from the snow I reflected on why I had so foolishly lost my concentration. I was an accomplished skier. I had taken it up when I played for a season in Zurich at the end of my football career, and the first time I got on a pair of skis I never wanted to get off them. I loved everything about it. The clear blue skies, the landscapes that looked as though the gods had spring-cleaned them each day, the snow that tumbled out of the skies like freshly sheared lamb's wool, and the après-ski. There is hardly anywhere else I would rather be in the world than in a pal's skiing lodge at the end of an afternoon down the black runs, a log-fire roaring and flickering in the wardrobe-sized grate, surrounded by my family – and inevitably clutching the evening's first glass of bubbly.

But my mind had been distracted that afternoon in a very big way. A few hours before I had set off on the run with a flare in my hand I had had a devastating phone call which had turned my world upside down. The contents of that call confirmed to me what I had already suspected. I had somehow managed to plunge my career into a crevice deeper than the one that encircled the landscape in front of me.

I had been expecting the call for a few days and I thought I was well prepared for the worst. I had been telling myself that I wasn't really bothered, whatever happened. I have always had enormous belief in myself, always looked on the bright side of things, never despaired at life's cruel tricks. For instance, imagine being an international footballer and being told at the age of just 27 that your career is over because your persistent back injury has become inoperable.

Throughout a tumultuous life of ups and downs, my wife Jill, without whom I would be nothing, has lived in dread that one day we, and consequently our three beautiful daughters, would end up on the scrap-heap. Well, I haven't been there yet – even though I will admit I have been pretty close.

My attitude to life is different to that of most people. I will never stay at a job if I am not happy. I don't care if it is well paid, or if ten other former footballers would sprint down the M1 to take my place. If I don't like what's going on around me, or people do not treat me with respect, I am happy to walk. I had issues with the top people at the station at the time. But they have since gone following a full scale takeover of the company. I have always been confident that something better will be waiting around the next corner. And usually I have been right.

But on this occasion, for many different reasons which I will go into, it was different, and I didn't feel very good about the present or the future.

I knew when I had gathered up the family and our skis a few days earlier and set off for Meribel that I had reached another of life's crossroads. And over the previous 72 hours the events of the week before had been gnawing away at me. So I was actually relieved when the mobile started to ring. I had had it switched off for the last three days, and even now I was taking calls only from those people I wanted to talk to. I knew a terrible bust-up was likely to have gone on after I left London, where there were a lot of very unhappy people. I saw that the call was coming from Mike 'Porky' Parry, my co-broadcaster at talkSPORT.

Officially, Porky was my boss, but I had never regarded him as such. Not through any disrespect, but Porky had two roles at the station: he was the programme director, and as such he was the boss man, but in his second role he was my sidekick on our award-winning breakfast show, and I really only knew him as the guy who had been sitting next to me between six and ten a.m. six days a week for the last five years. He had recruited me from television because he said he recognised in me the sort of personality and background on which the big bosses wanted to base the sound of the station. I had always had an accord with football fans. As a lifelong Celtic fan, I was one of them. And having enjoyed a football career that took me from Ipswich to Manchester United via Tottenham Hotspur, with thirteen Scottish caps and two European medals along the way, I had the right credentials to talk with conviction about the game.

To everybody else, then, Porky was the gaffer, but I could think of him only in terms of what we had been through working together on our breakfast show, which we had taken all around the world. I remembered him taunting the Germans after England's 5–1 victory in Munich in September 2001; how he tried to win a bet and nearly killed himself by attempting to dive into the Bosphorus in Istanbul; and how we drank dry the first-class compartment of a British Airways jumbo jet on a 'flight of death' to Washington DC. Closer to home, I once had to rescue him from an irate Newcastle fan who attacked him with a chair in a working men's club on Tyneside when he told 300 loud and boozed-up supporters that Geordie fans didn't care enough about winning. Between us we had created one of the most popular radio shows in Britain, and on the back of it I had built a lucrative new career as a broadcaster, an entertainer and an after-dinner speaker.

But those warm memories were as far away as outer space when I hit the button on the phone. I hadn't anticipated that our call was going to be so brief. There wasn't a flicker of warmth in his voice as he opened the conversation.

'Al, it's Mike,' he said. 'It's not good news.'

'Go on.'

'I've been conducting an inquest into what happened at Cheltenham.'

'And?'

'I am afraid that I've got to tell you that you are sacked. I am cancelling your contract.'

There was no way in the world I was going to get involved in a debate about the rights and wrongs of the situation. I'd occasionally seen Porky with his programme director's hat on before, and I knew he had made up his mind.

'Well, there's nothing I can do about that, Porky,' I countered, 'except to say that it has been great working with you.'

I detected a slight crack in his voice as he said, 'You too, Al. I'm sorry.'

The phone went dead. For some reason his last two words, 'I'm sorry', reminded me of the scene in *Top Gun* when the pilot who had cracked up while landing his plane on the aircraft carrier admitted he had failed and threw in his wings.

I was shell-shocked. I sipped at my champagne and reflected that here I was in one of the world's playgrounds for the rich and idle, and I had just joined the ranks of the unemployed and idle. But I refused to dwell on it. I had bounced back before, and I would do so again. I was irritated with Porky, though. After all we had been through and all I had done to build talkSPORT up from nothing, he had sacked me with hardly any emotion. At least that was what I thought at the time. I learnt later that, within a few hours of the call, he was being carried out of a hotel bar in central London, rambling drunkenly that he had shot his best mate.

There on the terrace of my hotel I did what I often do in times of crisis and ordered another bottle of champagne. I took comfort from the glorious surroundings, the beautiful flaxen-haired women whizzing by on their skis, and my wife and daughters, who I could see playing snowballs in the distance. I wasn't going to go broke today, tomorrow or this time next week, so why worry? But as I got stuck into the Moët et Chandon over the next hour I felt a growing uneasiness about how I was going to tell Jill and where I was going to turn now. I wished heartily that I wasn't at this juncture and started to reflect on how I had got there.

It had all started a week earlier when Porky and I set off after our breakfast show for the 2004 Cheltenham Festival, from where we would broadcast the show for the following three days. For me, this was the highlight of my year. Apart from Christmas at home with the family there aren't three (now four) better days in the calendar. I had loved horses and racing since going to Ipswich Town Football Club as a teenager from Glasgow. I started joining a few of the older players when they piled into their cars after training and headed off to some place called Newmarket that I had never heard of. It is, of course, the 'headquarters' of racing in this country, and from the first moment I walked into a trainer's yard and saw Ipswich centre forward Paul Mariner cradle the head of a horse that was named after him, I was completely captivated.

Over the years it became my passion, bringing me elation and desperation in equal measures – though anybody involved with horses knows you have more bad days than good. Goodness me, has it cost me some money over the years. And it's not just the horses themselves or the thrill of a bet that might make you thousands of pounds, it's the people in the industry that make racing and racecourses in particular such an addictive environment. The owners with their multi-million-pound fortunes; the trainers bearing the strain of every step their horses take; the bookies on the rails; the punters celebrating their big wins and sloping away in the misery of their even bigger losses; the girls tumbling tipsily on Ladies' Day; the champagne flowing in the hospitality boxes; the helicopters buzzing in and out of the course bringing the Arab sheikhs and their retinues to watch a horse increase its value to £10 million. The atmosphere is special, from the Roodeye inside the city walls at Chester to the vast expanses of Newmarket and the Epsom Downs.

But, for me, the best of the lot is Cheltenham and the National Hunt Festival every March. There are so many aspects of Cheltenham that are special. The location is stunning. Nestling in the beautiful Cotswolds, the course sits just outside the town in the shadow of a big, black hill called Cleeve Hill. The top of the hill seems to touch the sky. At that time of the year the clouds are grey and swirling and they furl around the course like a brew concocted by the witches in Shakespeare's *Macbeth*. It is dark and mysterious, but the whole place is lit up each year by the arrival of tens of thousands of Irish men and women. When they arrive they have bulging wallets, unlimited optimism and a huge sense of fun; when they leave they have nothing but empty wallets and swollen livers (one of the great landmarks of the Cheltenham Festival is the Guinness Village, a collection of black and white marquees inside the course that is a natural magnet to both the Irish flock and thousands of serious drinkers going racing that day). But they never lose their sense of fun. Although I am very much a Scotsman, the community I come from has an umbilical cord with the Irish. I have been a Celtic fan all my life, and that club and their supporters are immersed in their Irish ancestry.

The people who run Cheltenham have always been tremendously hospitable to me and talkSPORT. They are so happy to have us there that they insist we broadcast our breakfast show from the private box of Lord Vestey, the chairman of the course, way up at the top of the main stand. There are many advantages to this, but perhaps the best is that because of the illustrious company that will occupy the box later in the day we are always surrounded by a generous supply of the finest wines and champagnes known to man. Like most people who entertain guests at the Cheltenham Festival, the people who look after Lord Vestey's box are big on hospitality. Doing a breakfast show, the mouth can start to get a bit dry; it would be churlish to turn down the offer of a glass of bubbly as a heart-warmer to start the day. The time of day is no matter. This is Cheltenham, and this is the way it should be.

By ten o'clock, when the show has finished, word has usually got round that talkSPORT is on the premises and the invitations to join other members of the ruling classes quickly appear. The consequence of this is that, by the time we arrive at the Guinness Village, we have a distinct lead over the punters arriving for their first Guinness of the day. Many of them have been listening to Porky and me on their car or coach radios as they travelled down to the course. And before you know it there are six pints of Guinness for each of us on the bar. We never discover where they come from but, to whoever has bought them, can I now say, 'Thanks.' Porky and I never leave the tent before bunging £50 behind the bar for the barman to give away some free beer.

We always congregate in the same corner of the same marquee, and quickly merge into the company of those we call 'our own'. This usually comprises a host of ex-footballers like me, a good sprinkling of City brokers in their sharp suits and Rolex watches, old schoolmates from Holyrood School in Glasgow who now run successful businesses, and Ted the ticket-man and bookie who melts in and out of the shadows like a ghost. Talk about a man who lives on his wits. If you suddenly wanted to place a bet of £500 but couldn't be bothered to make it out of the tent, Ted would cover the bet himself. If your horse won, he would reach deep into the pockets of his white cashmere overcoat and produce your £2,000 winnings without a flicker of emotion. (Later on I'll tell you how Ted once spirited me into the five-star Owners and Trainers restaurant at the track in Chicago where the Breeders' Cup was being run.)

This fantastic atmosphere becomes more intoxicating the minute the Irish folk musicians start up outside the tent. Until then we will have heard the strains of the odd fiddle here and there, but when the band gets going the party is really underway. I'm in my element at just about the moment when the musicians break into the strains of 'The Fields of Athenry'. Even Porky, a 100 per cent Anglo-Saxon Englishman, gets swept away on the tide of emotion, belting out the only line of the song he's ever picked up: 'and he stole Trevelyan's corn, so the young might see the morn'. The whole tent is roaring away in song, the Guinness is going down as though it's more necessary to the body than oxygen, and nobody has yet seen a horse.

After a couple of hours I suddenly start to get the message from Porky that we have to leave. I could stay there all day in this wonderful warm atmosphere, but as usual I have accepted about half a dozen invitations for lunch and we have to do the round of the executive boxes. I don't know why it is, but when somebody invites me to a function, which happens every day, I always say yes because I hate disappointing people. The problem is, I don't carry my diary with me so I have to rely on my lovely daughter Michelle to sort out those I can go to and those I can't. She often has to try to work out how I can go to three events at once. But I can honestly say that I have never let anybody down by not turning up once I have given a commitment to attend.

Porky can nag like an old woman, and eventually I give in to his constant whingeing and reluctantly prise myself out of the tent and into the crisp spring air. We have to battle our way through thousands of in-flowing racegoers, cheery and buoyant about the day ahead. The smell of sizzling sausages and spitting bacon burgers mixes with the horsey smell of hay and manure as horsebox after horsebox arrives bringing the stars of the show to the track. The goodwill of the crowd is astonishing. Every few paces in the throng I happily sign somebody's racecard or pose for a picture. It's usually at about that moment that I realise I have probably had eight pints of Guinness and a bottle of champagne for breakfast. But *everybody* has beery breath, and the atmosphere, like the sausages, is sizzling.

Eventually we get to the first box of the afternoon and the party starts all over again. I'm surrounded by more ex-footballers, beautiful soap-opera actresses, high-flying journalists and the racing aristocracy. Every half hour we gather around the in-house television to watch the latest race and hear the roar, like that of aircraft engines, from the crowd on the track below us as the horses come home.

One year we were in the same box as championship-winning

ex-England international Peter Reid. Reidy won trophies galore with Everton, and Porky, who is a devoted fan of the Merseysiders, became his personal waiter for the afternoon. It was quite pathetic to watch my broadcasting partner, a grown man, following his hero around all afternoon with a bottle of champagne. Porky even offered to drive Reidy back to his hotel after the racing – one of his more stupid ideas as at the time he was so drunk he couldn't stand up without having his arm draped around the shoulder of a proper waiter.

Unlike most of the people with whom we mixed all day we had to drop out after the racing and go back to our hotel to have dinner and get our heads down. Our broadcasting team were all up again the following day at four a.m. to start that day's breakfast show.

Starting work at that hour after the revels of the day before would test anybody. There are few places in the world where I have felt so cold. At five a.m., wrapped in my huge Barbour overcoat, I would be out pacing the Cheltenham course, checking on the fences, chatting to trainers and jockeys out examining the course, and testing the radio microphones for the show ahead. Thoughts of the warmth and the comradeship of the Guinness tent a few hours ahead are already starting to circulate in your head, I can tell you.

The fateful day when it all went wrong started in just this way. Not only was it the last day of the Cheltenham Festival, it was also the national day of Ireland, St Patrick's Day, and, ironically, my wife Jill's birthday. How many more excuses does a man need to attack the black stuff with a passion bordering on lust? But the calendar had played a cruel trick on us. Shortly after we got to the Guinness Village that morning Porky reminded me of something I didn't want to hear. It was Thursday, the last day of the meeting, and the following morning's show was back in our studios in London.

I had been arguing all week that it was madness to close down the studio in Lord Vestey's box and that we should finish the week there. Otherwise we were going to have to leave before the biggest race of the week, the Cheltenham Gold Cup – the focal point of the whole meeting – to get back to London. The number crunchers in the capital were trying to tell us that it was 'only a two-hour drive', which illustrates how out of touch they can be. When 40,000 people pour out of Cheltenham at the same time it can take up to five hours just to get out of Gloucestershire. Porky had been banging on at the men in grey suits all week, but he had lost the battle with the financial director. Never mind the issue of creativity and quality, in my experience as soon as the question of costs arises, the argument is lost.

As a consequence, Porky was wearing his programme director's hat that day. As we trotted down to the Village he had none of the ebullience of the previous two days. His job was to get the whole team home early, and he knew I had no intention of going as early as him. He started moaning after just one pint. 'Come on, Al, make that your lot, we've got to get going.' He was sombre, and I wasn't. I was in my usual expansive mood. I was surrounded by a load of pals and I was enjoying myself. I wasn't going anywhere this early. I intended to have one more drink and then to start making my way back, after the first race.

The band had just struck up when Porky threw a fit. He started shouting that he was going and that I had better come with him otherwise I'd never get back to London for the following morning. The problem was that he forgot we were travelling in my car, and, when he remembered, he started hitting his mobile phone, trying to get somebody to take him off to the station to get the train back to London. All this was a source of great amusement to me and my band of Scottish mates, who spent the next half hour berating and mocking the man as he took to shouting down his phone trying to find somebody to take him away.

Porky is a shortish sort of a chap with a swathe of ginger hair (except for his crown) and a wild ginger beard that makes him look like something out of *Braveheart*. All my pals were goading him as a wild-eyed numpty. And the more they mocked him, the more angry he got. In my view he was overreacting. I am employed by talkSPORT only to present a breakfast show between six and ten a.m. each morning, so I was pretty short with Porky. If he wanted to go that was fine. I told him I would see him later.

With Porky gone, time inevitably started to drift by. The drinks were flowing, the party was in full flow. I was surrounded by ex-footballers, including broadcaster Chris Kamara and my old Celtic and Bayern Munich pal Alan McInally. We were also in the company of Jim Lewis, the owner of the horse of the moment, Best Mate, which was to go on later that day to win its third consecutive Gold Cup and establish itself as a true racing legend. Jim is a lovely man, softly spoken, with a shock of silver hair. He was surrounded by his family and friends, all of whom, like himself, wore Aston Villa scarves to show their support for the former European Cup-winning Midlanders. Sadly, since then, both Jim's wife and the horse have passed away.

I soon realised that there was no way I was going to be able to drive home that afternoon. But, again, that was not a problem. I planned to stay in Cheltenham that night, get up at 3.30 a.m. and drive to London the following morning. That might sound extraordinary to some, but my body clock was well attuned to it. For years I had been getting up at 3.30, showering and driving in to work from my home in Suffolk. Same routine, different location.

I went over to the executive boxes to say my farewells to a few people who had looked after us over the last few days, then rendezvoused with the driver I had fixed up to take me to my hotel. Unfortunately, because bedrooms are at a premium during Gold Cup week, I could only get myself into a country-house hotel in somewhere near to Moreton-in-Marsh, which on the map looked to be roughly in the right direction. It turned out to be one of those delightful little Cotswold villages with flower baskets hanging everywhere. As I checked in I had every intention of going to bed. It was about seven p.m., and I reckoned that seven or eight hours' sleep would do me fine before setting off for London the next day.

Then a twist of fate intervened which started to divert me from the plan I had very clearly constructed in my head. The hotel keeper was a big talkSPORT fan, and I signed a few menus for him. As he sorted out my key, he said, 'I suppose you've come up here to see your Scottish pal along the road, have you?'

'Who's that then?' I asked.

'Jim Steel.'

I shook my head in amazement. Jim Steel was a big rough, tough Scot who played for Southampton. We had both made it as professional footballers and bumped into each other occasionally on the celebrity golf circuit. Jim had also played with two of my good mates from the world of football and racing: Micky Channon, now a successful trainer, and Alan Ball, who will forever be lionised as one of England's World Cup winners. Now I had just been told that he was the landlord of the pub across the street from this remote little hotel at which I had arrived quite by accident.

There was one essential difference between Jim and me: I had played for Celtic Boys Club and Jim's lifelong dream had been to play for Rangers. We were from different sides of the divide. Though I was full of good intentions for an early night, I decided I'd just spend half an hour winding up my old mate.

I found his pub, and as I walked into the bar I saw the unmistakable figure of big Jim with his back to me, preparing a drink for one of his customers. To the shock of the whole pub, I boomed out, 'Hey, Bluenose, get me a pint of Guinness and make it quick!'

Jim, who had never been slow in sorting out problems on the cobbles, wheeled around, already tightening his fists, ready to sort out this loudmouth who had just walked into his pub bawling out insults. But as he saw me his face broke into a broad smile. He was incredulous. 'Baz, what the hell are you doing here? I can't believe it. Let me get a glass in your hand.'

We clasped each other like the old mates we were, and the wine started to flow. None of Jim's regulars had a hope of getting another drink that night without getting the full story of our respective football careers. As Jim got more and more intoxicated, his descriptions of me grew from 'this boy had a left foot like an Exocet missile' to 'the greatest young footballer in all of Scotland', and even up to 'the white Pelé'. Of course, it was St Patrick's Day and I goaded my old pal by leading all his loyal customers in a compilation of Irish songs.

It was party time again. All of Jim's customers joined in, and, though I was desperately trying to drink water, the usual battalion of drinks was marching down the bar. I eventually wrenched myself away just after ten o'clock, though in all honesty I could have stayed all night.

At that stage I didn't have any worries at all about making it back to London on time next day. I had once done it from York in the early morning, and that was a lot further away than where I was now.

But fate was to get in the way again. I had just acquired a new phone. It was one of those all-singing, all-dancing jobs which you open like a sunglasses case and which has a hundred different functions to send e-mails and receive pictures. I had never used the alarm clock facility on the phone before, but the process didn't seem overly complicated. I set it and put it on my bedside table. Just to make sure, I went downstairs again and asked the proprietor if there was going to be somebody around who could bang on my door at three a.m. (there were no bedside phones). He assured me that would be no problem. I went to bed, happy that I had covered all the angles.

Unfortunately, whatever could have gone wrong that night did so. I don't know why I stirred suddenly in my bed. It was pitch black and silent. Maybe it was instinct, but I suddenly got that uneasy feeling that all was not well. For a moment I managed to comfort myself with the knowledge that the alarm on my phone had not gone off. Neither had there been a bang on the door to get me up. I was now wide awake, and I became certain it was only about 2.30, in which case I would get up anyway and take a more leisurely drive back to London than I had planned.

I fumbled for the bedside light and winced as the bulb exploded into life. My watch – where was my watch? I was still wearing it. I squinted at it with one eye. I thought it said 4.25. Don't panic, I thought, you must have read it wrong. Maybe it had stopped or something. But I was panicking, and when I checked the time on my mobile it told me a similar story: it was just coming up to 4.30.

My head exploded. I was going to have to go like the clappers to reach London, break every speed limit known to man and hope like hell I could get there soon enough after six o'clock so that the listeners would not notice. Then my panic was swiftly replaced with anger. Why hadn't my phone gone off at three o'clock? Why hadn't the old geezer from downstairs knocked on my door? Why had I been let down?

There was no time for an inquest. I threw my clothes on, grabbed my bag and ran like crazy down the stairs. Not only was there no sign of the proprietor, but the front door was locked and barred. I couldn't get out. I started shouting 'Help, help!' as though I was being attacked or something. I didn't feel stupid, I just felt desperate. Every missed second was adding up to impending disaster. I was a desperate man; I felt like I was in prison. Nobody stirred despite my wild shouting.

Maybe there was a back door. But it was pitch black and I couldn't find any lights. I bowled down the corridor like a blind man and pushed open a door which I vaguely remember took me into the hotel's tiny lounge. It had French windows. I tried the handle but they were locked. But, thank you, Lord, there was a key in the lock.

I burst out into the bleak and freezing Cotswold morning but soon realised I was still in jail. I was in a tiny courtyard and the solid oak exit door was again locked, and this time there was no key. Another panic attack. I was going to have to climb over the eight-foot wall. Fortunately there was a bench near it. I summoned what was left of my athletic footballer's frame, hurled my bag ahead of me and scrambled over. Anybody witnessing my frantic exit from the hotel that morning would have been entitled to believe I was a fleeing burglar.

Just as I thought I was free I became aware of my next highly improbable obstacle: there was a milk float parked across the back of my car – the sort of old-fashioned milk float I hadn't seen since I was a kid. What was it doing here at this time of the morning? I had to move it.

But how do you drive a milk float? On the basis that it was the same as a golf buggy, I jumped aboard and stabbed the pedal. It shot forward like a kangaroo. There was a hideous crashing noise as crates of milk catapulted off the back of the vehicle and a river of milk started to cascade down the road. I had to paddle through it to clear away the broken glass with my feet. The way was now clear, but I was still in danger of shredding my tyres. I jumped into my car and gingerly reversed out on to the road.

Just as I was about to make my getaway, the milkman turned up and reached through my open window, trying to stop me from leaving. From his exhortations I gathered he thought I had run into the back of his float. But I didn't have any time to explain. I pushed him away, apologising profusely, telling him I had an emergency on my hands and that I would settle up with him later. Then I roared off down the village high street full of anger, bemusement and trepidation.

By now it was nearly ten to five. Could I by some miracle make it in time? I knew that, back in London, the set-up boys would be busily setting up the show. I tried to ring them so that they could work out a way of covering my absence, possibly for the first half hour, but my new phone was completely dead. Not only had it not woken me up, it was now about as much use as my racing binoculars in its ability to let me talk to the office.

I knew the game was up when I found myself on the Oxford ring road at 5.30. I decided there was no point in trying to kill myself or anybody else by battering on to London. As soon as I reached the M25 junction I would hit the capital's rush-hour traffic. I wouldn't even make it by seven. Nevertheless, I owed the boys a call, so I pulled into a service station to face my next challenge: making a call from a phone box.

I hadn't used a phone box since I was a boy. When you are a professional footballer you don't have to do anything for yourself, including using a phone. There is always somebody there to do it for you. And virtually since the day I retired from the game I had had a mobile, dating back to the very first ones which were the size of a brick and which you carried in a bag rather than in your pocket.

I went into the box but I couldn't figure out how it worked. What money do you use, and where do you put it? Do you use the money first or do you dial first? Then I realised that I didn't know the number of the office because it was programmed into my mobile, which was now kaput.

I felt helpless, and not a bit stupid. I enlisted the help of a passing lorry driver. But that didn't get over the problem that I did not know the office number, or how to find it. Fortunately, the lorry driver was a talkSPORT listener. He took the phone out of my hand, found talkSPORT's number, and got me through to the switchboard while I pumped coins into the slot.

Unfortunately, the man on the other end of the phone spoke

hardly any English. He was an overnight, £5-an-hour security guy and he was unable to understand me. The more I bellowed down the line, the less he understood. And the more panic-stricken he got at trying to handle this maniac on the phone at a quarter to six in the morning, the less tolerant I became.

'Put me through to Studio One! STU-DEE-O ONE!'

Suddenly there was somebody on the line, talking to me in English.

'Al, where are you? We're going frantic here!'

'I'm in Oxford. Look, I've had terrible problems. It's a long story, but—'

Beep, beep, beep, beep ...

I shouted over the pips, 'You're going to have to go without me. Tell Porky—'

And suddenly the phone went dead.

I was quite relieved, actually. I didn't want to get into long explanations. I'd done the best I could to tell them I wasn't going to be there. They'd just have to get on with it.

I wandered back to my car. Daylight was just starting to come up.

Then I started to feel uneasy. I had had a few run-ins with the management lately and I knew instinctively that I was in trouble. I'd missed a show a month earlier because I was worn out from a charity event I had been to the night before. And in the run-up to Christmas I had not been able to function on the very last day before the holiday. I had been to a party and had just stayed too late; I was struggling like mad the next day and had to retire after two hours of the show. As I motored back towards London I realised I would also miss out on interviewing Ken Bates, the then Chelsea chairman, who was due in the studio that morning. I always enjoyed interviewing him. He was frank and controversial. He didn't care who he upset and he made great listening.

I turned off the radio and put some music on. Rod Stewart started blaring out of the speakers, and I started to feel marginally better. I'm not the sort of bloke to be down for long. I couldn't undo what had happened so I figured there was little point in dwelling on it.

When I got back to London I received a message to take a few days off. I'd expected something like that. I grabbed my old mobile, hailed a cab and headed for my favourite wine bar on Ludgate Hill near Fleet Street. On my way there I rang Jill. When she answered she was in her usual state of panic whenever I run into a problem at work.

'What have you done?' she said. 'What will happen if you lose your job? What are you—'

'Jill, Jill, forget it,' I said firmly. 'I'm not in the mood. Get the skis out. We're going to Meribel.'

Then I rang my daughter, Michelle, who had skied for Britain, and asked her to organise the flights and hotels. She knew the routine. She didn't ask me what had been going on. She knew me better. She sounded happy, though, that we were going skiing as a family.

I arrived at the wine bar and was greeted warmly by the staff. Not surprising really. I am probably their best customer. Then I did what I always do in those sort of circumstances.

'Champagne,' I said.

The sharp popping of corks began.

CHAPTER TWO

COME BACK AL,
ALL IS FORGIVEN

*'We're getting about two hundred emails
a day calling me all sorts of names for
having got rid of you. Let's get together
for a sherbet.'*

WE stayed in Meribel for a week. I loved it, but Jill was just a bag of nerves, worrying about what I would do when we got home. I couldn't answer that, but I had had some serious setbacks in my life before, including the premature end of my football career, so I wasn't going to let this get to me. Nevertheless, as we set off for the airport I started to wonder where I was going to turn next.

I didn't have to wonder for long. Before we boarded the flight I took a call from the BBC who wanted me to do a show for them on Radio Five Live. This was a huge irony because at talkSPORT we had always regarded the BBC as the arch-enemy. Under our boss, Kelvin MacKenzie, we took every opportunity to berate and attack them. Kelvin hated them because they got £2 billion a year from the licence fee while we had to sweat blood for our revenues. They were not offering a daily or even a weekly gig, but it showed that I was still in the frame as a broadcaster. I was surprised, because the style Porky and I had developed on our breakfast show was a million miles away from the rather more staid style of the BBC. I was also heartened that they seemed very interested in talking to me even though the reasons for my getting the boot from talkSPORT had already been well publicised. Charlie Sale had written about my demise in his column in the *Daily Mail* with a lot of graphic detail. The news of my demise was written about at quite some length elsewhere too. I just don't know where the information came from. I just got phone calls from people who seemed to know an awful lot more about the situation than me. I didn't want – or need – the publicity. And fortunately any more recent bust-ups I have had with the authorities have not made the papers.

In fact, when I got home I discovered something else about MacKenzie that was deeply unpleasant. A letter had arrived at my house which was the official notice of my sacking. Fair enough. But in it MacKenzie described me as being a disgrace to my family. That made me very angry. If he had been a £10 cab ride away I would have gone and sorted it out with him.

When I had my various run-ins with the company MacKenzie would, for some strange reason, never deliver the bollocking personally. The message was always delivered second-hand through Porky or some other executive. He was very hard sometimes to understand. Sometimes I felt that the lifestyle I led was to be encouraged and sometimes to be frowned upon.

Only a few months earlier Kelvin, who had many qualities that I admire, came up to me after my show and told me: 'Thank you for saving my radio station.' It was invigorating working for a man with such energy and, though I didn't realise it at the time, he was of course, and still is, one of the legendary names in the media. Porky had worked for him at the *Sun*, and treated him with reverence.

I was no longer listening to talkSPORT. I couldn't see the point. Porky had shipped in a nice guy called Paul Breen-Turner from Spain to take my place. He was an industrious sort of a bloke who had been looking for a breakthrough in national broadcasting for years. Maybe now this was it. He had previously been our Spanish correspondent based in Marbella, where he had a share in a little coastal radio station that aired Jimmy Young-type programmes for the ex-pat

British community. He was an affable chap who had built up a fledgling operation into a very successful business called Spectrum FM. Whenever Porky and I were over there on a job he always fixed us up with good hotels and star guests from the showbiz and football world. I remember on one occasion Porky being transfixed by the magnificent new bosom of Bev Callard, the *Coronation Street* actress who plays brassy Liz McDonald. He couldn't keep his eyes off her deep cleavage as he interviewed her and completely lost his concentration, stumbling over his words and blowing her kisses.

I didn't hear from Porky in the days after returning from Meribel. I couldn't really blame him. What were we going to say to each other? Still, I hoped that once the dust had settled we might get together over a bottle or two to reminisce over the five years we had spent together on the road.

In the first few days back at home I was asked to do the show for the Beeb. After that, various offers started coming in from newspapers and the then-emerging area of betting websites. I also got asked to do some after-dinner speaking, and I started to write a newspaper column. A weekly TV show was also in the offing. As I had always thought, I was certainly going to be making a living, but in truth I preferred to have a more consistent pattern of work than the piecemeal arrangements that were now my fare.

I was happy, though, to be back on familiar stamping ground. I live in one of the most beautiful parts of Britain on the Essex–Suffolk border. It has the most captivating landscapes in the whole of the British Isles. It is truly Constable country. Just a few miles from my converted barn is the village of Dedham and Flatford Mill, the setting for John Constable's most famous works. My first night of marriage to my wonderful wife Jill was spent in the Maison Talbooth, a classic hotel overlooking Dedham Vale. Many, many times over the years I have driven down to Dedham and taken in the delights of the surrounding countryside, taking my three daughters to the historic locations of the paintings of one of England's greatest-ever artists. My little girl Stephanie was particularly intrigued by the picture-postcard quality of Willy Lott's Cottage, which features in *The Hay Wain*. And as the family grew up we spent many happy Sundays at the point-to-point racing at Higham, a few miles from our home, where we would while the afternoon away with a sumptuous picnic and a few bottles of bubbly.

Another favourite place of mine is Milsom's Hotel, just a few miles from Dedham in a village called Stratford-St-Mary. Over the years it has become something of a second home to me. Gerald Milsom, the boss, built it up from a little bed-and-breakfast into one of the finest country-house hotels in Britain and then developed other class restaurants in the area. He became a close personal friend over the years. He was a fanatical follower of Ipswich Town during my heyday, when we conquered Europe and were consistently one of England's top clubs. He was the sort of fan every club has, so close to the Ipswich players and officials that he was almost one of us. He travelled a few times on the plane with the team when we won the UEFA Cup in 1981, dispensing bonhomie on the way out and gallons of champagne on the way back. I remember in particular a huge celebratory trip home after we had battered St Etienne of France 4–1. To a lifelong fan like Gerald it was like being in heaven. The minute the plane landed we piled into a fleet of cars at the airport and headed straight to Milsom's, where we were still celebrating at dawn the following day.

Gerald had a close mate called Charlie Manning who used to travel with him. Charlie was an even more colourful figure than the hotelier. He was born in a gypsy caravan but through a combination of streetwise cunning and having an astute business brain, despite not being able to read or write until he was sixteen, he made himself a fortune. He started off with a hoopla stall on the beach at Felixstowe and within twenty years he owned every other property, usually an amusement arcade or a bingo hall, along the front of the Suffolk resort. He was an associate of Billy Butlin, the Canadian showman who arrived in this country after the war with five shillings in his pocket and went on to create the legendary Butlin's Holiday Camps empire.

Charlie, who raised huge sums for charity, drove around in a large black Bentley. As young footballers we weren't paid anything like modern-day players, and sometimes after a game he would give us the keys and tell three or four of us to go out and enjoy ourselves for the evening. We always found a willing driver, and it must have been quite a sight to see a gang of young international footballers being chauffeured around Suffolk in this huge Bentley. I always fought Paul Mariner for the front seat. He lived the part of the chauffeur-driven tycoon, always wearing dark glasses. For a laugh we sometimes used to stop when we saw a bunch of what were obviously Ipswich Town fans. Without engaging them in any banter I would ask, quite seriously, 'Hey, lads, do you know the way to Manchester? I'm signing for United tomorrow.' I'd register the look of astonishment and horror on their faces as they realised who we were – their footballing heroes – and what I had just said. The irony is that, in years to come, I ended up playing for Manchester United.

Not only was this a great flash motor to be touring around in on a Saturday night, it was also the best possible protection you could find. Everybody in and around Ipswich knew it was Charlie Manning's car, and *nobody* argued with him. Still, whatever he got up to in business he was never less than an absolute gentleman to us young lads and our girlfriends. If one of the players was getting married, cases of champagne or huge bouquets of flowers would suddenly arrive at the reception, sent by either Charlie or Gerald, or by both of them.

Mr Milsom was not only good to Ipswich players, he was also a great humanitarian. Long after I retired from football I was in his hotel one day when he introduced me to a fine young black boy who was training to be an opera singer. Gerald had had a house in Cape Town, South Africa, for many years. On his last visit he came across a young man – a singer with a special talent. The English hotelier was captivated by his fantastic singing voice, and discovered that the boy, the son of a Zulu tribal warrior, was trying to raise the money to go to a special school to train as a classical singer, his family being too poor to be able to help him fulfil his ambitions. Mr Milsom met the family and offered to sponsor the youngster through school in England, give him lodgings at his hotel, and help guide his career. In return, the singer would entertain guests at Milsom's by singing for them in the restaurant in the evenings. I have spent many a late evening at Milsom's with my family, entranced by the boy's fantastically powerful voice. The young South African spent three years in England and then went back to his own country where he is now pursuing a successful career. Sadly, Mr Milsom died suddenly at the start of the 2005/06 football season, though his son Paul is now carrying the business on.

Soon after I got back, I was sitting in the bar at Milsom's, the surroundings wrapping themselves around me like a woolly jumper. This was not just Constable country, it was also my racing territory. Although I made my name as a footballer and had had a good deal of success at club and international level, horseracing, as most people know, has always been a major factor in my life. In fact, these days it is a much bigger part of my life than football. My years as a professional player were magnificent, but they came and went, whereas my interest in racing, initially as a punter and more recently as a businessman, has grown each year. Newmarket, the home of racing, or HQ, as seasoned racing men like my pal Channel 4's Derek Thompson call it, is just a half-hour drive from my home.

Although I stayed right at the top of the game when it came to football, I think I am probably most knowledgeable these days on racing – and that has been the case for a few years. After you have been a professional footballer it is hard to retain that same buzz of excitement about the game when you move back outside. I had never really fancied coaching or management and wasn't really a member of that profession any more. But bloodstock had been in my veins since my first visit to Newmarket as a displaced teenager who had just got off the train from Glasgow.

From the moment I went along to my first meeting at Newmarket with some of the senior professionals I was absorbed by the whole business. The atmosphere of a racecourse has always captivated me. People win or lose when they go to the races, but they are mostly there to have a good day out, the girls in their summer frocks and the men showing early afternoon wear and tear in their shiny suits. And the animals themselves are a wonder to behold. Their grace and power; their human-like attitudes and temperament; the fire in their eyes and their bellies as they strive desperately for the winning post, manes flowing in the wind.

I also had a particular fascination with the colours of the silks the jockeys wore. Jockeys? Sometimes just tiny little men, but among the hardest I have ever come across. What guts you must need to climb up on the back of a half-ton horse, knowing that there's always a chance you are going to come a cropper. Jump jockeys in particular have my full admiration. I don't think there are any more courageous sportsmen. Even more so than Flat jockeys, they know that every day they go to work there is a chance they could be thrown off their beast going over a fence, or find themselves underneath the hooves of a dozen marauding horses.

As I sat in the bay window of the Milsom's Hotel bar sipping an early-morning glass of champagne, I started thinking that maybe horseracing rather than broadcasting was going to be where my future lay. I had a few outline plans to start a racing club, and that had already generated a lot of interest in the racing world. I was always being invited to meetings as a lunch guest to 'mark' the guests' cards, and it was something I enjoyed enormously. A smile came to my lips as I thought about the magic a race meeting held for me.

I was jolted out of my thoughts by my mobile phone ringing. Porky's name came up on the screen.

For a split-second I wasn't sure whether or not to answer it. I had nothing against the guy. He'd really had no option but to do what he had done, under direct instructions from MacKenzie. I just thought to myself fleetingly, 'Is that part of my life so far gone that I should now just close the book?' Nevertheless,

I thought it would be good to touch base with him.

I flipped open the phone. 'Yo, Porky.'

'Hi Al,' he said, hesitatingly. 'How are you doing?'

He sounded tense, but then I always did think he took his work too seriously.

'I'm fine,' I said.

'What are you up to?'

I explained a bit about the other work that had come my way, but I wasn't really interested in the small talk. I wanted to know why he had called.

'Well,' he said, 'I thought you might like to know that I have become public enemy number one. We're getting about two hundred e-mails a day calling me all sorts of names for having to get rid of you. People think I just sacked you for the benefit of my health. Listeners are sending death-threats in letters. Yesterday some bloke turned up at the station and wanted to fight me in a boxing ring, and if he beat me I had to reinstate you. I don't think any of us calculated for this sort of response from the audience. Taxi drivers give me stick.'

His language was littered with the F-word and, as he detailed his troubles, his voice got louder and more out of control. This was Porky at his stressed-out best. He had a demonic chairman above him who I knew wouldn't budge on the issue and the wrath of hundreds of thousands, if not millions, of listeners below who were hurling abuse and threats at him as though he were a war criminal.

'Let's get together for a sherbet,' he suggested.

'Is that wise?' I asked, surpassing the urge to laugh at my mate's clearly stressed-out mood.

'Yeah, but not in one of our normal places. Can you find somewhere around Liverpool Street or something?'

I agreed, and we set up a meeting for the following day.

I got there before Porky and picked a dimly lit corner of the cellar bar. A waitress brought over the obligatory bottle of champagne. I thought this was all a bit cloak-and-dagger, but Porky had insisted on a hideaway because I have a very distinctive appearance and I do get widely recognised. It didn't bother me who saw us, but I didn't know on what basis Porky was coming to see me. Did his boss know or not?

Porky arrived looking as though he was carrying the weight of the world on his shoulders. I'd seen him like this before. He slumped down in his chair and ordered a bottle of Chardonnay.

Without any preamble, he said, 'Al, you've got to come back.'

'Why's that?' I replied, chuckling at Porky's total absence of negotiating skills.

'I've become a pariah,' he said. 'Half the country hates me because you've gone. The abuse I'm getting is terrible. People are coming over to me in the street and bawling at me – in my face. My driver's mates have told him that he shouldn't bring me to work any more. The lad who makes up my baguette in the sandwich shop more or less throws it at me. And the listeners – it's like they are threatening to go on strike.'

Porky had already got through a third of his bottle of wine. Agitated wasn't the word. I was rocking in my chair with mirth at his discomfort.

'How's Paul doing?' I asked.

'He's doing great,' Porky replied. 'It's a hell of a role for him to take on, but he's gone at it full pelt. He's come out of himself. He's a class act. But the problem is, we have created such a monster with our breakfast show over the last five years that it will take at least two years to fill the void. You've got a lot of fans out there, and the way we're going there might not be a lot of them left as talkSPORT listeners unless I do something fast.'

'What about Kelvin?'

'Well, obviously I can't do anything unless he's up for it, but there's no point in going to him until I know whether you fancy it or not. And I can't tell him that I've approached you first. But I'm going to tell him that we need you back and hopefully he'll then think it's his idea to make the approach.'

I was still feeling pretty raw about the way I had been booted out, and the letter to my home, so I wasn't feeling exactly ecstatic about this turn of events. But it would be a good move to at least follow it through. So I gave it the nod. The relief spread visibly across Porky's face. We then got down to the serious business of demolishing the bar's wine cellar, bottle by bottle.

The next few days were a flurry of phone calls, furtive meetings with talkSPORT executives and stop-start negotiations. Porky and I started to meet in the same cellar bar in the City, and, as usually happens, we became very friendly with the staff. My breakfast-show pal and I had always loved the atmosphere of the wine bar or the pub, and we liked dispensing loads of bonhomie. We spent big and we tipped the staff even bigger. People started to recognise us and we would regale them with tales of the breakfast show. 'Are you going back, Al?' I was constantly being asked, while Porky was getting dog's abuse from pundits for being the cruel boss who had sacked me. I always answered in the same way. I told them jokingly, 'We'll see, we'll see. We're working on it. Porky's offering me a king's ransom and a written admission that he's a dickhead.'

One of the barmaids took pity on my beleaguered mate and started coming over to comfort him, stroking his hair and his hand. The more pissed Porky got the more beautiful this girl became. Mind you, she was a bit of a stunner. She was East European – Latvian, I think – in her mid-twenties with a swathe of dark hair and lovely high cheekbones that reminded me of Faye Dunaway. Her name was Karina.

Porky was a mug for a pretty face. I had seen him give away literally thousands of pounds over the years to women with hard-luck stories. On one occasion in a pub in Cardiff he signed a cheque for £700 to a woman he had never met before who told him she needed it for her mother's kidney transplant. Like you can buy a new kidney off the shelf.

One evening Porky and I rendezvoused as usual in the bar and we were in a particularly ebullient mood because that day an agreement had been reached for me to return to talkSPORT the following week. As we entered, Karina leapt on Porky, showering him in kisses. All the other girls behind the bar, most of whom were Latvians as well, joined in, mobbing my mate as though he were some sort of celebrity. I suspected he had promised to take the girl on a cruise or something. But it was much worse than that.

The previous night I had left the bar earlyish; Porky was ensconced in a dark corner canoodling with his girl. I knew he must have stayed on late because, unusually for him, he was pie-eyed during the breakfast show the following morning. I asked Porky what was going on and he just shrugged his shoulders. But the girls wouldn't leave him alone.

I went up to the bar to order some bubbly and asked the boyfriend of one of the other girls, who was also of East European extraction, why everybody was so excited.

'Hasn't Mike told you?' he said. 'He's marrying my sister.'

I started laughing, and so did the manager behind the bar. But it suddenly dawned on me that, while I thought he was having a joke, he was deadly serious, and he was celebrating.

I was pretty sure that Porky didn't know he was engaged to Karina. I waved my mobile phone in his direction, indicating that there was a call for him.

'You didn't tell me you were getting married, you tube,' I said once he'd reached the bar.

His face went into a confused and embarrassed smile. At first I could see that he hadn't even got half an idea about what I was saying, but then sudden realisation dawned somewhere deep in his eyes.

'What have I done?' he asked me hopelessly.

I put my arm around his shoulder and dragged him away from the bar.

'That bloke over there thinks you're marrying his sister,' I informed him.

'That's mad,' he said.

'Well, they don't think it is. Have you lost your marbles? How pissed did you get last night?'

'Not that pissed,' he replied sheepishly. 'Karina was telling me she's going to be thrown out of the country because she hasn't got a work permit, and I asked her if there was anything I could do to help. But I never asked her to marry me. I'm sure I didn't. Al, you've got to believe me. I wouldn't do that, would I?'

The celebration was now turning into a wedding breakfast, and lots of Eastern European people appeared to be joining in.

'Right, we've got to get out of here fast,' I said.

The only problem was that our coats, and Porky's computer

bag and phone were on the other side of the room and the celebrations were taking place between us and the door. Decisive action was needed. I told Porky to grab the gear and make for the door while I glad-handed some of the revellers. But he wanted to do it a different way. Porky has this strange streak of honour within him and he thought he should straighten things out with Karina first. Amazingly, he said he did not want her to think that Englishmen were dishonourable. He wanted to do the right thing. I sometimes despair for the boy. I told him it didn't matter; it would all be forgotten about in 24 hours' time and they'd never see us again. Despite my protestations, he insisted he wanted to sort it out.

He might as well have thrown a gallon of petrol over a fire smouldering in a gigantic grate.

He moved into the cheering crowd, took Karina by the hand and led her away into the corner. At first it seemed to go well, but then Porky must have got to the bit about not wanting to marry her. She suddenly screamed and started slapping his face and head. She was a tall girl and she was using her long legs to kick out at Porky as he cowered from her blows. In an instant the two of them were surrounded by the Latvian mob, which now numbered three or four sturdy-looking men as well as half a dozen girls. Everybody was shouting in an unintelligible language.

I knew this was going to get nasty. I had no option but to wade in. I grabbed hold of Porky, who was holding off one of the aggressors at arm's length. I put my full palm into the Latvian's face and pushed him hard enough to propel him over a chair.

'Get our stuff!' I barked at Porky.

One Latvian was screaming at us about 'honour' and a 'dowry'. 'You've got to give us money!' he kept screaming at me.

There was no way of calming things down, so I didn't bother to try. By now Porky had the precious bags and he was trying to fight off women who were slapping him and pulling his hair. Slap them back, I thought to myself, cursing the fact that he had been brought up in the English public school system. Fortunately, I hadn't.

There were now three burly Latvians between me and the door. I imagined them as three defenders barring my way to goal. I made a move to go right but then dropped my shoulder and lunged to the left. For the first time in years I was glad I was not at my playing weight. My eighteen-stone bulk hit two of them like a battering ram. One just bounced off me and was propelled across the other side of the bar while the other went down backwards, his head hitting the wall with a sickening thud. Summoning all the instincts that had got me through a fight a week as a kid in Glasgow, I raised my fists and bared my teeth at the third. He was having none of it.

By now Porky had wriggled away from the clawing and spitting women and we were away up the stairs. We couldn't run when we got into daylight. We were both too unfit, but luckily, as we hit the street we nearly ran under the wheels of a black cab. The driver recognised me immediately and could see we were in a bit of trouble. We threw ourselves into the back and the driver sped off without us even shutting the door, as raging Latvians started to emerge from the bar.

'Having a spot of bother, boys?' said the driver.

'Nothing we can't handle,' said Porky, still gasping for breath, as though he had everything under control.

I told the driver to head for the West End. No more cellar bars for me. We walked into Claridge's, and the maître d' greeted me like the old friend he was. I didn't even have to order. The Laurent Perrier arrived within minutes.

I was sticking to my old adage: when in trouble, double bubble.

As we raised our glasses, I leant over to Porky and told him, 'Next time you call off your engagement to a mad illegal immigrant who looks like she could have been a kick-boxing champion and whose family closely resemble the cast of *Gangs of New York*, you're on your own.'

It was OK, though. He knew he wouldn't be. We started work together again three mornings later.

It was just as well that we rekindled our working relationship when we did. Euro 2004 was looming and, in addition to doing our breakfast show together, we also had a series of lunch and dinner speaking engagements.

Sometimes these after-dinner events are a lot of fun, but sometimes they are not. To be honest, I'd rather not do them. I don't mind a question-and-answer session, and we did a lot of those in working men's clubs up and down the country when we were sponsored by John Smith's beer. But audiences can be funny: the delivery can be enthusiastically welcomed one night yet greeted with scorn the next. I remember one occasion when half the room walked out on us because Porky, a former war correspondent, made a passing reference to the Gulf War to which most of the audience objected. Most of the time, too, we were there for charities, or to represent the station, so we became a little bit disillusioned with the whole process, particularly as we weren't leaving an event until eleven at night yet still had to be back in the studio within six hours.

One function that does stick out in my memory is the time when we addressed Crystal Palace fans at their end-of-season dinner. Palace, as most people know, is controlled by Simon Jordan, a young, highly successful businessman who made a sizeable fortune in the mobile phone industry. A lifelong Eagles supporter, he eventually made enough money to achieve every ambitious schoolboy's dream of being able to buy his own club. It was clear from the start that he was going to be no wilting wallflower when it came to having a profile as a chairman. Managers such as Trevor Francis and Steve Bruce, who had tremendous records as players, came and went, and there was always talk that the manager, whoever it might be, had a permanently feisty relationship with the chairman. And Jordan didn't always have a cordial relationship with the fans, either, often hinting that they should be more grateful to have him around. But, let's give the boy his due. He risked a considerable amount of money on taking control of his club.

A previous attempt by a businessman to do the same thing at Palace had turned to disaster. Mark Goldberg was a computer mogul who took over the club and immediately adopted a 'schoolkid in a sweet shop' mentality. He decided that nothing was too good for the Palace. He approached Terry Venables, still a world-renowned coach, to become the manager even though the club was languishing mid-table in the division below the Premiership. Not only did Terry have great status in the football world but he had cut his managerial teeth at Selhurst Park, and done so well that the club was often referred to as young guns who would become the force of the future. According to what I heard, Terry very politely turned down the initial approach from Mr Goldberg, who then decided that there was no way such an eminent coach was going to reject the Palace. He went back with a mouth-watering offer which included a huge salary, big cars, big houses and quite a bit more. Terry could see the ambition burning in the heart of the new owner, and took the job.

But a year later it all turned to acrimony. Mr Goldberg had decided that he had no more resources to pump into the club after spending a reported £40 million. That might not sound like a lot in comparison to what Roman Abramovich spends at Chelsea, but remember this was before the era of the Russian oligarchs and Palace weren't even in the top division. A section of the fans turned on Terry because of his mega-bucks deal, but his response, quite rightly in my view, was that, if somebody offers you a job with a specific salary, do you take the job but ask for less money? You'd have to be quite mad.

Porky and I clearly had popular support among the Palace fans. Throughout the course of the meal they queued at our table – the top table – asking us to sign their menus, and we posed for dozens of pictures and spoke to relatives on mobile phones. While all that was going on, one Palace fan picked up my £250 felt-tip pen and I haven't seen it since.

There was a real knockabout atmosphere in the lovely marquee that had been erected over the pitch, and when we got up to speak there was a very loud cheer. I went first and reeled off a load of stories about playing against the Palace, and nights out with some of their star players from the past. I told them the tale about the Eagles player, who shall remain nameless, who was engaged to two girls at the same time, one of whom knew he was a footballer and the other who didn't.

Porky then stood up and decided to adopt his usual blunt approach to testing the resolve of the audience.

'How many of you hate the chairman?' he asked.

There was a lot of laughter, and some of the diners raised their hands.

'Because I've composed a little song here in tribute to Mr Jordan,' Porky went on. Then, to the tune of the ditty whose chorus is 'Did you ever see, did you ever see, did you ever see', he burst into song. It was incomprehensible but everybody laughed.

It was very amusing, and it absolutely caught the mood of the night. It wasn't malicious, it was pointed, and it was aimed at the chairman. The fans cheered because it was funny. Chairmen are always going to be the butt of the fans' jokes, and sometimes their anger, and this was actually quite an inoffensive and friendly dig at authority. Porky gave us two more verses but then couldn't keep going as he was laughing so much. The audience were laughing with him and as he sat down he got a huge cheer.

But clearly not everybody was happy. A few minutes later, as Porky and I were laughing along to the guest comedian, we realised that we had been surrounded by five or six very burly-looking blokes dressed in long leather coats and wearing leather gloves. One of them leant over me and whispered in my ear, 'Your presence is required in the boardroom.' I presumed it was an invitation to some sort of VIP reception after the dinner, so I thanked the man in black and said we'd see how late it was when the dinner ended. He leant over again and said, 'No, I'm sorry, you don't understand. You are required in the boardroom right now.'

I started to sense that all was not well, but I couldn't think why. The goons standing around us were now attracting attention, so I told the head goon to go away, take his mates with him, and we'd be up there after the comedian had finished.

A few minutes later we came off the raised dais and the men in black were in position to escort us up a very long flight of steps to the boardroom. We entered a long room with tables and chairs and there was only one person in there. He was another man in black, a scruffy-looking individual who was sitting in the chair at the top of the table. It wasn't the chairman, Simon Jordan.

The door was firmly closed behind us, and the man in the room started ranting.

'You have the audacity to come into my home and you insult us,' he said. 'You have the nerve to be invited here, to share our hospitality, and then you deliver your bile against us.'

I turned to Porky and said, 'Who's this clown?'

Before Porky could answer, the ranter was up on his feet and pointing in our direction. 'I'm the chairman's brother,' he said. 'I uphold the standards around here, and you have come into my brother's house and you have insulted him.'

I started laughing. 'What are you talking about, you idiot? You claim to be Simon Jordan's brother. You look more like his bag carrier to me. Simon's quite intelligent. As far as I'm concerned, you're a moron – and you look pathetic.'

Porky suddenly cut in and pointed out that, in every other boardroom in Britain we had ever been invited to, we had always been offered a drink.

'There'll be no more drink for you here, ever,' countered the ranter.

With that, Porky walked around him to a glass-fronted cupboard, took two bottles of beer, opened them and handed one to me. We flopped down on a couch and started swigging.

Raising his voice to new levels, the alleged brother screamed, 'I will not tolerate your behaviour in my home.' He then swore at us in very coarse terms.

I got up and walked over to a window. I opened it, turned to the ranter and said, 'Nobody speaks to me like that. You're going out of this window.'

Whether he gave out some sort of signal to the men in black outside, I don't know. But at that precise moment one of the leather-coated mob burst into the room. He indicated it was time for us to go.

'Give us a few minutes, boys, will you?' I said. 'We haven't finished our beers and we're still trying to work out what the missing link is going on about.'

There was a stand-off for a few minutes. Porky and I strolled around, swigging our beers, swapping a bit of conversation about the dinner; and then, when we were ready, we handed the empty bottles to the man who called himself Simon Jordan's brother, and left.

As we went down the stairs, four of the goons were following us. I tightened my fists and shouted to Porky in front of me, 'If any one of them comes anywhere near us, we are not responsible for our actions. If they want trouble, they're going to get it.' As we reached the bottom of the stairs, I turned to face them. I was ready.

But I was taken completely by surprise when the lead man raised his right hand in a 'halt' sort of gesture and said, 'Alan, I'm so sorry. The guy's deluded. He thinks he's starring in *Godfather IV*. Simon's not here and this one always tries it on when he's away. I'm afraid your car has come and gone because it couldn't find you, but I'll happily run you back into town. It's the least we can do.'

Some time later Simon Jordan did an interview in a newspaper in which he brutally slagged off the chairmen of a number of other clubs. Over the last couple of years he seems to have set out on a mission to become an unavoidable voice in football. He has even had his own column in a Sunday newspaper which has resulted in him facing FA charges. Among others, Jordan attacked Richard Murray, the vice-chairman of Charlton. He told the *Sun* that there was a running spat between the two men originating from Jordan's original newspaper claim that many football club boardrooms were full of 'tossers'. 'I apologised to Richard at the time,' the Palace boss related, 'saying that the article had had nothing to do with him, and he said that he had known me long enough to know what I was like. Four months later we go to The Valley. They equalise late on and we're relegated. As I go to leave, Murray says, "By the way, tosser, enjoy yourself in the Championship." My brother Dominic hears this and says, "Right, I f***ing want to have him." He goes downstairs to have it out with him. I catch up with them and Murray says, "You want to have a fight, do you?" I say, 'You're an old man. Why do I want to fight you?'

When I read this story I realised that Dominic was almost certainly, to my mind, the repulsive little squirt who tried it on with Porky and me that night in the boardroom at the Palace. The hot-headed bullying approach and the disgusting language were exactly the same.

Of the more recent story, I think Jordan is completely out of order to allow somebody representing himself to try to intimidate and physically threaten a man like Richard Murray, who is universally regarded as one of the most gentlemanly administrators in the game. I have been entertained at lunch by him and he is bright and cordial. Though of course he didn't become fabulously wealthy in the world of TV and showbusiness by being a wilting flower. If there had been a fight, I reckon he would have made mincemeat out of the loutish brother – and that would have raised a few cheers in the football world.

One of the other more memorable dinner events we have done was at Stamford Bridge. We have always had a love-hate relationship with the former Chelsea chairman Ken Bates, now in charge of Leeds United. Ken is a one-off. He simply doesn't care who he upsets when he speaks. But when he does go public it is not usually a meaningless rant against another club. I think he realises that tit-for-tat name-calling in football is wasted energy. In my experience, he goes public if he thinks it is for the good of the game or the good of his club. So, for instance, he was very vocal when the deal for the new Wembley Stadium was being put together because he wanted to make sure that the FA and football got the best deal. And, when it came to Chelsea, if somebody was dishing it out in a newspaper column against the club, they would get it back in spades in Ken's own column in the fortnightly programme.

I was one of the first to hear about the takeover of Chelsea by Russian billionaire Roman Abramovich. I got a call from somebody very close to Ken as the deal was being signed. The idea was to make sure that I was in the loop if it should leak out into a newspaper the following day. Sure enough it did, and I was able to reveal quite a few angles to the story that weren't known at that time. One of them was that Ken, though picking up a very substantial amount of money for his shareholding in Chelsea, was to remain as chairman of the club. This suited all parties: the Russians would benefit from having the club's patriarch around, and Ken did not want to suddenly pack his bags and leave a club he had transformed from a bankrupt shell into a force in the land.

Another benefit of remaining chairman was that he was able to continue with his tradition of 'Chairman's Suppers'. This was a once-a-month ritual of inviting along friends, fans and business contacts to break the bread with him and have a convivial evening in one of the glittering ballroom-sized suites at Stamford Bridge. He asked Porky and me to attend one such function and do a bit of Q&A with his guests after dinner. We were very happy to accept.

The proceedings were being chaired by a presenter from the club's in-house broadcasting network, Chelsea TV. Everything was going fine as we approached the stage after dinner and started the banter with the fans. But slowly I could see that Porky was getting irritated by the presence of the Chelsea TV man. He always thought he was a better anchor for these sort of events.

The three of us on the stage were sitting on tall stools which I always call 'ball-breakers'. No matter how you try to position yourself you always end up with your crown jewels looking as though they are trying to burst out of your trousers. I felt quite self-conscious and uncomfortable, so when I was asked whether I had an opinion on where the club should go next I muttered something about 'organic growth' and hoped the focus would move elsewhere.

The anchorman then asked Porky, 'Have you got any advice for the chairman?'

Porky replied, 'Yes. He's a fat get. He eats and drinks too much, and now that the Russians have taken over he should ask for a job in a Siberian salt mine so he can lose a few pounds. And he'd save thousands of pounds by getting free salt to put on those mountains of chips he stuffs down his grey-bearded gob.'

Nobody saw that coming, and at first the room was deadly quiet. But then one or two people started to snigger, and then there was uproarious laughter.

Ken wasn't going to take that without responding. He called over from his table for a microphone and gave it back to Porky with 100 per cent on top. It went something like this: 'Parry, you're the fattest bastard that I've ever let into Stamford Bridge. You're so fat we had to have a special door for you. You'd never get through a turnstile. You drink so much that every time you come here we have to plant a new vineyard near my home in the south of France – the sort of place, incidentally, where a bum like you would not be welcome – and I'm told the only thing that is stopping you from eating yourself to death is the fact that your mouth is never closed long enough to digest the hamburgers. Oh, and incidentally, I keep a picture of you on the fireplace to keep my cat away from the fire.'

Again, the room was in uproar.

Porky now wriggled off his tall stool and started wandering the room, delivering insults from every corner of it.

'Were you pissed when you signed Chris Sutton?'

And Ken, similarly, 'They're renaming the radio station after you. It's going to be called TalkBollocks from now on.'

It was all unscripted and made for great entertainment, but I had no idea how Ken had taken it. When I didn't hear from him for a few weeks afterwards I started to worry that Porky had blown it. But, actually, Ken is too big for that sort of thing. A couple of months later we were supping champagne with the chairman at his annual Christmas party. And Ken is still a very welcome guest on our station.

CHAPTER THREE

THE STATE OF AMERICA

It's a funny thing, but it doesn't matter how you're feeling before you go on air, the minute the red light goes on something happens to you. It's the best hangover cure I've ever encountered.

I FIRST started to think about it while drinking champagne in the Colony Club. I had lost a few hundred pounds on the tables and had retired injured to sit at the bar and take a glass of fizz while nibbling on a few peanuts.

The Colony Club in Mayfair, London, is one of the country's top casinos, and I had been going there for years. I loved the ambience of the place and the staff, who treated all their customers with great respect. I was a small-time punter compared to some of the people who came through the doors. I have seen household-name tycoons lose millions of pounds on a roulette table in less than an hour. A mate of mine, who was not quite in that league but who, nevertheless, was a wealthy property developer with big interests in Spain, once lost £400,000 in one afternoon. Five times he sent his driver to a bank depository to get him £80,000 cash at a time. He kept telling us all that he only needed one lucky spin of the ball to get his losses back and double his money. It was a high-risk strategy, and it didn't work. I'd seen him lose some big amounts over the years without it seemingly causing him too much pain, but he looked terribly wounded by his bad luck that day and was clearly shaken up when the time came to count up his losses. Maybe this time he really needed the money – and more – to stave off trouble. Whatever the case, a few days later he left town, his flat near to mine was vacated, and he cleared off. I've never seen him since.

As I was sitting on my high stool at the bar I was idly taking in the news on the flatscreen TV above the brandies. On it was a picture of a British Airways jumbo jet. I'd seen the same image a few times during the day. In the wake of the dreadful attack on the Twin Towers in New York on 11 September 2001 everybody was panic-stricken about travelling. I wanted to know what was going on, so I asked the barman to turn the sound up. The story was that flight BA223 from London Heathrow to Washington DC had been cancelled for a third consecutive day because of intelligence reports that it was a terrorist target.

I hated the idea that terrorists were stopping people in the free world from moving about. I hated terrorists and all they stood for. I was determined that my daughters were going to grow up in a society that put no restrictions upon them. I worked to give them the best life I could and some nutcase following a code that included blowing other people up was not going to threaten them.

I had been trying for some time to figure out what I could do as an individual to hit back against the terrorists. Now I had found a way: Porky and I were going to be on that flight to Washington the very next time it took to the skies. I rang him immediately and put the plan to him. He was well up for it. In fact, he liked the idea even more than me. During his newspaper career, Porky had worked as a Fleet Street journalist in America and had lived in both Washington and New York. He was very pro-American, so much so that we had once had a debate on our breakfast show that we should be the 51st state of the US rather than a country attached to the EU.

Porky dubbed it the 'Flight of Death', though I managed to restrain him before the following morning's show, when he had toned it down to 'the most dangerous airline flight in the world'. 'It's Brazil and Porky telling those cut-throat terrorists, "You don't frighten us, Osama!" We're flying British Airways. Catch us if you can.'

Within days we were sitting in the US Embassy in Grosvenor Square, London. It's only when you go to places like that that you realise what a very dramatic effect terrorism has had on all our lives. It was only a few months after 9/11, but already the building resembled a fortress. It was surrounded by huge concrete blocks, and entry to the visa section was achieved only after a rigorous security and checking procedure. Porky and I were grilled by American Secret Service agents. We had to convince them that the reason we were applying for entry visas was because we wanted to make a statement on the war against terror. Though they applauded our spirit, they were understandably a little perplexed. Mad dogs and Englishmen. We were going to take the following morning's Sports Breakfast show to Washington, which normally means terrible red tape and paperwork to get all our equipment out of England. But all the authorities rallied around – BA themselves were as enthusiastic about the mission as we were: after we contacted their PR people they did all they could to help – and within another 48 hours we were sitting in the first-class lounge at Heathrow waiting to board the flight. Providing it wasn't once again cancelled we would be on board the first British Airways flight into the American capital for five days.

We went through particularly extensive security checks and boarded the jumbo. On the way to the gate we were clapped and cheered by British Airways staff and loads of other passengers. It was quite surreal. Apart from Porky and me there was not another single passenger in the 'bubble' on top of the plane where you'd normally expect to see up to 30 other travellers. There were, however, some very nice young ladies from BA looking after us.

The plane was due to take off at eleven a.m. but we didn't actually depart until two because of the rigorous security checks. This was actually of great benefit: due to the extended time on the ground we drank nearly all the cabin's stock of champagne before take-off, and the crew had time to send out for fresh supplies.

The captain came up to meet us. He was wonderfully British and gave us great confidence in the journey ahead. Porky wanted to interview him on tape, but, unlike the rest of the crew, he wouldn't do it until we landed in Washington. This subsequently proved to be a bit of a problem because, by the time we got to the other side, we were all so tired and wrought with emotion that we couldn't enunciate any sensible questions.

As the mighty jumbo finally moved away from the apron at Heathrow and then thundered down the runway, I wondered what I had let myself in for. But the journey across was utter bliss. For me, the scourge of the modern age is the mobile phone. On the jumbo it was perfect. I could call anybody I wanted from the phone in my seat, but nobody could call me. Porky and I had lunch, then dinner, watched a couple of films and drank ten bottles of champagne and wine between us. We didn't once think that we were going to get blown out of the sky – though if we had been I don't think we would have noticed. The only bangs we heard on the journey were a succession of champagne corks bursting out of their bottles.

Dulles airport is about 30 miles outside DC. Before we left England a businessman who runs a worldwide limousine business had contacted Porky and told him that as he was a great fan of the breakfast show he wanted to provide us with a car and driver for the weekend. As we emerged into the arrivals hall we spotted a huge black man swathed in a full-length leather coat and matching leather cap holding up a sign the size of a barn door. In thick black felt-tip pen, the sign said 'Brazil and Pig'. I cracked up laughing, but Porky couldn't see the funny side of it.

Our driver, who was about six feet seven inches tall with dreadlocks down to his shoulders, had a very dramatic look about him. In fact, his face instantly reminded me of the actor Robert Guillaume, who played the butler Benson in the US series *Soap*, and in the spin-off *Benson*. I greeted him with that name, then immediately explained myself, hoping I hadn't offended him. But he seemed quite happy to answer to that name throughout the weekend. After we had introduced ourselves, Benson said, 'Good evening, gentlemen, and welcome to Washington DC. I will be looking after you guys for the weekend.' In the sort of accent that could have got him a part in *Hill Street Blues*, he added, 'You wanna go anywhere, you call me. You want anything, you call me. Anybody gives you any hassle out there, you call me.' A second man grabbed our luggage, and within a few minutes we were in a state-of-the-art stretch limo heading for the capital.

Whoever owned this car company certainly knew us well. Not only were there buckets of champagne sprinkled around the cavernous interior of the stretch, there were also half a dozen bottles of Porky's favourite Chilean Chardonnay in the fridge. I rubbed my hands together in anticipation. I just knew this was going to be a successful mission. Porky was like a kid at a school reunion. It was his old stamping ground, and he was immediately on the carphone fixing up a social rendezvous.

'Mr Brazil, have I got a surprise for you,' he said when he put the phone down. 'We're going to meet a few old friends.'

We didn't even get out of the car when we arrived at our hotel on Rhode Island Avenue. Benson summoned a porter to take the bags in and we shot off again. Porky had asked him to take us to a pub near the city's main station.

As the car pulled up I struggled to see the attraction. It was a pretty desperate-looking building in not such a great part of town. I was reluctant even to get out of the car – particularly as the temperature outside was minus fourteen – but Porky was insistent. One saving grace was that I noticed a Guinness sign above the door and a shamrock logo. It was clearly an Irish pub so it was probably the nearest thing they had in this town to an English pub.

Porky pushed open the door and I couldn't believe what greeted me. It was a mass of people cheering and jumping up and down, waving green and white scarves over their heads. The whole bar broke into a chorus of 'You'll Never Walk Alone', Celtic's traditional pre-match song (stolen many years ago, by the way, by Sassenach Liverpool). Porky had brought me to the equivalent of the Washington DC HQ of the Celtic Supporters Club. The walls were adorned in flags and pictures of my boyhood heroes. These guys knew that I was brought up at Celtic Boys Club. Though I had never graduated to be a first team 'hoop' I had won the Scottish jersey, so to them I was a hero. The Guinness didn't just flow; it was as if somebody had struck an underground well of the black stuff. We did the whole repertoire of Scottish songs while grainy old videotapes of great Celtic victories played out on a TV screen behind the bar.

Most of the people in there were ex-pats who had sought a new life in America. But there were some locals, including two young men who turned out to be officers from the sheriff's department. I didn't even know America still had sheriffs. I thought they had disappeared after the shoot-out at the OK Corral. So I started taking the mickey out of these two, calling them 'Deputy' and Dawg'. Fortunately they were pretty good-humoured.

Porky then had another brainwave. I kept asking if there was a piano player, because in this sort of atmosphere I like nothing more than to get around a piano for a rendition of 'Flower of Scotland' or 'The Fields of Athenry'. There wasn't one in the pub, but Porky had a mate who was the bartender in a piano bar in somewhere called Georgetown. Georgetown turned out to be the rock 'n' roll district of the capital, just up the road from the White House. I fancied the piano, but I didn't want to leave this great atmosphere. Then Benson solved the problem. Eight of the lads came with us in the stretch on the first journey, and then he went back and ferried another ten of them across town.

It was a magical night. Even more booze was flowing in the piano bar. I was in great voice. Microphone in hand, I was belting out all my favourites: 'And they stole Trevelyan's corn, so the young might see the morn ... the prison ship lies waiting in the bay ... Oh Flower of Scotland ...' Two young Scotsmen who were extremely polite and well spoken were also getting vociferously stuck in to the party. They turned out to be officials from the British Embassy, which was not very far away on Massachusetts Avenue. I didn't realise that Porky was a friend of the British ambassador, Sir Christopher Meyer, who later shocked the establishment with his revelatory diaries about diplomatic life in Washington.

I have to admit it was fast becoming a situation in which the shackles of an orderly day were being loosened. At times I remember having to reflect on what I was doing in this bar, what town we were in, and even what country. It occurred to me once or twice that we had come here to do a breakfast show, but I now had literally no concept of time. I had a watch on, but I can never work out whether Britain is five or six hours ahead, or whether we're behind. My watch, which was on American time, said eleven p.m., so I hoped it was about six o'clock in the evening in London. Porky seemed to have disappeared so I knew he would be getting on with business.

I had just launched into a verse of 'Scotland the Brave' and was at the same time quaffing a tumbler of champagne when Benson appeared.

"Fraid we have to go, Mr Brazil, sir,' he said.

'Yeah, yeah,' I said, waving my hand at him. 'There's plenty of time yet. What time is it in England?'

'I don't know, sir. I just know that Mr Parry says you have to be on the radio in four hours' time and I have to take you back to join him at your hotel.'

'Four hours?' I retorted. 'I normally make it by four minutes. Don't panic.'

I turned back to the piano, but suddenly felt my feet leaving the floor. As if by levitation, I was heading for the door. I thought I was flying, but in fact Benson had picked me up as though I was a child. He carted me outside, opened the door of the stretch and threw me into the back.

I was so stunned I couldn't say anything. Nobody in my life had ever manhandled me like that. Just as I was about to launch into a tirade, Benson turned around in the driver's seat and said, 'I am very sorry, Mr Brazil, but I am under orders to get you back to your hotel.' I learnt later that Porky had slipped him a hundred dollars to get me out of the bar. How underhand, I thought.

When we arrived back, my pal was in a typical panic, screaming down the phone in his suite. The engineers had gone ahead to the studio from where we were going to broadcast from just after eight a.m. English time, but it had turned out to be unsuitable. Technically, it wouldn't 'talk' to our studio in London. Porky advised me to get my head down for a couple of hours and he would send Benson to get me when we had sorted out whatever studio we were going to use. I nodded earnestly in agreement and patted my harassed partner on the back as he continued to try to sort things out.

Except that I didn't feel like getting my head down. It was nearly midnight in Washington. I didn't know when I was ever going to be in the American capital again and I wasn't going to waste the night. I didn't feel even a little bit tired, despite having been up for 24 hours, so I went down to the cocktail bar and ordered a bottle of bubbly. The strange thing about my constitution is that though I am a consistent drinker I don't very often get drunk. I knew I was OK because despite my Scottish accent I was having a perfectly sensible conversation with the barman about American history.

I arrived at the studio Porky had located in good time. We were just two minutes from going on air when our connection to London suddenly dropped. Our chief engineer, Ben, went white and started hitting an array of buttons. We couldn't hear any output from talkSPORT, which should have been coming to us through our headphones. According to our clocks it was 8.05 a.m. in England and we were due to come in live from Washington DC in one minute. I'm sure Ben was crying by now. He kept shouting 'Frame, you bastard, frame!' in a desperate attempt to bring the lines to the studios together.

My heart was thumping. Surely we hadn't come all this way to broadcast dead air? I was helpless to rescue the situation. It didn't matter what I said; nobody in London was going to be able to hear me.

The clock ticked to 8.06. The theme music for our show must have started now. I turned to Porky and raised my hands in the air in a desperate search for inspiration. He looked ill, and slumped forward with his head in his hands. Then, suddenly, the red light above the clock lit up like a beacon and a tidal wave of noise flooded into my cans. It took me a split-second to work out my timings, but I actually had no time at all. I sucked the air into my lungs and hit the intro right on the button.

'Good morning, ladies and gentlemen, and welcome to a very special sports breakfast show this morning all the way from the US of A. Yes, Porky and I are in the American capital this morning, just to remind you that, despite the threat of terror, life must go on. We flew over with our friends from British Airways last night and over the next four hours you're going to hear from some of the passengers and crew on that plane and from some of our American friends over here about their response to terrorism. OK, it's party time in DC, don't move the dial. You're having breakfast Stateside this morning with me, Alan Brazil, and Porky "my pal's the ambassador" Parry ... here on talkSPORT.'

We did a brilliant show, even though I say so myself. It's a funny thing, but it doesn't matter how you're feeling before you go on air, the minute the red light goes on something happens to you. I don't know if it's focus or adrenalin, but it's the best hangover cure I've ever encountered. Of course there have been one or two occasions when even that hasn't managed to make my tongue smaller in my mouth than it sounds, but by and large the minute I slip behind the microphone, it's like I have been cold-showered.

We received a load of calls from London congratulating us on a great broadcast. British Airways were delighted with the projection, and the bosses at the station, who were understandably nervous about the whole mission, were very pleased that we had pulled it off.

Now it was time to celebrate. We had completely lost touch with time, but Porky insisted we should get some sleep. I went to bed for a couple of hours but I simply couldn't nod off. I got up, went down to the bar and ordered a Budweiser. A few minutes later Porky arrived. He had been out walking. There is something wrong with that boy. It was -20°C outside, but he likes cold weather. He's the only person I know who goes to Iceland for his holidays. No joke.

After some breakfast we decided to do a bit of a tour. Benson took us down to Capitol Hill. I was staggered by the size and beauty of the building. I wondered what plotting and planning went on under that vast dome in this, the high church of the free world. It was a gorgeous January day, and as we glided down Pennsylvania Avenue towards the White House I could smell the power in this city. Up to my right was the HQ of the FBI; there was the Lincoln Memorial; over there was the Smithsonian Institution.

Before we got to the White House, Porky insisted that we took in the Vietnam Memorial. It was one of the most moving moments of my life. It is a long black marble wall with the names of the dead soldiers inscribed in gold paint. Next to each fallen soldier is his age. That song '19' that hit the charts in the eighties was right: most of the boys who died in that conflict were under the age of twenty. I had to bite my lip to stop myself crying as I witnessed parents at the memorial sticking pictures of their dead sons next to their name on the wall. I worked out that an eighteen-year-old soldier who had fallen in Vietnam in 1970 would have been older than me that day. Bloody wars, I thought, turning away from the monument with misty eyes. Look at the living I have done in all those years which was denied those boys.

Next stop was the White House, and by now I was getting a bit weary of the sightseeing routine. While Porky was boring Ben on the history of the West Wing, I spotted the Willard Hotel opposite. It was noon, it was freezing, and I fancied a drink.

Minutes later I was in the Round Robin bar. Unbeknown to me, this was a Washington powerhouse meeting place where government officials muttered coded messages to reporters from the *Washington Post* over a Jack Daniel's. It could have been a scene straight out of *All the President's Men*. I could imagine Bernstein and Woodward sliding into the bar any minute now.

Porky called me on the mobile. No, I wasn't coming back to the car, I was enjoying a drink. Ten minutes later he joined me. By this time I had struck up a conversation with a couple of newspapermen who had cottoned on to my accent. How come every American you meet has a grandparent in Dublin or Glasgow?

There was a very attractive middle-aged lady sitting at a table on her own. We both assumed she would be joined shortly by her partner, but after half an hour she was still on her own.

Porky wasted little time in getting on the pull. He drifted over and engaged her in conversation. When we were abroad I reckon he always told women he was a retired footballer and that he used to play for Manchester United because he once took a penalty at old Trafford in a charity match. She'd never heard of Manchester United, but she nevertheless warmed to his company, and very soon he brought her over to the bar. The three of us sat together on high stools supping champagne.

The conviviality was broken when Ben, who is openly gay, suddenly stormed into the bar and stood, hands on hips, wailing that we'd abandoned him and left him sitting in the car for an hour. 'There are places I want to go,' he remonstrated.

'Well, go, then,' I told him. 'Take the car and tell Benson to take you wherever you want to go. In fact, take the car for the rest of the day. Just make sure Benson picks us all up in good time in the morning.'

He was a happy bunny.

Meanwhile, Porky appeared to have struck lucky with his lady, Rhonda. The more champagne she drank – and it was coming across the bar by the gallon – the more she was spilling her heart out about her marriage and how her husband didn't understand her. She soon started stroking Porky's leg. She told him he was a lovely man, and then, just to prove she had had far too much to drink, she came out with the immortal phrase, 'You look like a love machine.' I nearly fell off my stool.

By now it was early evening, and we decided to head for a restaurant. Rhonda had called up two friends and we all rendezvoused in Smith & Wollensky's. Amazingly, there were three more single women in there, all sitting at their own tables. I had never seen this phenomenon before. In Britain I have very rarely seen a woman on her own in a pub, let alone in a restaurant. We were easily the most boisterous group because the three of us had spent all afternoon in the Round Robin. But we were, as ever, very good-natured, and we invited the three single women to come and join us.

There were now six women at the table plus Porky and me. It was like having Christmas dinner. When Porky started doing his impersonation of former president Bill Clinton, who he swore was a good friend, the whole restaurant became captivated. Inevitably, the champagne river was flowing again.

It's impossible to work out how long we stayed. All I know is that I hit the wall later in the evening and had to go back to the hotel. I must have impressed on the concierge the importance of getting up at 3.30 a.m. because the next thing I remember he was banging on the door. For once, I was downstairs first, waiting in the lobby and wondering where Porky was.

The lift pinged, the doors opened, and Rhonda strode out. She wasn't at all bashful. 'Oh, Al,' she said, 'you are two wonderful guys. This town needs more men like you two. I do hope you are going to come back and see us soon.' With that, she pecked me on the cheek, turned on her very high stiletto heels and was gone.

A few minutes later Porky arrived. He looked in remarkably good shape. He claimed that he had not been asleep at all and that he and Rhonda had just spent the night chatting in the bar and then in his room.

The problem was, where was the car? Just as Porky was about to hit the phone it drew up outside. The back door opened and out stepped a very tall and very senior-looking US Air Force officer. What was he doing in our car? Seconds later, Ben also emerged. The two men shook hands and the USAF guy strode off.

'What's going on here?' I said when Ben came into the lobby.

'Well, put it this way,' Ben replied. 'Saddam Hussein couldn't stick it up the US Air Force, but I did.'

I was momentarily shocked by his boldness, his exuberance and his total lack of embarrassment. But then we all started laughing. OK, I thought, if that's what turns you on.

We all bundled into the back of the car and headed for Dulles. The champagne corks were popping again as Porky led us in a rendition of the classic Beach Boys hit 'Help Me, Rhonda' over and over again, just like on a jukebox. We were in great spirits when we reached the airport. We should have been terribly tired, but the adrenalin had once again kicked in and we felt like we could go on for ever. And we soon realised we might have to, because a few hours after we were due back in England we would be doing our next breakfast show from our London studios.

Prior to going to Washington, as I mentioned, Porky and I had been to the US Embassy in Grosvenor Square to be interviewed for a working visa. We should have had no real problem as our visa application had been backed by British Airways, and Porky still held a US Social Security card and number from the years when he worked there in newspapers. Nevertheless, we had a four-hour wait and two separate interviews with officials before we got that coveted visa. So, bearing that in mind, perhaps I should have been a little more circumspect as we were passing out through security to get on board our plane in Washington.

We went through a beeping security gate and I was stopped by an official. There was a diagram of two feet on the floor, and he asked me to place my feet there. 'What's that for?' I asked.

It was a genuine question. The notorious story about a shoe bomber trying to blow up an aeroplane hadn't yet happened, and this was a new procedure to me. He just ignored me, and I became irritated. Without any sort of attitude, I tried again. 'Why do you want me to put my feet in there? Do I look like a terrorist?' I wasn't challenging him. I was just trying to engage this stony-faced official in conversation. I wanted a reaction because he was treating me with contempt.

Without any flicker of expression he asked me where I thought I was going.

'London,' I replied. 'Some people have a bit of personality over there.'

I don't know whether this enraged him or not. It was hard to tell. But he then said, 'If you don't put your feet where I tell you to put them, you are not going anywhere.'

I have never liked people threatening me, whether it was a kid in the school playground or an irate fan on the terraces. I said something like 'Get a life', and before I knew it I was surrounded by armed guards and officials. Somebody put their hand on my shoulder so I slapped it and pushed it off. More pushing and shoving, and now I could see this was in danger of getting out of hand. I had to defuse the situation.

'OK, OK,' I shouted, putting my hands above my head. 'Guilty as charged. Sorry, guys, no harm meant, but if this guy would just engage in a bit of dialogue we wouldn't be falling out with each other. Come on, we're all on the same side.'

To my surprise, a passenger behind me suddenly piped up: 'He's a very famous English footballer – leave him alone.'

'Scottish,' I interrupted, 'but he's right.'

Though the Americans have little feel for the game of football – or soccer – this was enough to calm things down. The cult bookmark 2007

TEMPEST PHOTOGRAPHY

of celebrity is massive in the US. If they think they are dealing with somebody famous they tend to back off. To them, fame is power. Now, far from being threatened with detention, we were given an escort to the first-class lounge.

Porky had gone white in the face. 'Al, why do you do these things to me?' he said.

'Stop whingeing,' I told him. 'When did the Americans last think you were so important that you got a ride on a golf buggy to the best champagne bar in town?'

That was not the last time I had dealings with security personnel in America. On a subsequent trip I went to Chicago as a guest of a couple of pals in the betting business for the Breeders' Cup meeting – the American equivalent of our Royal Ascot. It was another marvellous flight across the Atlantic with an endless supply of champagne. I had never been to Chicago before – and what a stunning city. It was colder than Washington had been, though. Chicago is on the Great Lakes, and the winds that whip off the water can drive temperatures down to minus 30 degrees.

I was there ostensibly for the racing, but on the first night we all got invited out to a theatre to see a musical show. I was quite happy with that as I like a good musical. It was also not as formal as a theatre, where everybody sits in rows. We sat at tables and drank champagne while watching the performers. I thought it was going to be a pure blues evening, which I was looking forward to, but mixed in with the Muddy Waters type of music was some sort of gospel-rock band. I had never seen a group of people singing spiritualistic songs before, and I don't think I ever will again. Because, although my mind went a bit hazy and foggy, I believe I had some sort of biblical experience that night which I've been trying to figure out ever since.

At about midnight I was beginning to feel the pace a bit. Not surprising, given that Chicago is six hours behind London, so that in effect it was six a.m. for me. We had just enjoyed a couple of hours of real rhythm and blues and we had been singing along when a gospel-rock combo came on stage. What with the late hour and the effects of the champagne, my eyes were really drooping, and I feared I was in danger of falling asleep. I didn't want to let my friends down so I rallied myself and tried to concentrate on the stage. The new group were a mixture of men and women all dressed in brilliant white smocks. My first thought was that they looked like a collection of angels. They started singing and dancing, and while at first they were only moving across the stage, they subsequently started flying in the air. I assumed they must be connected to wires, but I remember thinking it was a strange sort of performance: earlier in the evening we had been witnessing raw blues bands, now it was almost like pantomime.

All the time they were dancing the lights behind them were getting brighter and brighter. In fact they became dazzling, and I turned to my friends on the table to see if they were shielding their eyes like me. I couldn't see them, I assumed because of the impact of the powerful white light. It was as if I had glanced at the sun and been momentarily blinded. But then I looked across the room. I couldn't see anybody else at all. I wondered whether I had fallen asleep at the table or something and everybody had gone home. I wondered why they had left me.

I looked back at the stage. All the performers were now right near the front and they were beckoning me to join them, waving their arms in a 'come here' sort of gesture. I was really puzzled. I wasn't frightened or anything like that; in fact, I felt quite serene. My mind then filled with a sense of anticipation, because I wanted to know what happened next. That was when I woke up in my hotel. It must all have been a dream. But, if it was, then how did the night end?

Over the years I've done plenty of late-night champagne quaffing, but I have never been in the position where I couldn't remember things the next morning. Maybe it was the jet lag. But when I checked it out with one of my pals there were a missing couple of hours from the night for which I could not account. The gospel group had not been wearing white smocks but white suits and dresses. Apparently, I left with the others at the end of the show and three of us were given a lift home in the Jaguar car belonging to the manager of the theatre. We sat in the hotel bar for an hour before going to bed. I couldn't remember any of those details, yet according to my friends at no time was I 'out of it', rambling or incoherent.

The incident has puzzled me ever since. Was it some sort of a message from a higher calling? Was it a warning about my lifestyle? Was I hallucinating? Had somebody spiked my drink? One of my mantras when people start telling me that I'm cutting years off my life because I make sure I enjoy it so much is this: 'We're only here for a visit.' It's far too early yet for me to give up my visitor's pass, though I will wonder for years what exactly went on that night.

The visit to Chicago had only just started, and there were plenty of heart-stopping moments ahead. We went out to the track in a luxurious bus, and naturally there was plenty of champagne flowing. It was being served by a collection of very lovely young ladies. The more times I go to America, the more often it strikes me that many women in England do not look after themselves as well as most girls in the States.

My wife, Jill, is always immaculate whenever we go out, and she has brought up our three lovely daughters to be the same. At home I am constantly surrounded by make-up bags and shower rooms full of all sorts of potions, hairsprays and gels. The women in my life always look so well turned out, but that, to my eyes at least, is not always the case with much of the female population in this country. American girls just seem to have whiter teeth with broader smiles and better-styled hair. (I hope I don't find myself suddenly under attack for saying that. It's just an observation.)

Anyway, as we neared the track it occurred to me that I had not seen a single ticket for the venue. That's not a big concern when you are enjoying a bit of corporate hospitality, but you would normally have a badge or a pass to help you move around. I especially wasn't too worried that day because I was meeting up with Ted the ticket-man, our friend from Cheltenham.

Ted is an extraordinary sort of bloke. Nobody quite knows what he does, but he's never short of a few bob, and if you ever want a ticket for anything, from a West End play or an exhibition of Monet paintings in New York to an Ashes Test match in Australia or the Wimbledon men's final, one call to Ted is usually enough to solve the problem. He is also a bookie. He's a sallow, middle-aged character with his huge grey overcoat which has all the characteristics of a magician's cloak. From somewhere he pulls out an old-fashioned ledger and sets up business on the bar, taking and laying bets. At every big race meeting I go to I am likely to see Ted perched on the end of a bar somewhere, drawing up a book. This is particularly useful in places like the Guinness Village at Cheltenham. Whenever I have been there we have always got in first and therefore become wedged in at the front of a huge tent. It is virtually impossible to get out and back again in time for each race. This is where you would see Ted in action.

I admire a man who lives on his wits. Though there was one occasion when he didn't have his wits about him, and he consequently spent the night driving around the back roads of Suffolk looking for civilisation. I still chuckle wickedly when I think about it. I was holding a big party in a hotel a few miles from my home. Ted-the-ticket was working all that day, but eventually, at around eleven p.m., he turned up. By then my guests and I were just preparing to go back to my house on a minibus that was ferrying us around so that we could all have a drink. I told Ted to follow the bus and come and join us all at home. But for some reason he lost the bus and then found himself in pitch-dark in a rainstorm in deepest Suffolk with no address for me and a mobile phone that had no signal. He spent the night being chased off people's properties as he tried to find my home. It must have been like trying to find someone's vehicle in the long-term car park at Heathrow without knowing the make or the registration number. By the time Ted got himself into an area where there was a signal for his mobile, mine was nestling in the pocket of my coat in the cloakroom of my converted barn, while I and my guests drank and danced away on another floor. Ted eventually spent the night in the car.

Back in Arlington, as we pulled up outside the magnificent grandstand there was the man himself, hopefully with a pocket bulging with passes and badges to the track. But as we got off the bus he came towards me looking rather stern. I expected him to hand me some tickets, but instead he said, 'Just follow me. Don't ask any questions and don't stop walking.

Just follow me.' He then turned and set off at marching pace towards the main gate.

I had travelled up on the bus with Ted's friend. We looked at each other, shrugged our shoulders, and fell in behind Ted. He marched straight up to the Owners and Trainers' entrance and started shaking hands with any official in the vicinity. 'Hi buddy, hi guys. It's going to be a great day. London sends you its very best greetings.' He grabbed one very prosperous-looking racegoer by the arm, patted him repeatedly and said, 'How the hell are you? Haven't seen you since Syracuse – or was it Kentucky?' He hit everybody like a whirlwind. And human nature being what it is, most people tried to hide the fact that they didn't have a clue who he was. In fact, within a few seconds he was receiving as much goodwill as he was dishing out. 'Sure good to see you again,' said one man in a J.R. Ewing-style cowboy hat.

Ted surged straight for the double-door entrance while glad-handing anybody he could lay his hands on. A uniformed ticket-checker suddenly loomed into view and challenged him.

'Good morning, sir. Do you have your wristbands?'

'Wristbands? Wristbands? Do I look like I need wristbands?' answered Ted, following that with a very convincing and dismissive laugh.

'Well, sir,' began the man on the gate.

'Don't worry, I know you have got your job to do,' said Ted. 'But so have I, and I've got to meet your chief operating officer. I'm already late. But, don't worry. My girl is already inside and she'll come down and sort everything out for you.'

The gateman hesitated, but then decided that this eccentric Englishman could be somebody really important and let him through. We followed.

I breathed a sigh of relief. I could never have had the gall to pull off a stunt like that, and I was cringing at the thought that had we been properly challenged I could have been ceremoniously ejected from the whole event. Ted clearly didn't have any tickets at all for this event, but he had got us in.

But that was only the start of it. Just as I was thanking the Lord for helping us to avoid detection, Ted said, 'Now look, fellas, that was the easy bit. We've now got to get to the fifth-floor restaurant where there should be a few spare seats on one of the best tables at the track. The problem is, we have to go up through each floor by escalator, and every time we do they'll ask us for a different coloured band. So don't break stride, just keep close behind me.'

I was dreading this. I had always been used to being invited to events like this on a legitimate basis, or, if necessary, paying big bucks for the right table. I had visions of being slung out of Arlington by armed security guards or, worse still, being arrested as a fraudster. But I had come all the way over from England and I had no choice but to follow Ted.

At the top of the first flight he pulled back the sleeves of his big grey overcoat and pulled his shirt cuffs out. He said to the security guards, 'Let me give you a bit of advice, boys. Never, ever buy your shirts in Jermyn Street in London again.' Then, thrusting his arm out, he went on: 'Feel that. Go on, feel that. Shocking, isn't it?'

The man holding the radio was completely perplexed. He wasn't sure what to make of Ted.

'Have you got your wristband, sir, for this floor?' he asked.

'I'm so sorry, young man,' Ted responded, 'but our host who is entertaining us on the fifth floor – you know, the table in the window that overlooks the finishing post – has gone up in the elevator and taken all the bands with him. I'll have them sent straight back down to you.'

We moved on. We glided through the second floor, and at the third Ted suddenly pulled me forward and said to security, 'This is a great day for you, boys. I want to introduce you to Alan Brazil. That's right, Brazil. He's the great Scottish soccer star, and he is so named because he is the nearest thing Europe ever had to the great Pelé. If we had a football here, now, this man could bend it right around the Arlington track.'

What the security men made of this, I don't know. Fifteen years after retiring from the game I wasn't exactly at my playing weight. I smiled, shook hands, and said the first thing that came into my head. 'Yes, I was here commentating for Scottish television at the World Cup,' referring to the tournament that had been played in America in 1994.

We negotiated the fourth, too, and then found ourselves on the escalator approaching the fifth floor. This was the level on which the very cream of American bloodstock aristocracy were going to be spending the afternoon, and I steeled myself for the fact that this might become our Waterloo.

Instead of shouting out goodwill messages and blustering as we approached security, Ted went deadly serious and quiet.

'Do you have your wristbands, sir?'

Ted exploded. 'Wristbands? Do you know how many horses I have brought over from England for this meeting? Do you have any idea of the scale of operation that's gone into getting here? And do you know how many owners are waiting through that door for advice from me about their animals, which are worth millions of dollars? And you want to talk to me about wristbands?'

It was so explosive and specific that even I believed Ted was legitimate. So did the gateman. He released the clip on the red rope and ushered us through. I was writhing inside.

The only problem now was to find a table. But that was no problem for Ted. He walked in, pointed to a table for ten by the window, and told the waiter, 'We're sitting there. My friends are a bit delayed but they'll be here shortly, so if you could open an account for me for the drinks and bring us some champagne, I would be very grateful.'

My pal and I couldn't believe we were in. But we were both still worried that any minute now the real occupants of this table would arrive and we would be slung out. When I voiced these fears to Ted he simply waved his hand around and told us to leave it to him. The champagne duly arrived and, as always, after a few glasses my fears about being slung out started to evaporate. I don't know whether Ted had been party to some inside information, or if the waiters were primed to keep him informed, but we spent two hours at the table completely on our own.

Then, just as I thought we were going to get away with it for the afternoon, a group of people arrived at the door. Ted seemed to know instinctively they were the genuine group. With his usual consummate style he moved towards the figurehead, who turned out to be a Canadian multi-millionaire, shook his hand vigorously and started giving him the sob story about the terrible mix-up with the arrangements. Three more chairs suddenly appeared around the table, and within minutes everybody seemed to be best friends with each other. I don't know who Ted told the Canadian he was, but at regular intervals the Canadian would introduce Ted to a friend as 'one of Great Britain's top land-turf agents, specialising in chancery'. Whatever that meant.

For the first time that day, I relaxed. And Ted's run of luck hadn't yet come to an end. He had genuinely set up a tab for all the drink, starting with the champagne that we drank earlier and taking in all the drinks for the party of ten. He figured that as we were on one of the top tables, with the best views, for which we hadn't paid a penny, he should at least foot the drinks bill. But as we left the track he was beaming from ear to ear. He had settled the drinks bill and it had run into thousands of dollars. Remarkably, the method of payment was not an electronic machine but one of those old-fashioned roller-type devices that imprints the details of your credit card on three carbon copies of the invoice. Amazingly, the waiter who was sorting the bill gave Ted his credit card and all three copies of the bill. Ted couldn't get out of there fast enough. The restaurant didn't have any record whatsoever of the payment, and once we had left there was no way they could have recovered it because they had no electronic record of Ted's account. No wonder the champagne was still flowing on the way back.

I had a glorious return flight to England. That trip to Chicago would have been almost perfect except for a disappointing surprise that greeted me when I arrived home.

At the time I was part-owner of a number of horses through my love of racing. One of them was a colt called Indian Haven which I thought had every chance of entering the highest ranks of racing – Group One. Unfortunately, my two co-owners did not share the same optimism. While I was away in Chicago they received an offer on the horse, and took it. It was, in my opinion, a wrong move as I was very confident the horse would make a top three-year-old. But I had to accept I was out-voted. As far as I was concerned we had lost the prospect of owning a great horse and, just as importantly, winning a good deal of money from it. Sadly, I was to be proved right.

CHAPTER FOUR

CONTINENTAL CAPERS

*I feel in much better form with the
remnants of a beautiful bottle of Merlot
in my stomach than if I have had an early
and stone-cold sober night. Some of my
flattest shows have taken place when I
have been behaving like a choirboy.*

I HAVE been involved in several campaigns in Europe. In two of them I won a UEFA Cup medal; in the last of them, I like to think that I won a lot of listeners for talkSPORT and spread our gospel around the continent – though with varying degrees of success.

When I started at the radio station we had just converted ourselves into an all-sports station. To give the bosses their credit, they soon put their money where their mouth was, investing big sums on rights to English teams in Europe. To back that up, they started to send my breakfast show to the Continent to promote the coverage.

On of the first times Porky and I ventured into Europe was in February 2002, when we went to Holland for England's friendly against the Dutch in Amsterdam. Porky was acting like my minder because this was a new venture for the company and, as he was the programme director, he had to make sure it all went well. On the night before the game he suggested we have dinner in the hotel and a 'quiet' night. Porky was always up by 4.30 and in the studio for five o'clock for a six a.m. start. To me, though, that is a waste of valuable sleeping time. I have always been able to assimilate facts and figures very quickly. I can get the grip of an argument more easily by learning fast, not by labouring for twenty minutes over a dozen different sources of information. But on this particular night I decided for once to give the early-night routine a go. I had been invited to join a card school with some pals I had met through Frans Thijssen, my Dutch former team-mate at Ipswich. But I knew that would mean a very late one, so I declined. I could always get a couple of bottles sent up to the room.

Porky and I had dinner and then retired to the lounge for a couple of glasses before going to bed. There was nobody in the lounge, a huge room with high, draped windows. It was pretty lacking in atmosphere so I was happy enough to turn in. But then, as so often seems to happen in my life, an unforeseen twist steered the night into a totally different direction. Just as we were about to get up and leave, the doors of the lounge burst open and dozens of Fleet Street sports writers started to pour into the room. A celebration had been organised to pay tribute to the last-ever international match to be covered by the legendary John Sadler, the veteran *Sun* scribe who had decided after more than four decades to hang up his pen. One by one the hacks came over to greet us. Many had reported on me in my glory days or followed me with club and country, and Porky had worked with dozens of them during his years in Fleet Street. Before long there was a party going on and the atmosphere had been completely transformed. I went up to the bar and started swapping stories with some of the biggest names in back-page sport. I could see the slow realisation in Porky's face that there was absolutely no chance now of me making that early night.

The boys only stayed for an hour before they went off en masse for a celebratory banquet, but it was a power-drinking hour and it gave me the taste. In fact, as I reasserted my right to stay up as long as I wanted to, I felt quite ashamed of myself for being cowed earlier by Porky's plan for an early night. I should have told him to get lost.

This may sound odd, but early nights don't suit me. A few years ago Chris Evans, widely regarded as one of the greatest radio broadcasters of our generation, admitted that he was often the worse for wear when broadcasting. He was involved in a court case, and, while putting his case forward, he said that being intoxicated was not a problem, and in some cases it actually improved his ability to perform. Though I would never advocate being drunk on the air, I agree with some of what he said.

Broadcasting is about being on the edge. It's an instant challenge, and there is no way back. Unlike writing a newspaper column, where you can adjust your words, you can't change your words on air once they're out. Once you have spoken, that's it. This makes for a challenge and an adrenalin rush, and for me it works better if I have had a good night before going in to the studio. I feel in much better form with the remnants of a beautiful bottle of Merlot in my stomach than if I have had an early and stone-cold sober night. Some of my flattest shows have taken place when I have been behaving like a choirboy. One week I couldn't have a drink for four consecutive days because I was on antibiotics for a chest infection – they were some of the flattest shows I have ever done. I certainly felt so, and so did people working around me. It's not a question of being dependent on drink, it's just whatever suits the individual. Some people get the same feeling after going for a ten-mile run. There are a lot of people in the broadcasting business who can't operate unless they snort cocaine, which is much worse than champagne. I've never knowingly taken a banned drug in my life.

So, to get back to my point, I decided that night in Amsterdam that I would go to the card school after all. I taunted Porky to the point where he had to come with me. In these sorts of situations he doesn't know what to do. If he comes with me he knows he could end up getting more smashed than me; but he also knows that if he doesn't come with me he has no control over where the night will go and, more importantly, what time it will finish. Secretly, I know he would like to be a dilettante like me when it comes to observing accepted procedures. But there is something burnt into his soul which makes him respectful of the rules.

I dragged him into a taxi and we shot off to my pals' place in Rembrandt Square. It was a gentlemen's gaming club. Before I could find them to organise some credit, I approached a roulette table. I needed some cash quick.

'Porky, give me some money, quick.'

He tried to protest.

'Come on,' I said. 'I feel a lucky moment coming on.'

He reached into his pocket and pulled out a wad of notes. I grabbed the lot and gave them to a young lady, asking her to get me some chips.

'Al, for Christ's sake, that's the advances I drew from the office this morning. What the hell are you doing?'

'Stop panicking,' I said.

The girl brought me my chips back. I put Porky on the spot.

'What colour, red or black?'

Porky was gobsmacked.

'Come on,' I said. 'Red or black?'

Looking completely panic-stricken, he spluttered, 'Black.'

I placed the chips on the table. Next to scoring goals for Ipswich and Scotland, this was the best feeling in the world. I loved the sound of the silver ball rolling around the rim while the wheel was spinning in the opposite direction. The anticipation was like finding out whether the jury was going to find you guilty or not guilty.

The ball fell on to the wheel and clattered around a few times. It hopped and bumped, and then settled on a number. It was red.

Porky went white, but before I could give him the chance to say a word I launched into him. 'Look at that, Porky, you've lost us all our money. It's all gone. Why did you choose black? That's your prejudice against Liverpool showing.'

He was speechless. Then he started trying to get angry. 'You irresponsible idiot,' he barked. 'You've just lost us all our money.'

'No,' I countered, 'you lost it. It came out of your pocket and you called black.'

I couldn't keep up the mock anger, and I just burst out laughing. Porky was completely floored. He'd just lost all the company money. I couldn't have cared less. I expected to get that and a lot more back over the next few hours.

'The trouble with you, Al, is that you have the responsibility factor of a sixteen-year-old,' Porky said.

I was laughing even more now at his indignation. He'd had enough. He turned and walked out. Later, I found out he'd had to walk back across town because he had no money.

For me, the night was young. And it was dangerous. Not only did I now have the 'taste', but I had the gambling bug as well. The following morning's breakfast show seemed a very, very long way away.

I had a great night at the tables. I met my pals, we drank a load of champagne, and I listened in admiration to a Frank Sinatra impersonator who was so good that when I closed my eyes it sounded like the real thing. I never looked at my watch, but the moment came when I could sense it was time to go home.

Back in my hotel room, I was just about to get into bed when the stillness of the early hours was disturbed by a fierce knocking on the door.

'Come on, Brazil! Get yourself out of bed, you idle get!'

I looked at my watch. Blimey, I had completely misjudged the time. It was 4.30 a.m. Porky was already up and about. I grabbed an eau de cologne spray and gave myself a few squirts. Assuming an air of total confidence, though wearing only a green pair of boxer shorts, I snatched the door open.

'What's all the noise?' I said. 'You'll wake everybody up.'

I completely took the wind out of Porky's sails.

'You're up,' he said, incredulously.

'Of course I'm up. I've just got out of the shower.'

'Great, well, that's marvellous. I'll leave you to it then,' said a delighted Porky. 'Remember, the studio's just down on the left.'

'No problem,' I said.

I closed the door and started laughing again. My mate wasn't half a mug, I thought.

I climbed into bed. I reckoned I could grab a quick hour and still appear bright and fresh for the breakfast show. The next thing I remember was more hammering on the door. The champagne had clearly taken effect because for some reason I thought it was Sunday. I don't know who the door-knocker was – probably one of the production boys – but I told him in no uncertain terms to sling his hook and rolled over.

It could only have been a few minutes later, but it might as well have been hours, when there was a new and more concerted battering on my door. I still thought it was Sunday,

Above: Victory for Celtic Boys Club in the Amateur Scottish Cup Final. I'm at the back. Holding the cup is Roy Aitken who went on to be the captain of Celtic and Scotland.

Below: Celtic Boys Club at the end of another successful season. I'm at the back again!

Left: Getting the better of my good pal Gordon McQueen as Ipswich trounced Manchester United 6-0. I later played with Gordon at United.

Above: Pre-match meal with the boss, Bobby Robson. I owe him a lot for shaping my career.

Left: Even as a kid I was lucky enough to be picking up trophies. My mum and dad still have this collection.

Left: At Foxhall Stadium. Hitching a ride with Dave Langham, the star rider with the Ipswich Witches speedway team. Bobby Robson would have had a heart attack if he'd seen this.

Below: My first sponsored car – a Talbot, embarrassingly with my name painted on the side. But it was my first real motor and I was very proud of it.

Right: I created a club record at Ipswich when I scored five goals against Southampton in one game in February 1982. Happy supporters escorted me off the pitch.
(© Popperfoto)

Left: Here I get the better of Southampton stalwart Nick Holmes on the way to another goal when I grabbed five against Southampton – including a seventeen minute hat-trick
(© Popperfoto).

Right: Posing with the ball after I scored my five-goal salvo against Southampton. The picture was used on the front of the programme for the next home game versus Everton.
(© Popperfoto)

I loved playing night games under lights. Here I am battling with West Brom defender Brendon Batson, who was until recently the Deputy Chief Executive of the PFA. (© Popperfoto)

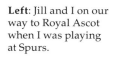

Left: Jill and I on our way to Royal Ascot when I was playing at Spurs.

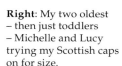

Right: My two oldest – then just toddlers – Michelle and Lucy trying my Scottish caps on for size.

Left: Balance was an important part of my game and here I get the better of West Brom's Bryan Robson, who remains a firm friend to this day.

Right: The day after I scored my five goals against Southampton I met one of the world's most famous ever racehorses – Shergar – in his box at Newmarket. Shergar was later kidnapped and never seen again.

but this time it was the unmistakable voice of Porky bellowing out. I could hear he was going mad, and the mists of confusion slowly started lifting. I looked at my watch. Crikey, it was seven minutes to six.

'OK, OK,' I said. 'Sorry, Porky, I just dozed off for a few minutes while catching up with the news. I'll be right out.'

But as I tried to lift myself out of bed I realised my back had locked up. I had been forced out of professional football at the age of 27, and every now and then my dodgy discs still floored me. This was going to be tough. I was never going to make the start of the show. I thought about just giving it up altogether and going back to bed, but I wasn't totally uncaring about Porky's predicament so I pressed on.

I had to literally crawl on my hands and knees to the studio. When I got there I was absolutely exhausted, floating around in a world of my own. Thank God there was a couch for me to lie on. I lay there watching Porky trying to get the show out on his own. He was struggling. I could see the seething anger in his face. He should have been concentrating on broadcasting, but he was gnarled up about me. I've got a wicked sense of humour, and I found it all quite amusing.

On the coffee table in front of me was a big bowl of sweets. I fancied a bit of chocolate so I picked up the dish, balanced it on my stomach and started nibbling away. I was in a very mischievous mood. Whatever sin I had committed, it was now too late to put it right. To wind up Porky, I started throwing sweets at him at crucial moments. Just as he was about to introduce the traffic I would whack a coffee cream at the bald patch on his head; when he was about to cross over to our reporter at the England camp, ping, a chocolate-covered raisin hit him right in the eye.

At the first break he ripped off his headphones. After a brief exchange of views it was decided there was little point in me joining the show. He demanded a meeting downstairs at midday.

After a few hours' sleep I had a shower and spruced myself up to take the flak. Thankfully, my back had settled down and I was much more awake now, feeling remiss for leaving my pal in the lurch. Nevertheless, I could not be putting up with lectures.

Porky was just about to launch into a 'how dare you' tirade in the lobby of our hotel when a delegation from the FA appeared. Porky's a terrible groveller to the footballing authorities, so his attitude immediately turned to charm and friendliness. This gave me the opportunity to defuse his anger, and before he could get into his stride again I had steered him across the road from the hotel to a little Italian restaurant we had used the day before.

As we walked in we were greeted like heroes. That was probably because we and our crew had drunk the place out of Pinot Grigio. Luckily, our arrival coincided with the arrival of new stocks, one poor fellow having to stagger up the street with two cases balanced on his shoulders. I got a few glasses down my partner's throat and, as ever, he started to calm down. He'd clearly had a hard time from London.

As the wine started to flow in quantity, our conversation began to turn around in circles. We weren't sure whose fault it was that I missed the show that morning. Maybe it was the hotel for not giving me an alarm call, or perhaps Porky should blame himself for leaving me in the casino the night before? We were soon best friends again. It turned into a friendly and sociable afternoon with all sorts of other journalists and broadcasters popping in and out of the restaurant.

When it got to seven p.m., we remembered we had a football match to go to. The whole purpose of us being there was for the Holland v. England game in the Ajax Amsterdam ArenA, which was due to kick off in two hours' time. We grabbed a cab and set off. I knew that Porky had completely lost it when he started leaning out of the window of the car singing 'Three Lions on My Shirt'. Every time we passed a group of England fans he urged the cab driver to hoot his horn while he punched the air and chanted 'Angler-Mania', which somebody had told him was Dutch for 'English'. I tried to shut him up because my previous experiences of Holland were that the riot police belt you first and ask questions later.

Sure enough, when we arrived at the stadium there was a huge police presence. When I was playing for Scotland, one of the bonuses of going abroad was to see the Tartan Army in their thousands around the football grounds. They built up a reputation over decades of being well behaved. But England fans had done completely the opposite. Bad behaviour down the years at club and international level had made them the pariahs of the Continent. Whenever we went to an England game there was always an uncompromising attitude towards the boys who were swathed in the flag of St George.

The driver dropped us on the road to the ground and there was the usual cacophony of noise and mêlée of people that surround a football ground. Above this, I was suddenly aware of a tremendous noise to my left. When I looked up, I saw a full-scale baton charge of mounted police almost on top of us. I pushed Porky in one direction and threw myself back in the other. That was it. I wasn't going to stick around in this sort of atmosphere. I mean, I had to be coerced into watching England games at the best of times.

It was a cold and windy February night, and the hotel bar and a TV screen seemed a very sensible alternative. As a result, I got an early night. But the same could not be said for Porky. He got in with a group of fans after England and Holland drew 1–1, a result that clearly hadn't pleased my pal. He was there in plenty of time the next morning, but I could tell from his non-stop talking that he was not fully compos mentis. As the show got going he seemed normal enough, but then I asked him probably the simplest question of the week: 'So, Porky, what's your verdict on last night's game?'

I wasn't looking at him as I asked the question; I was adjusting the volume levels on my headphones. I thought I must have turned them down too far because I couldn't hear his reply. But when I looked at him I realised he had lost it. His eyes were staring at me and they were completely blank. There was nothing going on in his brain. He wasn't at all sure about the question. Battling to plug the gap, I said, 'I know you weren't happy with England's performance here in Holland, but surely it's not rendered you speechless?' That kick-started his head. He started laughing. It was a false laugh to me, but he was trying to even up his silence with the audience. To give the boy his due, he has remarkable powers of recovery. Once I had pushed a cue sheet on the game in front of him, he was away. I spent the next four hours trying to shut him up.

The reason my broadcasting partner had lost his momentum over the Holland result was because he had wanted revenge against the people he called 'the cloggies' for a 2–0 defeat in England the previous August. Porky is the very worst sort of arrogant England fan who believes that his nation have a God-given superiority and a right to rule the game. As far as he is concerned, the World Cup is 'permanently on loan to pretenders to the Crown'. So you can imagine what he was like in Germany – a few months earlier – when England achieved their stunning 5–1 victory on their way to the World Cup finals in Japan and South Korea.

I had left the stadium in Munich a quarter of an hour before the end of the game and I was safely locked up in my room well ahead of the first English fan arriving back at our hotel. Porky, apparently, stayed in the ground for a full hour after the final whistle, delirious at England's admittedly brilliant performance. The English victory I could take, but Porky's boasting I could not. He stayed up all night in the lounge of our hotel with hundreds of fans, liberally dishing out the bubbly. Several times our co-commentator at the game, Alvin Martin, tried to make it to bed, but each time Porky persuaded him to stay 'a few more minutes' to share with the fans the glory and the honour of representing his country. In the end, Alvin, a naturally modest and unassuming man, paid the night porter to lock Porky in the champagne cellar while he made his getaway.

***

Most European cities have something to offer, in terms of their culture, their architecture or their people, but there is one place that for me will always top the list of 'best places to go'. Monaco.

As far as I am concerned, this little principality in the south of France is *the* place. I hope one day that I can pack up my bags and maybe persuade Jill to move there for good. So you can imagine how delighted I was when I discovered that we were heading out there for Chelsea's Champions League semi-final against Monaco in April 2004.

The previous year I had been invited out there for the Grand Prix, which must easily be the most glamorous sporting event ever staged. I spent three days on a pal's yacht doing absolutely nothing except drinking champagne, soaking up the sun and indulging in a modicum of gambling. I have to steer away from the casinos in Monte Carlo because there you are dealing with some very high rollers who can lose my annual earnings with one throw of the dice.

It is a privilege just to be there. You can scent the money wafting around in the air. I don't know who invented the expression 'the beautiful people', but I can tell you that they all live in Monaco. I am unashamedly in favour of wealth and consumerism. I sit very happily with the culture of Rolex watches, expensive cars, large drink bills and the company of the rich and the famous. That is not because I want to hang on to these people's coat-tails. Far from it. They inspire me to want to become one of them. And anybody who has made him- or herself a fortune sizeable enough to be able to live in this opulent community usually has a very interesting story to tell. Also, once the rich have consolidated their fortunes, they gravitate towards the famous, so you find yourself sitting in a restaurant next to Sir Roger Moore or Sir Elton John. Believe me, that is a better experience than finding yourself in a burger bar in the middle of Workington – with the greatest respect to that fine Cumbrian town.

On the yacht one year I spent an afternoon with Audley Harrison, who was then an up-and-coming boxer. I was at the front of the boat with a glass of bubbly in my hand talking to a couple of pals who were London financiers when suddenly the sun seemed to have gone in. When I looked up I realised it had been blotted out by the arrival of a huge man who I did not at first recognise.

He fired a question at me: 'Are you Alan Brazil?'

I nodded.

With a look of slight disdain on his face, he added, 'From talkSPORT?'

'Yes,' I said, starting to worry about what was going on here.

'And you work with that muppet Parry?'

I nodded again, starting to feel a slight sense of relief that this giant of a guy wasn't homing in on me but on Porky. 'Oh, yes,' I said. 'Yes, I work with him, and, yes, he is certainly a muppet.'

Porky, who thought he was an expert on boxing, had been slating Harrison ever since he won his gold medal at the Olympics in Australia in 2000. He had accused him of being too old to become a top professional and ridiculed his ambitions to win the world heavyweight crown.

'Yeah,' said the big man. 'You tell him that Audley Harrison would like a little word with him if he would like to pop around to my gym.'

With that he burst out laughing and offered me a gigantic spread of five fingers of muscle and bone. I, too, erupted into laughter and shook his hand warmly.

Our talkSPORT trip to Monaco in April 2004 didn't really start in the style I would have liked. I prefer to go there on a business class flight, sipping champagne to get me warmed up for the fun ahead. Unfortunately, this time it was to be easyJet. But, what the hell. Porky and I stocked up with our own champagne before we got on the plane, and, after a quick word with one of the lovely hostesses, we fixed ourselves up at the back of the plane with a couple of spare seats. I wasn't asking for any special treatment because all the other passengers had presumably paid the same for their tickets as we had for ours. The plane was full of football fans heading out for the big game, and through having been a player and now hosting the talkSPORT breakfast show, I was a very well-known figure. I love meeting the fans, signing their autographs and posing for pictures, but on planes in particular that can be very disruptive, and the crew understood that.

In our little conclave at the back we were with Frank Lampard senior, father of the Chelsea star, who was with other members of his family. There were also a couple of chaps from a big sponsorship company. It was a good job that Porky and I had thought ahead on the booze front because the flight is less than two hours and the drinks trolley was starting at the front of the plane. It was going to be a long time before it got down to the back. To the relief of those around us we produced the bubbly and a couple of bottles of white and red wine.

Everybody happily got stuck in, except for one guy in the window seat one removed from Porky's aisle seat. To this day we have no idea who he was, but it was obvious from his attitude that not only was he not a football fan, he clearly disapproved of those who were. In fact, he seemed to disapprove of almost everything. He had taken his own brown wholemeal bread sandwiches out of his holdall and was nibbling them while sipping water from a bottle that was labelled 'distilled'. He was hunched forward over his table reading some sort of biblical book, and every time a fan came up and asked me or Frank Lampard for an autograph he looked up disapprovingly. He clearly also disliked the popping of champagne corks and the consumption of any form of alcohol, judging by the dirty looks he gave us whenever we laughed at each other's jokes. You couldn't help but take the mickey. I started referring to him in hushed tones as 'the evangelist', while Porky branded him 'Joe 90', because his thick black-rimmed spectacles made him look like the puppet character from the show we all watched as kids.

Sooner than we would have wished, we were all told to take our seats for landing. My heart lifted as the plane tilted to the right to reveal the sparkling Mediterranean Sea below us. As I slid into my seat I handed a full glass of red wine to Porky and asked him to finish it off. At that precise moment the plane banked to the left and dropped very suddenly. It was only for a split-second, but it caused everybody's heart to skip a beat. There were no casualties ... except for the evangelist. Porky had been holding the red in his left hand, and as the plane dipped and then dropped the wine shot out of his glass and went all over the evangelist's face. It also hit the ceiling above him and soaked his book, and what was left of his wholemeal butties.

We watched as a very fine red Merlot dripped off the ceiling on to his head. He couldn't see through his Joe 90 glasses because they were smeared. The wine was also dripping off the end of his nose; he looked like a little kid with a snowdrop on the end of his hooter in winter. The poor guy seemed to be in shock. His body had reflexed as though somebody had put an ice cube down the back of his shirt. His mouth was opening and closing like a fish but nothing was coming out.

Everybody burst out laughing. This was not stifled amusement. This was Benny Hill and Tommy Cooper all rolled into one. I could not contain myself. I had to take off my seat belt otherwise I was going to choke with convulsions.

The only person showing a modicum of concern and restraint was Porky. He had grabbed a white serviette from somewhere and was trying to wipe the evangelist's glasses for him. He also started mopping down the man's white shirt, and tried to dry out his book. Porky was still apologising profusely when the plane came to a standstill. The evangelist still hadn't said a word. Porky reached into his pocket, stuffed a pile of notes into the guy's hand and said, 'That will help with the dry-cleaning.' Then, as the doors were still opening, he grabbed his bag and bolted off the plane. We weren't far behind him.

The following day we were up at 4.30 a.m. That can be a problem for me in the wilds of Suffolk in November, but it is no problem in Monte Carlo. We had set up a broadcasting studio in a suite in a hotel on the front. I stood on the balcony as the light came up and the view was everything I'd been thinking about over the past week. I'm sure there were more yachts berthed in the harbour that morning than you would see vehicles in a Tesco car park in Birmingham. They were all shapes and sizes: sleek, white-hulled vessels, some with sails, many just giant motor launches, and others that looked more like cruise liners.

In the middle of this opulent array, one yacht stood out. It was clearly too big to come right into the harbour so it was anchored out in the bay. There was no problem about getting ashore as there was a tender tethered to its side and a helicopter sitting on a pad above the deck. It was the *Pelarus*, the biggest boat in the fleet belonging to Chelsea owner Roman Abramovich. Clearly he was in town for the game that night – but, wow, talk about arriving in style. I wondered how any one man could acquire enough wealth to be able to maintain a fleet of yachts. I had read somewhere that it cost half a million US dollars just to fill the

Pelarus up with fuel. Would I want the responsibility of that sort of wealth? I wondered to myself. For about half a second. Then I decided, 'Yes!'

Porky and I produced a wonderful show, even though I say it myself. We had brought out the old Chelsea record 'Blue is the Colour', and for four hours we became honorary Chelsea fans willing them on to victory that evening. The minute the show finished I was popping a cork into the clear blue sky. We were due to go to lunch with a bunch of high-rolling Chelsea fans in the Café de Paris in Casino Square. I hoped we would bump into Terry Venables and Ken Bates because they had invited us out to dinner the night before but we had arrived too late to be able to go.

Ken has always been great to me and I hated letting him down. He had moved to Monaco after selling Chelsea to Mr Abramovich. He received £17 million for his shareholding, and a few days later he told me over lunch in Langan's Brasserie in London that he intended to spend a million a year until he died. But he was 72 then, and as he expected to live until well over a hundred he joked that he might have to get a job as a radio broadcaster to fund the shortfall. Thank goodness he's back in the football business with Leeds. What a character.

Lunch in the Square lived up to every expectation. On our table was one of the boys who made up the singing group Tenors Unlimited – a class act if ever I heard one. These guys performed all over the world. He gave us a short rendition of 'Nessun Dorma', but being a professional singer in a busy open-air restaurant he didn't want to perform the whole thing. I could accept this. When I was a professional I would not have played football in the streets, for all the obvious reasons. But some of the guests on our table urged him to sing more. He clearly didn't want to, and just as the situation was starting to become tiresome Porky put on his diplomatic hat and decided to defuse the situation. The problem with Porky is that after a few glasses of wine he thinks he is smarter than the average bear. He suddenly jumped up from his seat and shouted out, 'Come on now, let's be fair. The guy's given us a rendition and we should be grateful for that.'

So far, so good. But I wasn't anticipating what happened next.

'You want to hear singing, I'll give you singing.'

Alarm bells started ringing in my head. All of a sudden there's my broadcasting partner up on the table delivering his version of the Beatles classic 'When I'm Sixty-Four'. I tried to get under the table to avoid the embarrassment, but there wasn't room. Porky was off. 'When I get older, losing my hair, many years from now, will you still be sending me your Valentine, birthday greetings, bottle of wine ...'

I didn't know what to do. Here we were in the centre of the most affluent and sophisticated city in the world surrounded wall-to-wall by zillionaires, and my mate was belting out a Beatles song to keep them entertained. I thought about grabbing his leg and throwing him off the table, but the fat get might have landed on somebody and hurt them. I tried to look away.

'If I stayed out till quarter to three, would you lock the door ...'

It was excruciating. I had to leave the table. Strangely, though, the lads who were with us were enjoying this impromptu performance and clapping along. And as he finished off with 'Will you still need me, will you still feed me, when I'm sixty-four?' he got a rousing ovation from the crowd in Casino

Square. It was a pity Porky had got up on the table, though, because we all got up and drifted off and he was left to settle the bill. And lunches for twelve don't come cheap in Monaco. Weeks later I remember seeing Porky arguing with the finance director in the office, trying to convince him that the £3,000 bill was actually for the hire of a studio rather than a lavish lunch, overflowing with wine.

There was another problem on the company credit card which Porky also had to deal with. On the way back to our hotel I diverted the taxi to one of my favourite hotels in the south of France, La Reserve de Beaulieu. I've been captivated by it ever since I first went there as an Ipswich player. From the bar it has a wonderful sweeping view of the sea, and you can sit out on the rocks and enjoy a delightful glass of red with the breeze coming in off the water. And there's a particular label of red wine there that I believe is the best in the world.

Porky and I settled into our seats and the waiter arrived with the magic bottle. Porky agreed it was indeed a fine bouquet. So much so that he insisted on ordering another.

'Are you sure?' I said. 'It's quite an expensive wine.'

'Rubbish,' said Porky. 'It tastes great, and you have to pay for quality. What's a few bob when you're looking after your palate?'

The second bottle duly arrived, and then, unfortunately, so did the bill. It was £500. The problem was that Porky had miscalculated the price when he ordered it. The price was in euros, but he was the only person in France still working in francs and he had divided the figure by ten. I was back in the taxi laughing my head off and urging him to hurry up while, for the second time that day, Porky argued the toss with a French waiter over a drinks bill.

***

From a personal point of view, my most enjoyable foray into Europe was in May 2003 when we went to Spain to broadcast from Seville, where my beloved Celtic were contesting the UEFA Cup final with Porto. It was a bittersweet trip, because though it was marvellous to be among my own people in the sunshine of Spain, we lost the match to the team being coached by Jose Mourinho. It was little consolation that Porto went on to win the European Cup the following year. We didn't know it in Seville, but the legend of Jose Mourinho, 'the special one', was about to be born.

Seville was a nuisance to get to. I couldn't figure out why a final was taking place in what looked like such a small and remote town. We had to fly in and out of Madrid to get there, and Porky was thrilled when we twice flew over the Bernabeu and got a majestic perspective on Real Madrid's ground. Even I was impressed by the place. I had made my European debut for Ipswich at Barcelona's Camp Nou, which is still the best stadium in which I ever played, but looking straight down from the sky at the Bernabeu, with its sheer sides and three-tier-high stands, I knew I would have loved to play there just as much.

Memories stirred in me of the ultimate European competition and the Lions of Lisbon. We were flying south towards Gibraltar, and with my rough schoolboy geography I reckoned we couldn't be more than a few hundred miles away from the Portuguese capital. Strange thoughts, I know, but that's what happens when you're still a fan.

The hairs first started to bristle on the back of my neck when we started our ascent into the town. I'm not sure what we were looking at below, but it resembled a huge green and white tablecloth laid out in the middle of a desert. On closer inspection it became clear it was a campsite full of Celtic fans which had been set up on the edge of town. My people. I hadn't been camping since I was in the boy scouts, but right now I wanted to be down there with them. I would forgo a warm shower and a soft bed for one night to be around the campfire with the boys. Well, almost.

Actually, as we landed, I realised how much I was looking forward to reaching the hotel. It had been a very long day. Porky and I had been up at four a.m. for the breakfast show, we'd been part of a presentation team to potential sponsors at lunchtime, and we'd just completed a five hour split-flight to Seville. And in a few hours' time we would be doing another breakfast show.

The problem was, the moment I walked into our hotel I was greeted like a long-lost son by a huge group of Celtic fans. Among them were some old school friends and also some mates from the City of London who wouldn't normally be found in the middle of a crowd of well-lubricated football fans. Tartan bonhomie was flowing everywhere. So was some rather average-tasting sparkling Spanish wine. I came back to life, and within an hour we were in a piano bar somewhere singing 'Flower of Scotland'.

Seville had been taken over by thousands of Scotsmen and their green and white shirts and flags, many of whom clearly didn't have anywhere to sleep. When we got back to the hotel bar Porky peeled off to bed, but within a few minutes he was back down in the bar with a face like thunder. He was complaining that there were two drunken Scotsmen sleeping in his bed and demanding that the barman find the manager. He said it was a disgrace and an outrage. I took him to one side and broke the bad news. On our tour of the bars that evening I had bumped into an old Glaswegian mate. He had with him his 76-year-old father-in-law, a former coal miner who suffered from emphysema. Neither of them had a bed for the night, so I took pity on the old guy and gave them Porky's room. Porky was raging. 'Calm down,' I told him. There were two full-sized beds in my room and he could have one of those. But that only made him half-happy. He knew there was always the chance I might invite a few pals up to the room for a nightcap. He stormed off to bed. In the event, that would have been too harsh, and I too called it a day.

The following morning after the breakfast show Porky and I went drive-about. We had to do a reconnaissance of the stadium for the game that night and work out a route back home that would not take hours. Following a back road, we came across what looked like a farm building from which emanated the sound of a noisy gang of Scotsmen. Curious as to what was going on, we followed the trail through to what looked like a mini bullring. It transpired that we were actually at a rearing farm where young bulls were trained in the art of facing matadors.

In the middle of a high wooden ring there was one of my countrymen facing a bull. The animal must have been very young because it was no more than three feet high. But instead of standing in front of this mini-beast with a cloak, the Celtic fan in the middle was bending over, pulling up his kilt and baring his backside at the animal. The fact that he was holding a half-empty bottle of sangria in his hand gave us some indication of the fact that his judgement may have been impaired. The little bull galloped around a few times, then headed straight for him. He led with his head and smashed straight into the man's behind, propelling him right off his feet and very rapidly about ten yards forwards into the wooden wall. Everybody was helpless with laughter. It was one of the funniest things I have ever seen. If you tried to stage it in a television show it could never be as funny.

The drunken 'toreador', stunned by his collision with the wall, staggered to his feet, and, in a mad attempt to try to regain some dignity in front of his helpless mates, he lined up to take on the bull again. This time he was going to face it. He crouched down like a man in a rugby scrum with one hand on the ground to steady himself. With the other hand he beckoned the bull forwards, but at first it showed no interest. It just trotted around the edge of the ring. But then, as the Scotsman's quiet whisper turned to a roar, the animal responded and charged towards him. Amazingly, the Scotsman, whose reflexes had clearly been slowed by drink, attempted to head-butt the bull, but his body was still arched back when the animal trampled all over him. He was left a writhing, moaning mass on the dusty floor, but in distinctive style he never released his grip on the bottle.

I don't know whether the 'toreador' ever made the game that night, but I'm happy to report that two young lads did. Porky and I were back at the hotel that afternoon when we came across two youngsters aged about sixteen who had hitch-hiked across Europe to the game. They looked like they had been on the road for a week. Their Celtic shirts were torn and they didn't look as though they'd had a decent meal for days. We bought them food and drink and discovered that they had come all this way without even a ticket for the game. I looked at them and realised that I could have been looking at myself at their age. I dragged Porky away and put a suggestion to him. He agreed. We called the lads over. I will never forget the look on their faces as long as I live when I handed them our two tickets. They both started crying.

Porky and I spent the rest of the afternoon calling in favours from the gentlemen of the press. An hour before the game, we managed to blag our way into the press box. Unfortunately, Celtic lost 3–2 after extra time. And, believe me, sparkling Spanish wine isn't anywhere near as good at numbing the pain as the real thing. Where was that bottle of Bollinger when I needed it?

CHAPTER FIVE

ON THE GALLOPS

By the time I left the course I was carrying my money in four Sainsbury's carrier bags. I had a total of nearly £40,000 in cash. Going back over the Pennines, our car looked like it was carrying the proceeds of the Great Train Robbery.

I WAS sure that death was imminent. My only consolation was that I was going to breathe my last on Newmarket Heath. I had long believed that if there is a heaven on earth, then truly it is on these sprawling green acres at the HQ of the racing industry. But at that very moment there was nothing pleasant about the turf beneath my feet, for I was speeding over it at a hell of a pace on the back of a horse that was out of control.

For some reason, Blackie, an old hack that was used by trainers to follow their strings while exercising them, had suddenly gone mad. I had been pootling around in the early-morning mist on the edge of the heath when the horse suddenly decided we were going on an unplanned journey. It bolted, and started to gather pace. 'Whoa, boy, steady, steady!' I shouted while trying to contain my panic, to show the horse that I wasn't frightened. But Blackie was having none of it. In fact, things just got worse. The horse veered to the left, gathered even more pace, and headed down the slope towards the main road at the bottom.

I pulled hard on the reins but it had absolutely no effect. I was sitting on half a ton of horse that by now seemed to be completely out of control. It was like being in a sports car with a steering wheel that wouldn't turn, an accelerator jammed to the floor, and no brakes. Alarm turned to blind panic as the beast galloped along. It was impossible now to hide the fear in my voice. 'Stop, Blackie, stop! Please don't do this to me!' I had to resort to expletives too.

They say a drowning man sees his life flash before him as he goes under for the third time. That was happening to me. At the time I was a professional footballer at the top of my career and I was about to be killed by a mad horse that looked intent on either leaping or crashing through the fence at the bottom of the hill on to a busy road. I thought about my wife and children. Would they lose the house? What was my manager Bobby Robson going to say about losing one of his star strikers to a riding accident? He'd go mad, because we were banned by our insurance policies from taking part in anything dangerous. I had been the subject of an awful number of newspaper headlines over the previous few years, and I could see another one in my head now: 'Brazil Killed in Bolting Horse Terror'.

Fear and panic had indeed turned to terror. I was screaming for help. I heard myself shouting to Blackie, 'I'll give you carrots, boy, a big bag of carrots, if you will just bloody well stop!' I think horses can reach a maximum speed of only about 30 miles an hour, but I honestly reckoned Blackie was doing about 60. I was hanging on to his neck looking down at the ground, and it seemed to be flashing by at a very rapid rate. I thought about trying to throw myself off, but I'd seen too many jockeys suffer crippling injuries in falls and figured that, even if I survived, it would probably spell the end of my football career.

Then a string of horses came round the turn at the bottom of the hill. Thank God, I thought, they'll rescue me. But, as I went bolting past them, waving one arm and shouting, 'Help, help, my horse is out of control!', they all fell about laughing. They were stable lads and apprentice jockeys. Couldn't the bastards see I was in perilous danger?

The fence loomed in front of me. I tried digging my heels into Blackie's rump as though I was a cowboy in the Wild West with spurs. I attempted to block his sight, but nothing worked.

I suddenly remembered I was a good Catholic boy and started praying to God. I don't know if I should thank the Lord or whether it was just coincidental, but, seconds later, Blackie suddenly stopped and I was thrown forwards out of the saddle on to his neck. I instinctively grabbed his head, but he lowered his neck and I slid straight over his ears and nose on to the ground. My heart was pounding as though I had just run three lengths of a football field, and I was drenched in sweat. I was lying there looking up at the beast and I am certain I detected a look of contempt on his face. I don't know if horses can smile, but Blackie pulled his gums back and showed me a full set of teeth. I was just glad to be alive.

Years later, I shuddered when I read the story about *Superman* actor Christopher Reeve being paralysed from the neck down after coming off his horse. He had tangled up the reins in his hand as he went to ground and landed flush on top of his head, crushing his spinal cord. He described it as like a hammer hitting a nail perfectly on the head. That could so easily have happened to me, I thought.

I lay on the ground on the heath as the trainer came cantering over. After enquiring whether I was all right, he said, 'You've been out too long. Blackie was just telling you that he wanted to go home for his breakfast.' If only horses could talk, I thought.

From that day to this I have never sat on a horse. On one occasion there was an event at talkSPORT which involved promoting a show we were broadcasting from York races. I was asked to get on the back of a horse, but I refused. I would rather have lost my job. In the end I posed for photographers on the back of one of those 'bucking bronco' game machines – while it was completely static, of course.

The experience didn't, of course, affect my love affair with horses and racing, which, as I've mentioned, began after I arrived at Ipswich as a kid and started taking days out to Newmarket with some of the senior pros. Prior to that I had absolutely no interest in the turf. If ever I was housebound as a youngster with the flu or an injury I would flick the telly on but I would watch anything other than racing. It simply never appealed to me. That all changed when I started making very-early-morning forays to Newmarket Heath.

Because of its proximity to the horse-racing world, there were always people about at Ipswich who in one way or another were attached to the bloodstock industry. They would range from multimillionaire owners through very successful trainers down to stable lads who in many ways are the backbone of the industry and who, mostly, love football almost as much as they love horses. After games at Portman Road there would always be somebody around in the lounges who would invite a few of the players over to their yard in Newmarket – or, better still, to their lavish homes on race days.

On a day off I would usually go over to Newmarket in the morning with fellow Ipswich players Eric Gates, Paul Cooper and Kevin O'Callaghan. I would leap out of bed at five a.m., rendezvous with the boys and be in Newmarket by six. Some trainers took their first lot of horses out just as the sun was coming up, and there is no finer sight for me than to see a string of horses emerging from the misty early-morning shadows on to the heath. In the summer the skies are invariably clear over

Newmarket and a fierce wind can whip through the air. It is like being desanitised of everything else you do in life. You focus on the landscape and the majestic bloodstock and the men on their backs who guide them so skilfully across the turf. Often when I am looking at a horse in full flight I suffer a visual mirage, and the animal doesn't look as though it even has legs. It just seems to drift at lightning pace through the atmosphere, nose straining out in front. For me, it's a picture of utter magnificence.

Once on the gallops the horses would pound away, their manes flowing horizontally behind them as their trainers tried to bring them to peak fitness for a forthcoming race.

It's one of the most magical sounds in the world for me, the rhythmic beat of horses' hooves on turf (I have a Clint Eastwood movie at home on DVD which I often put on just for the sound of an army of horses approaching from beyond the ridge). An hour after the first horses a second string would appear to be put through their paces. The trainer would always sit majestically on his hack watching the progress of his steeds.

As a young footballer there were not a lot of people I envied in life, but a trainer was one of them. Some of the boys I knew were so involved with racing that they had ambitions to go into the game when they finished with football. Many tried and failed, but there are two notable exceptions. Former Newcastle and Coventry striker Micky Quinn runs a yard almost single-handedly in Newmarket, and to this day I love having a few drinks with him on a Sunday in a club in the centre of the town. Considering his limited resources he has had tremendous success, with a regular stream of winners. Micky was a tough, bustling centre forward who played successfully for fifteen years, and he puts all the passion and energy he displayed then into racing today. He works with us sometimes at talkSPORT, and could do a lot more in that field with his Merseyside wit and humour, but he loves the racing world.

The other massive success story is Mick Channon, one of the most successful trainers in this country. He controls a massive spread at West Ilsley, near Newbury in Berkshire. The famous story about Mick is that his manager at Southampton, Lawrie McMenemy, was once giving the team talk before an important cup game. Mick was sitting in the corner of the dressing room reading the *Sporting Life*, which was then the bible of racing. McMenemy shouted at him and told him to pay attention. The international star striker got up and said, in that rural burr of his, 'Gaffer, how many times have I got to tell you, football is only my hobby.' Some hobby. He played 46 times for England.

But, for me, while I was still a footballer, getting involved in the horse-racing business was just a distant dream. For the time being I just wanted to soak up the wonderful atmosphere of its culture.

After we had seen two lots of horses on the heath we would retreat for breakfast. Often we would go to the home of top trainer Clive Brittain. His yard was called Carlburg, on the Bury Road near to the Bedford Lodge Hotel. Mr Brittain's principal owner was a Greek shipping magnate by the name of Captain Marcos Lemos. He was a regular guest at Ipswich Town FC. That was the way in which connections were made between the racing industry and football. We would arrive at about eight o'clock and the sound of sizzling bacon and bubbling sausages greeted us as we entered the yard. That and the smell of sweating horse flesh as the animals returned to their boxes are, for me, the aromas that most signify the racing business. In that huge kitchen we'd be served the best cooked breakfast I have ever had anywhere in the world. Often it was done by Mr Brittain's wife, Maureen, or it was served up by one of the maids. Full of fried tomatoes, eggs, mushrooms, bacon and sausages, we would then make our way back on to the heath for the final lot of horses to be brought out, at around 9.15.

All this, and the day had not really even begun. We would return to the house and go into one of the reception rooms for a few glasses of champagne to discuss what we had all seen on the gallops that morning. Then other guests of the trainers and his owners who were there for the day's racing would start to arrive, and if they wanted to talk football we were always very happy to oblige.

Sometimes, if it wasn't a race day at Newmarket, I would receive an invitation from an owner or a trainer to join him in his helicopter to go off to a track where he had a horse running that day. The first time it happened I was hesitant. It wasn't that I didn't want to go to a race meeting. I loved them. But the previous year I had been on tour with Ipswich to Canada, and in the ski resort of Whistler I had taken a helicopter ride that was so terrifying I vowed never to fly in one again.

I was being taken for a trip over the mountain while the boys were training because I had twisted my foot. The moment I arrived at the aerodrome I didn't like the look of the machine at all. I had never been in a chopper before, and this one, close-up, looked like nothing more than a bubble with a rotor blade on the top. It looked so fragile to me that I couldn't believe it wasn't going to be blown all over the place by the winds that swirled around the mountain. I made my fears known to the flight organiser, but he was dismissive. 'There is no safer aircraft in existence,' he said. 'You look at the records. Flying is safer than driving your car, and helicopters are safer than aeroplanes. And, anyway, I've got you Alain as your pilot. He's my best man.' Not wanting to appear to chicken out, I reluctantly agreed to go.

I regretted it the minute the machine lifted off the ground. It was as if we were just floating. You didn't feel like you had the security of a floor and a wall and a window around you. It was just one great big glass bowl, and the pilot appeared to be flying it by whacking a gearstick around. The sooner this was over, the better. The higher we got, the more my stomach seemed to sink. It went too high to feel that I would survive if it fell to earth, but not high enough to give me the confidence that it was a proper flying machine that belonged in the air.

As we approached the mountain, coated in fir trees, we suddenly dipped forwards and started losing height.

'Goddamn it,' said Alain, more in irritation than concern, 'looks like we've hit a bit of down-draught.'

I was petrified. I held on to something on the roof, though I'm not sure that would have done me any good had we crashed. I just needed something to hang on to.

We were now clearly heading for the mountain. I was just as petrified as I was that day I was on Blackie, but at least I had some sort of control on a horse. I could kick my stirrups into it and wave my hand in front of its eyes. The most terrifying thing was that Alain, instead of concentrating on flying, had his head turned to me and through the earphones was trying to discuss football with me, like we were sitting in a pub in Ipswich. With his baseball cap pulled down over his head and his shades on, I couldn't see any expression on his face.

We were heading towards a cliff, yet he seemed completely unconcerned. Was this guy on drugs or something?

I patted his shoulder frantically and pointed out front. 'The cliff,' I said. 'The cliff. We're going to hit the bloody cliff.'

He didn't react, but at the last moment he flipped his stick and the nose of the chopper lifted and just cleared the rocks. 'A good job I shaved a few inches off that last week,' he remarked, as if to comfort me.

I remembered a fairground ride I'd once been on called the Pirate Ship. It's a wooden boat on a huge bracket that swings to and fro and almost tilts over itself. At the critical point where it reaches its maximum height you get a sense of weightlessness, as if you are not connected to anything solid – and that was exactly how I felt in that helicopter. I was so frightened I thought death might be a better option.

I didn't think things could get worse, but they were about to. Suddenly the copter went into a spin. I don't know if helicopters can loop-the-loop, but that's what I felt the pilot was doing. I was going to be sick, so I stuffed my hanky in my mouth to stop myself from vomiting. 'Please, take me back,' I said when I'd regained the power of speech. I tried to close my eyes but that just made me feel more ill.

Alain must have noticed by now how ill I was looking. 'Don't worry,' he said, 'it's just a bit of fun to liven up the day.'

Mercifully, we soon returned to base. As I got out on to the Tarmac I was literally staggering, weaving from side to side in a manner that had never happened to me when I was drinking. I spent the rest of the day lying on the couch in my hotel bedroom with the curtains drawn.

It was only when the rest of the lads got back from training that I realised I had been set up. Alain was no ordinary pilot.

He was a stunt flyer of both helicopters and aeroplanes who ran his own flying circus. He'd worked on dozens of films, including two James Bond movies. Somebody had told him I was an adventurer who wanted to experience some flying tricks. I tell you, if I'd found out that day who did it I'd have taken him to the top of that mountain and thrown him off it.

But back to Newmarket. I did take the helicopter ride, and then many more after that, because the machines were always at least four seats. They looked more substantial than Alain's bubble, and if you didn't want to look down, you didn't have to.

Another magnificent house we were often invited to belonged to a Lloyd's underwriter named Charles St George. To this day I have never met anybody who has turned themselves out as well as Mr St George. He was a tall, imposing man with a shock of steely grey hair. He wore very expensive dark suits, had beautifully manicured hands and impeccable manners, and carried himself like an emperor. He had a summer house in Newmarket next to the Tattersalls sales ring. It was a magnificent Georgian building, and at that time I had never been inside such an impressive house. It was daunting. A butler always opened the door, and another would be circling with a tray of champagne flutes.

Best of all for me was the fact that in those days Mr St George had connections with the jockeys Lester Piggott and the young American Steve Cauthen. Piggott was and still is the greatest jockey there has ever been. Even to be in the same room as him, let alone engaged in conversation with him, was the stuff of dreams. I sometimes found it hard to believe that it was actually me, a boy from Simshill, who was standing there talking racing with a man who was a living legend. He'd probably been asked a million times before, but he still seemed interested when I enquired about his Derby winners, the greatest horses he had ever ridden, and his most treasured memories. And, of course, you couldn't find a much higher racing authority when it comes to discussing the present day. Jockeys are not allowed to give you tips on horses, but it is fascinating listening to their expert knowledge of the going, the mindset of horses in the stalls, and how certain animals like certain tracks.

I remember once we saw Lester on the opening day of the Craven meeting at Newmarket. I regard the Craven as the proper start of the Flat season, and we must have had a day off from training the following day because on that occasion I remember we were drinking champagne. I don't think Lester sipped more than a tenth of an inch from his glass. He was riding that day, but he always said it seemed more sociable when mingling with the owners to have a glass of champagne in his hand, even if he wasn't going to drink it. He had a little boy staying with him at the time called Christopher, and Paul Mariner and I would play football with him in the back garden.

At the races that afternoon we went to my father-in-law's box. Roy Davis, my wife Jill's dad, was a larger-than-life character who had built up a successful building business. He loved his racing, and his football. He would invite all sorts of celebrities into his boxes at both Newmarket and Portman Road. On this particular day I remember that Robert Sangster, the legendary racehorse owner, spent some time with us. Another guest was Charles Benson, the renowned racing writer, known as 'The Scout' of the *Daily Express*. At the time he was the biggest name in racing journalism, but he was also famous for another reason, one that made him one of the most intriguing men I have ever met. Charlie was a member of the Mayfair set of gamblers that included the billionaire business tycoon Jimmy Goldsmith and the notorious Lord Lucan. Lucan, of course, was at the centre of one of the biggest murder mysteries of the last century. Benson was said to have been with him, playing cards with a group of friends, on the last night he was ever seen.

I've always wondered whether Charlie Benson took to his grave the secret of what happened to 'Lucky' Lucan. He was a real character. Once, when we had both had a few drinks, he challenged me to a tennis match. I had just retired from football at the time but I was still pretty fit. Charlie was a bear of a man, and the idea of him prancing around a tennis court was simply ridiculous. The only exercise I could envisage him ever taking part in was sprinting to the bookies and back to place a bet. I assumed he had had too much to drink; it was preposterous that he could compete with me on the court. I had been a professional athlete for about twelve years and I was quite useful with a racket because I had played a lot when Ipswich were on the road. So I turned him down, in the same way I would turn down the challenge of a boxing match by a ten-year-old kid. It wasn't fair to allow a man to involve himself in something in which he would get massacred. Naturally Charlie wanted a wager on the outcome of the game, and he was calling high stakes. That was another reason I turned him down. But he was very persistent, and kept raising the stakes. In the end I agreed to play him, but I insisted that I be handicapped. I had to win each set by four clear games.

On the day in question quite a big crowd of onlookers gathered at a country house just outside Newmarket. I warmed up with a couple of bottles of bubbly before the game. As I stood on the baseline waiting to take Charlie's first serve I was looking at my watch. There was a big race I wanted to watch on the telly in an hour and I felt sure he would have packed it in by then through exhaustion.

I heard a shout from across the net, and then a sound rather like a muffled gunshot which seemed to have come from somewhere around my feet. When I looked up, Charlie was moving to the other side of the court. I was still trying to figure out what was going on when the umpire shouted, 'Fifteen-love.' Very slowly it dawned on me that Benson had sent his first serve down and I hadn't even seen it. What was going on here? I wondered. Then his second serve came whistling down. This time I saw it but I had no hope of getting to it as it kicked up at the very corner of the court. I peered across the net. What the hell was going on? Charlie was wearing a baseball hat with a big peak that obscured most of his face. I was so puzzled that I wondered whether he had put somebody else in to play for him.

I lost that first set after taking only one game. When we changed around, I put it to him that he had obviously played before. 'You didn't tell me that,' I said.

'You didn't ask,' he replied.

It turned out he had in fact been a junior Wimbledon champion and might have turned professional if the lure of the turf had not won out in his affections. He couldn't move around much on the court, but his serves were unreturnable, and he positioned himself so well that I could never get a ball past him. He beat me with ease. I felt like a complete fool and had to shell out on our sizeable bet, though in fairness to Charlie he spent most of it on champagne that afternoon – which was entirely typical of the man.

On another occasion Charlie was around when Robert Sangster invited us to his home in Moulton, just east of Newmarket. It was another magnificent home. There were loads of dignitaries there, many people from Sheikh Mohammed's organisation and one of the greatest pop stars of all time, Rod Stewart. Rod had come because he was a big friend of Mr Sangster, but his biggest interest in life was football, not racing. And when he learnt that a few of the former Ipswich lads were going to be there, especially the Scottish ones, it was an extra incentive to come along. Among other things, we reminisced about the time when we met at his villa near Malaga during the 1982 World Cup in Spain.

It was a memorable afternoon. I think it rates as one of the greatest social events I have ever been to. We sat down to lunch at the side of the swimming pool. There were waitresses all over the place serving lobster and caviar and bottles of Dom Perignon champagne. It must have been a wonderful atmosphere because I didn't even want to go to the races, which is very strange for me because I love the racetrack. Nevertheless, a fleet of stretch limos arrived and ferried us to the Rowley Mile course, to Mr Sangster's private marquee. Rod was with me all afternoon, and we just talked football.

Some celebrities use football as a vehicle to make themselves more roundly popular, but Rod is a genuine soccer nut. I've been invited a number of times to play on the full-size pitch he has had laid out at his home in Essex, but I have never been able to make it. I'm not surprised, though, that he has his own team. I was in a black taxi once in London when I got chatting to the driver, who revealed that he played for Rod's team. I remember his name was Johnny, and in his spare time he was a stand-up comedian. He did a very good impersonation of Sir Trevor Brooking.

The longer I played football, the more I became involved in the racing scene. I suppose that was because I learnt more about the business as I grew older, and each year a new contract would bring you more money and you became more confident about what you were doing with it. It paid off for me in a big way once when I went to York races with a fellow professional who was, and still is, a footballing legend.

I was playing for Manchester United at the time and the close season had just begun. My pal came over to my place with a driver, and we set off across the M62 for the track. It transpired that my fellow pro was about to take delivery of a brand-new sponsored car and he didn't need the immaculate Jaguar we were travelling in. He asked me if I knew anybody who was looking for one. I loved the vehicle. It was very opulent inside – more so than a Mercedes or a BMW – and I told him I would think about it.

Any race meeting is a great day out for me, but I was going to this one focused on one horse in particular about which I had received good information. I had a bundle of notes, some £4,000, bulging in my pocket. The horse was a filly called Rye Tops, and she was being ridden by Pat Eddery, who for me was the top jockey of the day. But in the hours before the race Eddery got stuck in a traffic jam on the A1. There had been a big crash, and the tailback was huge. Mobile phones were not really in popular use in those days, but somebody had picked up a message that the jockey wasn't going to make it.

This was a really big blow. I wondered if it was better just to forget the whole thing, but then I managed to get hold of a mate in Newmarket who knew the replacement jockey, Brian Rouse, really well. He said that Brian knew the horse as well as anybody and had ridden it out many times, which was very important because the filly had one great asset that needed to be managed really carefully. She had a terrific burst of speed, but it was very short-lived and had to be kicked in at exactly the right moment. If the horse went too early she would fade before the post.

When the race got underway I had put every penny on her. Any punter in my position will tell you of the agony of watching such a race. You live every pace. Every stride is a nightmare because in your mind you think you've seen something that could make her pull up. Have the other horses boxed her in? Is there an unknown animal out there that is going to surprise us all? In circumstances like that I often wish I could lie down in a darkened room for about five minutes and only emerge after the race is over so that I won't have to go through this agony.

Halfway through the race Rye Tops was in fifth place, sitting on the shoulder of the horse in front. It wasn't that long a run, but I was praying that Brian would wait before he went. Suddenly I saw his knees jerk out and back in again. He was going for the front. She sailed majestically past the fourth, third and second horses. Was it now time to hold it up again? But there was no holding her. As I had been warned, she sprinted on. She was soon out in front. But there were still two furlongs to go. Could she be caught?

The second horse was gaining ground. Just as I had been warned, our horse had run out of puff and was losing her lead. She was two lengths ahead, then one length, then half a length. I was shouting myself hoarse from the box above the winning post, and praying. 'Please, Lord, don't let her lose her lead. I've got children to feed.'

The winning post was suddenly in the picture, and we got home by a head. Praise be to the Lord. It was one of the most frightening but ultimately euphoric experiences of my life on the racecourse. I had a huge bundle of money coming my way, and needless to say the champagne was flowing. My footballing pal, though not into racing in anything like as big a way as me, had also cashed in big time.

But our good fortune for the day had not yet expired. I met a trainer, and after a conversation with him I thought I had a pretty good idea about which horse would have a chance in the last race. And I had plenty of dosh. I didn't go mad because the horse I had my eye on was a very big price. It came home easily, and the pot swelled with another wheelbarrow full of cash. By the time I left the course I was carrying my money in four Sainsbury's carrier bags. There was simply no other way of transporting it. I had a total of nearly £40,000 in cash. To put that into perspective, at the time I was earning between £2,000 and £3,000 a week at Manchester United. It was before the tidal wave of money Sky TV brought to the game, but even so it was a very good wage in those days. I had won twelve times my best weekly salary in one afternoon. For an average Premiership footballer these days the equivalent figure would be about half a million.

My pal had also done extremely well and was himself loaded down with the spoils of the day's events. The only problem we had now was what to do with all these banknotes. Going back over the Pennines, our car looked like it was carrying the proceeds of the Great Train Robbery. I have to confess that my wife Jill had no idea that I dealt in such large amounts of money when I went to the races. Neither did the wife of my pal. Far from being delighted by my good fortune, my wife would figure out that if I could win such huge amounts at a racecourse, I was also capable of losing them. And, of course, she'd have been right.

It was far too late to stick it into a bank. We stopped at a pub and discussed the serious possibility of putting it in a left-luggage locker at Piccadilly Station in Manchester. But then we discovered that because of IRA threats they didn't have the facility any more.

Eventually we had to take it home. The plan was that my pal, who had not won sums as big as mine, would tell his wife that he had got his money from me because I had bought his Jaguar. Then he would bring the car over to my house the following week, I would take possession of it and give him a load of my money, and he would then deposit it in a bank.

But that still meant I would be arriving home that evening with tens of thousands of pounds. I got the driver to drop me off at the end of my road. It was twilight, so I crept up to the house and went behind the garage. I was in luck: the connecting door to the house was open. I stuffed the bags full of money into a plastic bin full of leaves. Then the door slammed shut on the lock behind me leaving me stuck in the garage. I knew Jill was in because her car was parked on the drive. It was going to look a bit odd if I arrived home by emerging from the front of the garage. Just as I was climbing out of the side window, Jill appeared in the garden and saw my leg waving about. I had to do a sort of mid-air flip to make out I was trying to climb into the garage rather than climbing out. I said I had lost my keys and that I thought she was out. I know she didn't believe me, but she clearly couldn't figure out what I was really doing. She put it down to me having had too much champagne.

Buoyed by my success, I went back to York for the next two days of the meeting. My pal duly turned up the day after that with the Jag. Unfortunately, by that time, I had lost all the money I had won over the last 48 hours. It didn't really bother me. I have a great sense of 'easy come, easy go', and I got two more tremendous days at the races out of it. But it left my pal in a pickle. He couldn't take the Jag home because he had told his wife he had sold it to me. That, after all, is why he'd arrived home with bundles of cash. Now all my money was gone and I couldn't buy it off him. He was panic-stricken, but I found the situation so absurd I couldn't stop laughing. It was like the Jag was a stolen car. It was hot. How do you get rid of a brand-new luxury car like that? I think he took it to some car dealer who knew a few of the boys and settled for a knockdown price.

On another memorable occasion, after retiring from football, I went to two great race meetings 135 miles apart on the same day and pulled off an amazing betting coup – completely by accident. I first went to Newbury on the train because I had to myself what I thought was some great and exclusive information on a filly (it always seems to be the ladies with me). I didn't want to attract any attention so I stayed away from my usual haunts in the champagne bars and boxes. There would be plenty of time for that after I had fleeced the bookies. Then, fortunately in hindsight, I was spotted by my old pal the England World Cup winner Alan Ball.

Bally was a great racing man and we had become big buddies over the years. He had an infectious personality and was an excitable, non-stop talker. In fact, the only time I ever shut him up was during an Ipswich v. Southampton game in February 1982 when I stuck five goals past his team.

As soon as he saw me he said, 'I know why you're here. You've come for that filly, Miss Bagatelle, haven't you?'

My cover was blown. But I didn't realise that this was the best thing that could have happened to me all day.

Mick Channon soon joined us, and I learnt from both of them that there was a locally trained horse that was going to pose a big danger to Miss Bagatelle. I was so convinced about my information on the filly that I didn't at first want to listen. But Mick was already becoming a top racing man, and Bally, who's the sort of pal everybody would want, kept warning me about throwing my money away. I had my normal wedge of £4,000 in my trouser pocket, and I was torn as to what to do with it. By now Miss Bagatelle had taken serious money so her price had come down quite considerably, but I still thought she would win. The horses were being put in the stalls when I finally made up my mind. On the rails, I placed two grand on each horse.

They were off. Miss Bagatelle was clearly completely out of the race early on. Thank God I hadn't squandered all my dough on her. The danger horse swept home at 4/1. I had won £8,000, even though I had planned my whole day around a horse that never got into the reckoning. How lucky a break was that?

But, for excitement, my day had really only just begun. I bumped into a friend, Barry, from Coventry. He too had had the word on Miss Bagatelle so he'd had a poor day so far. As I was talking to him another friend of mine came into my sights. It was Willie Carson's pilot. I asked him why the champion jockey was flying, and it was because they were going from here after the last race to the evening meeting at Newmarket. I established that there were two spare seats on the plane, and I asked him if we could hitch a ride. He said, 'You'll have to ask the boss.'

The pilot also told us that the owner of Willie's horse in the race that was just about to begin was expecting a victory. I ran down to the start, stopping on the way to place a few hundred quid on Willie's horse. As he was about to take his ride into the stalls, I shouted over to him and asked if we could come on the plane to Newmarket. He agreed, and told us to be at the finishing post because he was leaving immediately the race was over. I told Barry we were on our way to HQ. He threw the keys of his Mercedes car to his brother and asked him and his two friends to set off right away and meet us there.

Willie's horse won, and within twenty minutes of the race ending we were airborne from the strip in the middle of the course. It was a four-seater, and for part of the journey at least Willie was at the controls.

As we came in to land in the middle of the Newmarket course it could not have been a more perfect evening. There was a beautiful blue sky and the course below us looked immaculate. The only people I felt sorry for were those we had seen trapped in a traffic jam on the M25. I hoped that Barry's brother had somehow got around it.

Before we left the plane the pilot gave me another tip, on a horse called Sheriff's Star in the maiden race being ridden by Paul Eddery. I had not even had a chance in our fast-moving day to look at any form for Newmarket so I had no idea how Sheriff's Star was rated. Being a maiden, of course, the horses don't have much history. I went up to a bookie I knew on the rails and asked him about the horse. He replied, 'The dogs are barking.' I took that to mean that it was an odds-on favourite, and as I had won more dosh already that day than I expected I decided not to bother with a bet. I would have had to put a few thousand on to get any sort of worthy return anyway.

I was soon in a tent with a load of people, and they were all asking me what I fancied in this race. I told them about Sheriff's Star and said it looked like a cert, but added that I wasn't sure they would get a very attractive price. The race went off but I wasn't taking much notice because I was having a glass of bubbly with a trainer. But the noise in the tent got louder and louder as the horses progressed towards the finishing post. There was an explosion as they crossed the line. People were coming over to me and shaking my hand; women were kissing me; glasses of champagne were arriving by the dozen. I couldn't understand it. With the greatest of respect to the people around me, I couldn't see that any of them would have risked more than £50. And with an odds-on SP their money back might have only amounted to about £40.

I was staring up at the telly when the result flashed up. Sheriff's Star had come in at 33/1. No wonder everybody was ecstatic! What on earth was the bookie on the rails doing telling me that this horse was, at best, evens? I could have made myself a fortune if I'd known the real price. I found a race card and tried to make some sense of it. It took me about two and a half seconds to work out what had happened. Sheriff's Star had not been rated by anybody, but the favourite for the race was called something like Shareef Afar. When I'd approached my man on the rails he had clearly misheard me. The two horses' names got crossed over. Maybe it was a combination of my guttural Scottish accent and a few glasses of champagne that had caused the confusion.

I should have felt furious. But I didn't. I'd had a very good day, and perhaps this was God's way of telling me not to be greedy. And, to be perfectly honest, I got a tremendous sense of satisfaction at seeing the sheer elation of some of the punters around me who had enjoyed their biggest-ever wins.

Barry's brother didn't get to the course until just before the last race. He had got stuck in the traffic we had seen from the plane. But he was as good as gold about it and certainly wasn't as fed up as I would have been if I'd had his nightmare journey. I didn't know it that night, but that was the last time I saw the boy alive. Six months later, on 2 December 1988, he was aboard Pan Am flight 103 when it was blown apart by a bomb over the little Scottish town of Lockerbie. He was going to America on his honeymoon. He and his bride were among the 259 people on the plane and another nine on the ground who perished in what, at the time, was the worst terrorist attack in history.

CHAPTER SIX

THE COACH
FROM HELL

I nailed him in a courtroom.
But, though that was some form
of retribution, I knew I would never
be able to expunge my hatred for him.

I WAS enjoying a day at York races when I spotted him. His big white pasty face was burnt on my soul. I have only hated one person in my life, and it is him. My blood started to boil. He was walking in my direction but it was in a throng of racegoers. One minute he seemed within punching distance and the next moment I had lost him.

My fists had tightened together in the way they used to when I was a kid about to take somebody on outside the school gates.

My quarry had spotted me and he was away. But he was a bloated, overweight creature and I was a former professional footballer. I would get him. I pushed on through the throng with an urgency that should have come from a man who was fleeing, not one in pursuit. 'Excuse me, excuse me,' I was crying. 'Please, get out of the way. Get out of the bloody way!' But there were too many people and my quarry was soon putting distance between us.

I concentrated on what I could see of his dark suit. He had always worn a dark suit. He was going to make the gates, and he would be away. But I was sure I knew the racecourse better than him. I turned around and decided to make my way along the big wall that runs down one side of the course. I knew there was a gate on the corner where the officials came in. If I could get there I could probably cut him off on the road on the other side.

I got out on to the road and scanned the crowds pouring out of the track. I couldn't see him. After a few minutes I realised he had gone. I was panting with the physical effort and the emotional turmoil into which I had just been thrust. What was he doing here? I wondered over and over again. Surely he wasn't mad enough to be stalking me? He knew that I had vowed to kill him if I ever saw him again. And I swear I still would to this day.

The loathsome individual who had triggered my explosive behaviour was a man called James Torbett. I had to cast my mind back 30 years to the incident that blighted my life. When I was thirteen, Torbett sexually assaulted me. It scarred me for decades and it may have changed the course of my football career and prevented me from playing for the team I had loved all my life, Celtic.

As a kid, my parents had trusted this man to guide me as I took my first steps in football, and to look after me when I was in his care. He was the boss of Celtic Boys Club. A highly respected figure at Celtic Park. A millionaire businessman in the Scottish community. A so-called pillar of the Establishment. In fact he was a dirty little pervert who preyed on me and other little boys whose confidence he had gained. Our mums and dads had happily let us go off to the boys club, never reflecting for a minute that we could be in any possible danger from anybody connected to the mighty Celtic Football Club. It was a worldwide institution, and at its helm was Jock Stein, the man everybody in our country regarded as the embodiment of Scottish values: decency, family, and consideration of others. And that is probably why Torbett got away with his despicable acts for so long.

Many years later I nailed him in a courtroom when his

misdeeds came to light. But, though that was some form of retribution, I knew I would never be able to expunge my hatred for him. While he is alive, the shadow that has blighted my life will still be there.

I think the proudest day of my life was when I passed the trials to be admitted to Celtic Boys Club. It was a dream come true. It was such a great institution. But from the first moment I met Torbett I knew there was something funny about him. My antennae told me to be wary. Torbett was the general manager of the boys club. It was never really clear what football experience he had. He didn't look like he had a footballing past, and I often wondered why he was involved. He tried to be this fatherly figure, but I didn't like it. I didn't like the fact that he was always taking a gang of us off for hamburgers after training or after a game. And he would always be giving lifts to the lads, even though he lived miles away from their homes. Even in my early teens that seemed a bit odd to me. We could all get there under our own steam, and a lot of us liked to go as a gang on the same bus. It was great for the camaraderie and it was strength in numbers. Our Boys Club blazers often attracted trouble so we tried not to travel alone.

He would often invite a group of us to his home, too. That was the thing I really didn't like. He would give us ice cream and biscuits; he even had boxes of toys which I thought were meant for kids much younger than us. I never saw a Mrs Torbett when we went there. That might sound quite naive now, but in those days in Glasgow everybody had a mum and a dad. Your dad went out to work and your mum was at home washing and cleaning. My mum always smelt of polish, and our front step was always scrubbed. But Torbett lived in a dingy council flat, and it was untidy.

On one particular occasion we were all at his place because there was a very big European youth tournament coming up and he said he wanted to talk to us about tactics.

All the lads would move around his flat – some in the kitchen or the hall, some of us in the lounge. The man who was supposed to be the head of the Celtic Boys Club would be putting his hands all over the lads, kissing them, giving them little pecks. Not for the first time I wondered what was going on. What went through my mind was that the lads he was paying all the attention to must be related to him. He must be their uncle or something. Why else would he be doing that?

He found me sitting on the sofa on my own in the lounge. I was feeling pretty bored and I wanted to go home when Torbett came and sat down next to me. He sat close to me, much closer than was comfortable, and without any warning he put his hand between my legs. I froze. He started kissing my head and trying to touch the outside of my trousers, but I was wriggling away from him. I remember his horrible swollen face next to mine. He was smiling. He thought this was fun.

I had never felt like this before. I was frightened and very confused. The only relationship I had ever had with a man up to that point was the father-and-son relationship with my dad. He was good and solid, and I felt very safe with him. Now I felt threatened. I leapt off the couch and headed for the bathroom because I knew it had a lock on the inside. I just wanted to get away from him.

I slammed the door shut. I thought he might come after me. I had my back to the door and I was trying to figure out in my head how far the window was from the ground, because if he tried to get in I was planning to jump. My heart was thumping like mad. I started to think carefully to make sure that I had not imagined what had happened.

After a few minutes I realised he wasn't pursuing me, but I was too frightened to leave the lavvy. Then I heard the voice of my good pal Davey Gordon in the corridor outside. I wrenched open the door and grabbed him.

'Come on, Davey, we've got to go.'

'Hang on, Baz, what's the rush?' he said.

I raised my voice. 'Come on, we've got to go. We're late.'

I grabbed my coat and bag and ran out of the flat and down the stairs in case Torbett was following. Davey was behind me. I didn't ease up until I got to the bus stop, and then I went home. Davey and I sat next to each other in silence until we got to our respective stops.

I didn't know what I was going to say to my parents. I wondered if I was very flushed. I worried that they might be able to tell that something had happened. I wasn't going to tell them. I couldn't. I got in and went straight to my bedroom. I shouted out that I'd got hit by a ball and I was going to lie down. I was unusually quiet over dinner. What had happened to me was not the sort of thing you spoke to your mum and dad about over dinner.

Over the next few weeks I learnt from coaches at the club that I had lost my place in the squad for the European youth tournament. It's obvious why I was dropped. I had already had my picture taken with the squad, though, so it appeared in the programme for the event.

From then on I did not go to the club as often as I used to. My mum and dad were very surprised because usually they couldn't keep me away from the place. Instead I would put my blazer on and pretend I was on my way, then stop behind the school instead and play football there. I was always home earlier than I used to be. I just said I wanted to get on with my homework. When I did go, I stayed right out of Torbett's way. He did no coaching. He just floated around all the time. It was easy to avoid him, and I never again went out for hamburgers. And certainly not back to his place.

It never once occurred to me that other boys might be in danger.

On the odd occasions when I found him in the vicinity I always avoided eye contact. When I think back now, I'm astonished at how child molesters like Torbett can so brazenly pursue their evil ways. Amazingly, he would ring my house and try to get me to come to extra training sessions. He even put to me repeated invitations to go out for hamburgers again, and ice cream. But ice cream was one thing I would never eat again: when he assaulted me it was immediately after he had dished out bowls of ice cream with raspberry topping. Whenever I see that now it makes me want to throw up.

I always said that I had too much homework. I couldn't bring myself to address the real reason. My parents started to realise that something was wrong, but I assume they thought it was a football-related matter. I did take my game very seriously after all. Presumably, Torbett knew that I would never tell anybody. I realise now, of course, that that is the classic behaviour of a paedophile. First they wheedle their way into a position of authority in places where there are plenty of children. Second, they win the trust of the youngsters, and then the parents. And then they bank on the fact that children are almost always too frightened and confused to spill the beans – which makes these sorts of crimes doubly disgusting because the children are completely defenceless. Torbett was a successful businessman who ran a chain of shops that supplied cups and medals to football clubs. He was a friend of members of the board at Parkhead. He must have known that if a little boy suddenly alleged he had been touched up, nobody would want to believe it.

What these attackers do worry about in their warped minds is that as the child grows up and turns into a man, will they revisit the horror of what happened to them when they were little and decide to try to do something about it? I will forever wonder whether that was why I was more or less thrown out of Celtic when I was the star player in the boys club.

For most of my schoolboy career I had played anywhere on the left-hand side of the team. In those days, and it's still the case today, a good left foot was a rare attribute. You didn't necessarily need a left-footed forward, but you did need somebody with that skill at left-back and on the left side of midfield. So I was moved around quite a lot – good for experience, but bad for consistency. In one way it was a tribute to my skills, but in another I had never been able to stamp my authority on a team by commanding one permanent position. When I was fifteen I got fed up of being moved around and decided I wanted to play up front. I thought that with my speed and my ability to get past players it was my best position. And I was proved right. I scored 62 goals in my final season with Celtic Boys. It was a club record I held for many years. Surely my dream of being taken on as an apprentice at Celtic would come true?

But it didn't. Lots of the other lads had what was called an 'S' form, an indication that they would be taken on by the club. I realised I was not going to get an offer. My disappointment was eased by the fact that, by then, I had been for trials at a number of the bigger clubs in England, and I had visited

Ipswich three times. I really liked Ipswich, and I was happy to go there. I have never regretted that. But I wish I could go back in time, eradicate Torbett, and see where I would have gone without his odious interference in my life. Before my departure for England at the age of sixteen, people around me asked me the same question over and over again: 'Why aren't you signing for Celtic?' There was nothing I could say, except that I had not had an offer.

In the 1981/82 season, when I was a star in the English league, I returned to Celtic Park to play a testimonial match. A club director called Mr Farrell singled me out after the game and said to me, 'How did we ever miss you?' For the first time I was tempted to say something, but as I was then at the peak of my career I bit my lip and shrugged my shoulders. 'I'll always be a Celtic man in my heart,' I told him, which was in every word the truth.

I didn't worry every day of my life about Torbett, but I often reflected upon it. By the mid-1990s, a couple of decades after the event, it was slipping further and further to the back of my mind. I had been forced out of football with an incurable back problem at the age of 27, and after a few years of uncertainty I had settled down to work in the media. I had been involved in some unfortunate business projects, but then had found my level as a co-commentator on football for Sky Television. I was developing a new career and felt the past was better left behind. But then I received a phone call that reignited the whole business and brought me into the limelight in a way I could never have imagined as an innocent thirteen-year-old.

When I picked up the phone it took me a few minutes to work out who was on the other end. It was a demented Scotsman who was wailing down the phone. I couldn't make any sense of what he was saying, though I thought he was trying to tell me he was haunted. I soon realised it was my old boys club pal Davey Gordon. I hadn't spoken to him in over twenty years so it was no wonder I didn't recognise his voice. And, anyway, he was in a very high state of agitation.

I calmed him down, and the full story spilt out. He had been approached by a newspaper that, after all these years, was investigating Torbett. Up to that moment I had no idea that Davey had suffered the same fate as me. He was very distressed and frightened. He had never made it as a footballer; he'd been driving a taxi in Glasgow. The effects of his schoolboy ordeal had preyed heavily on him over the years and he couldn't face reliving it all now. I told him I would do whatever I could to help.

I had been away from my home town for some twenty years, ever since I left for Ipswich, but when I started to make some enquiries I realised that rumours and innuendo about Torbett had been rife for most of that time. At one point Celtic manager Jock Stein, who most people regarded as the embodiment of all that was right and proper about the Scottish way of life, threw Torbett out of the club. But when the big man left, the pervert crawled back from under his stone and wheedled his way back in.

Eventually, the *Daily Record*, which at the time was the unmatchable tabloid market leader in Scotland, decided to investigate. They did a thorough job of trying to track down boys who could have fallen into Torbett's clutches. One of the others was a lad called John McCluskey. He was the brother of George McCluskey, who was a Parkhead favourite. John was singled out as a brilliant footballer. He was Celtic's youngest-ever signing when he joined them at the age of thirteen. The previous year Jock Stein himself had promised the youngster a place on the groundstaff the minute he left school. The account of his ordeal was even more horrifying than mine. This is what he told the paper:

We were on a tour in Norway when I was thirteen. Unlike other coaches, Torbett was staying in the dormitory as he always did when he was away with the boys.

He shouted to me to go into a side-room to check that the strips had all been laid out properly for the following day's game. But when I got in there the kit had already been laid out.

Torbett followed me in. He sat me down on the bed and put his hand inside my pyjamas. Then he fondled me. I was terrified. I did not know what to do.

I was away from home and I couldn't do anything. I just let him do it to me. When I think about it now it makes me sick.

He left, and I cried my eyes out. I didn't want to go back among the boys and I didn't want to be by myself. I was very scared and I didn't know what to do. I crept back to bed, pulled the covers over my head and sobbed myself to sleep.

The next morning I didn't know what to think. I thought there must be something wrong with me, that I must have enjoyed it to have let it happen in the first place. And I was too terrified to complain to anybody.

My life had changed when I got back from that trip, but I still madly wanted to be a great footballer.

I stayed away from Torbett. The other lads were always going to his house but I had only been once and I was never going to go again. I saw him slapping and punching a boy that I didn't know. I thought he might have been his son or

*something because he treated him terribly, but the boy did
not hit back.*

John was very unlucky in pursuit of his football career. He
became a hero in Scotland when he scored the winning goal
against England in a schoolboy international at Wembley. It was
live on television, and he seemed destined for a magnificent
future. But, before he could establish himself in the senior
team, he received a kick in training that caused a blood clot in
his leg. It never cleared up, and it ended his budding career.

He took to booze. It was partly to ease the pain of a football
career that had evaporated, but mostly, he said, it was to blot
out the memory of Torbett's abuse. John decided to come
forward in the wake of the Dunblane massacre when sixteen
little children were murdered by a pervert called Thomas
Hamilton. The kids were herded into the school gym and shot
by the maniac after he was relieved of sporting duties involving
coaching young boys. His behaviour had been drawn to the
attention of the authorities, and in his sick mind he took his
revenge against the defenceless children, then killed himself.

I was approached by the newspaper and I was happy to
give them my own account of my torment. The publication
of the *Record* investigation caused a sensation in Scotland,
and not unnaturally the police soon became involved. But it
was two years before the case came to court. I kept in touch
with developments, though, and I was looking forward to the
pervert receiving justice.

Apart from the opening day, the trial wasn't reported in any
detail in England so I kept in touch by phone with friends
north of the border. Then I got a call from a reporter who had
been working on the case. Apparently there was no certainty

that Torbett was going to be convicted. His crimes had taken place a very long time ago and the witnesses had been very emotional when trying to give their evidence. Some of them were broken men as a result of the assaults. The defence had dwelt on the details of the offences and some of the men were unable under cross-examination to get all their facts right and remember precisely what happened to them and when. I was asked to go and testify as a witness for the prosecution. Once I learnt that Torbett might get off, I had no hesitation.

I left the newspaper office in London and went straight to the airport. The trial was at such a crucial stage that I was needed in court that day. I urged the taxi driver to put his foot down on the way to Heathrow. Somebody met me at the airport and thrust a ticket into my hand. I sprinted for the gate, but as I was pounding down the walkway to the aircraft I saw the door starting to close. I shouted wildly, then threw myself into the plane. At Glasgow, I ran off the plane and headed for the taxi queue. As I came out through the doors I was hit by a barrage of flashing lights. For a moment I assumed the photographers were waiting for somebody else. But they weren't. My expected arrival had already made the local radio news.

The taxi driver was highly excited about the prospect of taking me to the court. 'I admire you, Alan, for what you are doing,' he said. 'It can't be easy for you raking over all that terrible business when you were just a laddie, but we all want that bastard to go down.' He wouldn't take any fare from me as we turned the last corner on the banks of the River Clyde.

It was only when I got to the court that I appreciated for the first time the incredible interest that had built up in this case. I couldn't get out of my cab because the photographers were pushed up against the door by those behind them. One young reporter who had spotted me first had his face pushed hard up against the window by a TV crew behind him. He had a notebook in his right hand, but he was having to use his left hand to stop his face from being flattened. As a result his red biro had gone right up his nostril. I feared he was going to kill himself.

Two policemen pushed their way through the mêlée, created space and escorted me into the building. The barrage of photography was the most intense I have ever experienced in a life of being in the spotlight. When I was safely inside I couldn't see anybody properly as my eyes were full of black dots and bright blue rings. I made a mental note that if I ever had grandchildren I would make sure nobody ever took a picture of them with a flash camera.

I was briefed in an anteroom by the prosecution lawyers and barristers. They made it clear that my evidence could be vital. I had absolutely no fears. I was very confident that I could deliver. After a few moments I was called in to court, and I entered the witness box. I had never been in a court before. I was impressed by the high ceiling, the pillars, the polished wood and burnished rails. The room was packed with people; some were even sitting in stairwells. I had played in a few full-house stadiums in my time but I had never seen one that was as proportionately as full as this court.

The jury were right in front of me. To my left was a lady judge, who was in fact a sheriff, and to my right, in the dock, was Torbett.

At first I don't think he recognised me. Maybe the prosecution had not told his people they were calling me. I had put on a few pounds since my playing days ended and he'd last seen me face to face when I was fifteen. To start off with, he looked smug. His balloon-like face oozed confidence. I stared straight at him and he couldn't hold my gaze for more than a tenth of a second. Disgust was clearly etched all over my face because the usher had to ask me several times to identify myself while I was lost in the mists of time, thinking back to what that bastard had done to me. Seeing my determination and fortitude, Torbett slumped forwards. His face sagged. He knew he was done for.

The prosecution asked me several basic questions, and then to outline my account of what happened. I was very composed. I had in fact wondered whether this day would ever come. I'd never envisaged ending up in a courtroom getting my revenge. I thought it was far more likely that, if I ever saw my assailant again, I might not be able to contain myself and I might lay into him. But public exposure like this was better. Now the whole world would know him for what he was.

At the end of the prosecution questioning the barrister said to me, 'Do you see that person in this room?'

'Yes,' I replied. I swivelled to my right and pointed my arm straight at Torbett in a way I might have pointed to the corner flag in my playing days to indicate it was 'our ball'. 'That's him, there, sitting between those two policemen.'

There was an audible gasp in the courtroom. Torbett looked away. Some of the women in the gallery clutched their chests as though they had just been informed they were in the company of the devil. In my opinion, they were.

The defence barristers then cross-examined me. I don't know how previous witnesses had shaped up in the box. It was a very traumatic event for everybody concerned, but when it was over I knew I had performed well. The defence did not really come at me as strongly as I thought they might.

I assumed they would challenge every word, but they didn't. In fact, the cross-examination was brief. At all times I kept full eye contact with the jury.

When everybody had finished, the judge complimented me on being a 'good witness'. She then asked if I would like to leave the building by the side door. I turned down her offer because I didn't want to hide. I wanted to be as public as possible. I had absolutely nothing to hide. I had just given an honest account of a hideous incident. Why should I try to slip away unseen? I wanted as many people as possible to know about the evil wretch who was sitting in that box. And I wanted the jury to know that I was standing by my evidence and that anybody in the world could challenge it. It was the truth.

When I got outside there was an even bigger bunfight going on than there had been when I went in. The police had to intervene and open up a corridor for me to get to a waiting car. I have dealt with a few reporters in my life, but this lot were manic. They were trying to hang on to my shoulders, though I don't know why. There was nothing more I could tell them that I hadn't told to the court.

I jumped into the car and it sped off to the airport. It was the shortest journey I had ever made to Scotland. Carloads of reporters were following me. They chased me into the terminal building. I knew that by law I couldn't speak to anybody about the case because the trial was still going on, and I did not want to be seen in the company of newspapermen. I approached a security guard and started to explain, but he already knew what was going on. He whisked me off to a VIP suite. Solace after a long and fiery day.

I reckoned I deserved a drink, and within a few minutes a waitress had put a champagne glass in my hand.

A week later I was driving to a job when I got a call on the mobile. After seven hours of deliberation, James Torbett had been found guilty of three charges of shameless and indecent conduct. That was for attacking Davey Gordon, me and another lad called James McGrory. I did wonder why the jury had taken seven hours. To me it was clear Torbett was as guilty as hell. I also found it disappointing that he was allowed to walk from the court at the end of the hearing while the judge considered his sentence. He eventually went down for just two years. I wish he had been locked up for life. The newspaper reporter told me later that my evidence had finally nailed Torbett.

I was lucky in that I managed to recover from my ordeal, and because my football career worked out I was able to do so much in my life that was successful. Psychologists would say that because I was able to achieve high self-esteem I had the strength to put the experience behind me and I didn't let it torment me and drag me down over the years. But, for some of the other lads, their lives were literally destroyed. You have to wonder, for instance, whether the reason they never made it as footballers was because of what happened to them at Torbett's hands. And, as I said, I will always ponder on whether or not this evil man manipulated me out of Celtic even though as a youngster I was breaking records. Could he, for instance, have passed comment about me to others that I had an attitude problem, or that I had shown disdain for Celtic, the club I still love? I will never know.

CHAPTER SEVEN

FOLLOW THE HOOPS

*I can remember to this day the thrill of
being part of the green-and-white army.
I had an identity. I was in love with my
team, and I was now part of the
pilgrimage to pay homage to them.*

I WOULDN'T have been anybody's favourite choice to end up behind a microphone when I was at school. And no wonder. One of my classmates at Holyrood in south Glasgow was Jim Kerr, who went on to become the lead singer of one of the biggest bands in the world, Simple Minds. The guitarist from that group, Charlie Burchill, was also a mate. I quite fancied being a rock star too. From what I could make out a singer like Rod Stewart, one of my heroes for his devotion to Scotland, had the perfect life. He was adored by millions, had his pick of girlfriends, drove flash Lamborghinis and had all the money in the world. I did once contemplate it because I had a good voice. There was, however, one very big complication. I was going to be a footballer. I was going to play for Celtic and Scotland. I was going to make my mum and dad proud of me.

I was born just up the road from Hampden Park, the national symbol of my country's football heritage. When I kicked a ball around in the streets it was under the watchful eyes of the ghosts of Scottish legends like Hughie Gallacher, who I am sure I saw once or twice riding through the air in a chariot. From my bedroom window I could see the games at Hampden. Throughout my youth there were so many big matches between Celtic and Rangers there, and I could follow the progress of the game by both observing and listening to what was happening inside the stadium. If there was a roar that was almost deep-throated, it was coming from the far end of the ground, which was covered and always occupied by the Rangers fans. It meant they had scored. But if the cheering appeared to be much louder and dust started to rise from the open end nearest to our house, it was the Celtic fans who were jumping up and down to celebrate a goal.

It was the first football ground I ever went into. But it wasn't an international game packed with 130,000 fans (as the stadium could be in those days), it was a more modest affair in front of a few hundred spectators. For Hampden was not just the national stadium, it was also the home of Second Division Queen's Park. It was an eerie feeling, being at the home of Scottish football, watching a match and hearing your own voice echoing off the roof above you. But it still helped fuel my ambition. I was going to become the hero of hundreds of thousands of school kids just like me. I went to bed every night literally dreaming of wearing that green-hooped shirt and scoring against Rangers at Celtic Park.

I have been Celtic mad as long as I can remember. I went to a Celtic school, I come from a Celtic family, and everything in my life was about the team from the time I could walk. When I was kicking a ball around with my mates in the street outside Hampden I pretended to be the wing wizard Jimmy Johnstone, who, God rest his soul, died while this book was being written. I used to look up at that magnificent towering stadium with walls like a medieval castle and reflect that only supermen got to play on the inside of this 'cathedral'. I hoped so much that one day it would be me, but I wondered how I was ever going to become a giant of the game, like Johnstone and my other hero, the Scottish sorcerer Denis Law.

When I was just seven, Celtic won the top club trophy in the world, the European Cup, and, from that moment on, the impossible dream of becoming a footballer was awakened in the heart of every school kid in Scotland. You didn't have to be a Celtic fan to marvel at their achievement. It was folkloric. If you had invented the story and put it into a boys' comic it would have seemed too fantastical to be true. A group of football-crazy lads, many of whom went to the same school – some had gone to mine – had moved through the ranks of junior and senior football and emerged as one of the most powerful forces Scotland had ever seen. They were ordinary young kids, some with holes in their trousers and others with the soles coming off their shoes, who played with a tennis ball in the terraced back-to-back streets where they were brought up; like every kid in the area they ate football for their breakfast and dinner; boys who had a dream and little else to steer them through life.

All the Lisbon Lions were brought up within 25 miles of Celtic Park. They weren't just a team. They were best pals. They played their hearts out for each other, and for the fans they recognised as their brothers, their school mates, even their teachers. They had good Scottish names like Lennox, Auld and Gemmell. And Johnstone. Some of them had never even travelled abroad before breaking through to Celtic's first-team squad and competing in Europe. Nobody in our neighbourhood in Glasgow had ever been abroad, but we'd heard about some people who had. 'Rich' people could get on aeroplanes and go to places in Spain where they would lie on a beach all day and waiters would serve them drinks.

Those players were crowned the best when the rest of Britain was only just beginning to learn about the Continent. We knew about these Continental teams because they came to Scotland to play Celtic and Rangers. Their players were exotic.

They looked like bandits out of Western films. They were dark-haired and dangerous. They wore vividly coloured shirts and had hairy legs. They celebrated goals dramatically. Like girls sometimes, hugging and kissing each other. Most of all, they were mysterious. Surely they were too good for a group of lads from *my* neighbourhood?

But sure enough, in May 1967 we were in the final of the European Cup, against Inter Milan, in a place called Lisbon in some country called Portugal. I literally prayed under the sheets in my bed every night that my dad would somehow find some tickets to be able to take me on this great adventure overseas to see my heroes do battle with Europe's finest. I even plotted with my mates that we should run away and go to the game ourselves. But I wasn't even allowed to go to Celtic home games on my own in those days.

We watched our team achieve the ultimate glory on a little black-and-white TV set with friends and neighbours all crowded around it. The pictures were terribly grainy and waves kept floating up and down the screen, but we saw Celtic win in the bright sunshine, and it was the first time I realised that grown men can cry as well as children.

Amazingly, nearly four decades later, when I was covering the 2004 Euro Championship with talkSPORT in Portugal, I met a Scotsman whose father had never gone home from the European Cup final. During the course of the tournament we bumped into a young fellow called Andre. He was Portuguese, but he didn't look anything like the rest of his countrymen. He had dark skin, but he also sported a shock of ginger hair. He was a striking-looking boy. He told me over a few beers (quite a few) of how his father, Jack, who worked in the fruit markets in Glasgow, had arrived in Lisbon for the final with a bunch of mates. They were euphoric for days after the famous victory and they all decided to chuck their jobs in and spend the rest of the summer on the beach. They worked in bars and as labourers in the developing hotel industry in the Algarve, but when autumn arrived they gradually drifted back to Scotland one by one.

All except for Jack, who had been brought up in a children's home and who had never enjoyed such balmy, sun-kissed days in all his life. He had met a Spanish girl, Antonella, who was working in the south for the summer season. He went back to Barcelona with her, where Andre was born, and always intended to return to his native Scotland. But Antonella did not want to go, fearing that she would not be able to tolerate the cold Scottish winters. Eventually they compromised by setting up home in the Portuguese capital, Lisbon, which Jack said was his spiritual home. He then worked for the next 30 years as a taxi driver until he died of a heart attack. Andre told me his father was not the only one who never made it back to Scotland, and that there were still Scottish taxi-drivers from 1967 working in the city, though I never encountered another. This was the sort of passion that was being burnt into my soul as I sat cross-legged on the floor of our lounge watching that famous victory.

It was the beginning of the most glorious chapter of success in my club's history, and thank goodness I was just old enough to appreciate it. Celtic had, amazingly, only won the Scottish title four times in the previous 40 years, the fourth time being just the year before, 1966 – which, of course, gained us entry to the 1966/67 European Cup competition. But, from that 1965/66 championship on, Celtic took the title nine seasons in a row. We even reached another European Cup final, in 1970, though we were beaten on that occasion. Many years later I was reminded of this 1970 defeat when I was part of a soccer forum in a working men's club in Glasgow. The great Tommy Gemmell was on the panel and I asked him in front of a boozy crowd of several hundred fans, 'What was it like to score that goal in the European Cup final?' The fans started shouting and screaming as though I was a referee who had just given a 50-50 decision against them. When they quietened down, Tommy narrowed his eyes behind his steel-rimmed glasses and spat at me, 'Which one?' I had forgotten that the greatest left back in the history of Scottish football had not only scored when we won the big trophy in 1967, but also against Feyenoord in 1970 in the narrow 2–1 defeat.

It was within this late-sixties wave of white-hot euphoria – the revival of Celtic, their astonishing European success, and the realisation that any kid on any street might have a chance – that I decided it was football for me. And when I say 'decided', I really mean that. There was something spiritual about my belief that I was going to become a footballer. Teachers are always asking their pupils what they are going to do with their lives. I always replied, 'I am going to be a footballer.' 'Yes, Brazil,' the teacher would reply, 'of course you are. But if that rather narrow ambition does not work out for you, as it almost certainly will not, what then?' I would refuse to retract. I just kept saying 'footballer'. I really believed it.

Immediately after I saw Billy McNeill lift that huge trophy, I was out on the streets with my pals. We all wanted to be Tommy Gemmell or Bobby Murdoch. We re-enacted that most special moment – the winning goal – over and over again. The chorus from an army of mothers throughout the neighbourhood trying to get us home to our beds was ignored over and over again. It was the biggest day of our young lives and it only reinforced the dream I had had since birth to play for Celtic.

We were always out playing football anyway. In the summer nights we would play behind King's Park Secondary School, and when we had the chance we would climb over a fence on to a well-maintained hockey pitch. Before long the call would go up, 'The jannie is coming!' And the janitor, in his brown coat and looking for all the world like the chap who did the same job in the TV series *Please, Sir!*, would suddenly appear, waving his stick. We must have been the bane of his life. Often when he thought he had got rid of us we had actually climbed through an open window into the gym and we were playing five-a-side. He would eventually spot us through the big-walled window, but we just used to stand there laughing, knowing it would take him five minutes to get through all the doors with his collection of jailer's keys.

I'm sure I developed my body swerve from evading him. When he eventually made it into the gym he would announce haughtily, 'Right, boys, I've got you now. There's no way out except through me. Line up, and we'll get your parents down here to get you home. I hope your fathers are in a better mood than me.' Then three of us would run at him from different directions, swerving and diving around him until he spun around and fell on the floor. My dad never swore at home, but the poor old jannie certainly knew some ripe language.

I must have stood out as quite a good footballer at school because from the age of twelve I can remember scouts coming to our house to talk to my mum and dad. I was too young to go to England for trials, though; they were just putting their marker down.

Ironically, the first time I was called for a trial to Celtic – the call I had been waiting for all my short life – I couldn't go because my love for the club had got me into terrible trouble with my parents. Celtic were playing on a Wednesday night in a vital cup game at Dundee. Because I was a good footballer I played with older and bigger boys, and I was then part of a gang who were all a lot older than me. The night before the game they were all talking about going to Dundee. I was determined not to be left out. As I said, at that stage of my life my mum and dad would barely even let me go to Celtic Park on my own. I was, after all, only thirteen. But the following day I just walked out of school and met up with my pals. I'd saved up some money for a new pair of boots and I was going to use that for my turnstile money and rail fare for the two-hour journey to Dundee.

I can remember to this day the thrill of being part of the green-and-white army. I had an identity. I was in love with my team, and I was now part of the pilgrimage to pay homage to them. I had never felt anything like this before. I had seen hordes of Celtic supporters passing our house on the way to cup finals at Hampden. I had yearned to grow up quickly so that I could be a big boy and be one of them. Now I felt I was. Now I felt I was a fully paid-up member of a movement around which I wanted to shape my life. People talk about sectarianism in Scotland, but that wasn't a word I ever used in relation to the community in which I grew up. I was just one of them, and I was going to be one of them for ever. At that age every young lad is looking for an identity, and, particularly in Scotland, there is a clannish aspect to life.

Strangely, considering how I acquired a taste for it later in life, I turned down several attempts by my pals to get me to drink on the train. I swigged from a bottle of beer as we packed ourselves into the goods van, but I spat it out. It was the worst thing I had ever tasted. I couldn't imagine how grown men could possibly drink pints of the stuff. Now I understood why my dad never took drink. I figured that when I grew up I was going to be the same. How daft does that sound now?

As the train pulled in to Dundee there were lines of policemen waiting on the station with yapping Alsatians straining on their leads. As the doors to the train were thrown open there was an outburst of noise unlike anything I had ever heard before. 'Celtic, Celtic, Celtic!' rang out the chant from a thousand voices. The sound shot into the air, hit the station roof and came back to us again. As we made our way through the station the dogs barked louder. Beery breath and expectation were all around me as I immersed myself in the fanatical green-and-white wave.

My ecstasy increased when Celtic won the game in extra time. Dixie Deans scored the winner. Even though all drink had been taken off the boys as they passed through the turnstiles there were still plenty of bottles about, mostly whisky. Every time we scored we all leapt into the air and I got showered in Famous Grouse and Johnnie Walker.

When the final whistle went I reflected for the first time on the fact that I was going to have to go home to face the music from my dad. A little tremble went through me, particularly as extra time meant I was going to be later than ever. I had told one of my classmates to go to my house on the way home from school to tell my mum that I had gone to the match. I told him to say that I'd been offered a lift by the father of another pal to try to make out that I was in adult company, and that I couldn't get home to tell them because I would have missed football practice.

As we started to leave the ground, the atmosphere changed to something a lot more intimidating. Though I was willing to face the wrath of my dad for going to the game, I wasn't going to get myself into further trouble by getting into a scrap. Crazy images went through my head of me being arrested and being up in front of the beak the next morning. That would have sent my folks into space. I came from a good middle-class background. To bring such shame on the family would be unthinkable. So as we left the ground, and I could see all my mates spoiling for a fight, I decided to make my own way back to the station. In my naivety I thought that by breaking away from the main group I would be less visible and therefore wouldn't attract any trouble. It was one of the worst decisions I ever made in my life. I still shudder when I think of what happened next, and whether I should thank the Lord every day for surviving.

I strode off towards the town, but within a few minutes I started to feel terribly self-conscious. It was dark and cold, and gangs of youths were milling around on every street corner. I tried to walk by with confidence. I wasn't wearing any colours, but I was conspicuous simply for being alone. That's not normal for a fan of my age leaving the ground. Something on my face was giving out a message. As I walked past one group of youths decked out in Dundee's colours, the biggest one of them moved in front of me, looked me straight in the eye and asked, 'Where are you from, son?'

I knew that the moment I opened my mouth my accent would give me away as a Celtic fan. There was only one course of action. I was a budding footballer who was already starring for Celtic Boys Club. One of my strengths was my speed. The other was my body swerve. I was going to have to use them both right now. I smiled at my inquisitor, dropped my right shoulder and sprinted past him on his left.

The shout immediately went up: 'Get him! Get the Glasgow bastard! Get the kid with the curly hair!'

But I'd taken off like a shot and I was very fast. There were probably ten or twelve of them in pursuit of me and I hoped that among that number there wasn't a national schools' sprinting champion. The problem was, I didn't know where I was going, and I was starting to attract the attention of other gangs on the main road. One lad, realising what was going on, came at me from across the street, but again my body swerve held me in good stead. Nevertheless, the numbers of those chasing me was growing. I made a quick turn down a side street, hoping to shake them off. It was a mistake. There was another gang of rival fans at the bottom of the road, and for the first time I started to feel really scared. It looked like I was trapped.

I bolted down an alleyway, hoping like mad that there was an exit. But there wasn't. I was running straight towards somebody's back gate. I didn't bother to see if it was open, I just leapt up on top of it without breaking stride. I was now in somebody's densely black garden, kicking bins over while the Dundee fans were coming over the wall. They were all shouting and screaming, and one got to within a few feet of me before I whacked him full in the face with a dustbin lid. A light went on in the house which threw out just enough illumination to let me work out that there was a path along the side of the house to the front, where there was a hedge. I set off again and went straight through the hedge. It tore my coat, a branch scraped along the top of my eyebrow, and blood started running down my cheeks. But I was now back on a road and

I was running like hell again, still being pursued by at least a dozen people shouting blood-curdling threats at me. I felt like a fox being pursued by hounds. The longer I ran and the more I evaded the kids chasing me, the more angry they were getting. My heart was thumping, but thanks to my football training I had plenty of puff left in me. I was sure I was going to outrun them, but I was in the heart of enemy territory and they seemed to be pursuing me in relays.

Before long I found myself on the edge of the town. I saw a sign that I thought said 'Station' and I took comfort in the fact that if I could make it there I would be safe in the midst of the green-and-white army. I hared around the corner, and there was the station. But it wasn't the railway station, it was the bus station. I was getting tired now, and the pursuing Dundee fans had still not given up. I sprinted into the huge building but I couldn't see any way out. In blind panic, I dived under a double-decker bus. I was lying on a mattress of oil and sawdust and I could feel the underside of this huge vehicle on the back of my head. My heart was thumping so fast I feared it might be echoing around the building.

I heard the mob come in and I could see their feet from where I was hiding. Many of them were wearing Dr. Martens boots, the heavy leather footwear of 'bovver-boys'. I knew that if I was discovered I had a very good chance of finding out just how much damage those boots could do to a human face. My pursuers began jumping on and off buses in an attempt to find me, but nobody seemed to twig that I might be under one. After what seemed like an eternity they all gave up and drifted away.

I stayed under the bus for a few minutes longer and was readying myself to depart when the most horrendous thing happened. The bus suddenly started up. The engine roared into life and something started bouncing up and down on the back of my head. I have never before or since been so frightened. The roar of the engine was so loud that it disorientated me. I was frozen with fear. If the bus moved, I feared my head was going to be squashed or I was going to get my legs run over by one of the huge tyres. But I didn't dare move in case the bus did at the same time. At least if it went in a straight line and I stayed still I *might* survive. I was praying to God for help.

Then I heard a great clanking noise that I knew from travelling to school each day was the sound of the driver putting the vehicle into gear. I had to move, I realised; it was now or never. I scrambled out from under the far side of the bus, and just as I drew my feet clear it rolled backwards. Those huge, heavy wheels missed me by a few inches.

I think I must have been in a state of shock because I just sat slumped against the wheel of another double-decker for about ten minutes, just trying to get my senses together. A conductress spotted me and came over. She thought I had been in an accident – which of course I nearly had. I can't imagine what I looked like. There was blood caked on my face and leaves and twigs in my hair. My clothes were ripped and the whole of my front was like an oil slick flecked with sawdust. On top of that, she probably thought I was drunk because I smelt of the drink the lads had showered over me when we had scored. I thanked her and scrambled away.

I now felt very homesick. I even for a minute contemplated heading for a police station. But then I discovered that the railway station was just a few minutes away and I found new resolve to press on. By the time I made it there my pals had been there for nearly half an hour. Fortunately, the train home had been delayed. That was good news, and bad. I wasn't going to be stranded, but it was now going to be the early hours before I got home.

All my pals burst into laughter when they saw me. I told them my tale with a trembling voice, but I got little sympathy. I did gain a bit of respect though. Blood on the face was very important for your street credibility, even if mine had come from a branch in a hedge rather than the fist of a rival fan. The others had had a bit of confrontation on the way back to the station too. They'd had a police escort, but there were a few times when gangs of locals tried to steam into them. They all said that they'd enjoyed the aggro. I certainly hadn't.

It was after two in the morning when I finally walked through the door at home. My dad went ballistic and clipped me round the ear. He would probably get arrested for that these days, but back then it was the way parents punished their kids. That was fair enough for me. My mum nearly fainted when she saw the state of me and made me have a bath before bed.

The following morning at school I felt brilliant. The memory of being under the bus still sent a shiver down my spine, but I felt like I had entered a new world because I had completed my first great adventure following my club away from home. I hadn't spoken to my dad that morning because he had gone off to his shop early. I didn't care what punishment he was going to dish out to me as long as he wasn't going to stop me playing football.

My desire to be a footballer had increased dramatically some time earlier when I had played in front of a big 'crowd' for the first time in my life. There was a Celtic v. Rangers cup final coming up at Hampden and thousands of fans from both sides were queuing for their tickets. There was a red ash pitch right next to the stadium, and on the day the tickets were on sale I was playing there. For the first time in my life I was performing in front of a crowd. The experience was fantastic. When I did something good I got a big cheer from the fans, and when I messed something up there were groans and a few cruel comments. But that just spurred me on to show them that I could do things better. I loved the atmosphere and the sense of competition. It was fantastic to think that through my own actions I could draw such a passionate response from people.

At around this time, as I said, I had been accepted to play for Celtic Boys Club. As far as I was concerned that was like entering the Kingdom of Heaven. I wanted for nothing more. I was a bright kid at school and did well in all my exams, but I didn't care about that because I was going to be a footballer. So, for me, being allowed into Celtic Boys Club was the equivalent of a pilot receiving his wings. There was a tremendous tradition about the boys club. Although it wasn't the official academy of Celtic it was very much their 'feeder' facility. All the Celtic greats had been groomed there, and as far as I was concerned this was all part of my life plan.

On training nights, if you turned up in anything other than the smart grey slacks and green blazer with the club's badge on the pocket, you weren't allowed in. But in a divided city like Glasgow the uniform could always give you hassle, though I was so proud to wear it that I was happy to fight to defend what it represented. The area in which I grew up was Simshill in the southern part of the city, where there were more Rangers than Celtic fans. Celtic Boys Club was in Barrowfield in the east end, not far from Parkhead. From the town centre I had to get a number 64 bus out to the training ground, and it went through mixed areas of football support. I used to have a fight every few weeks. Fortunately there is not a lot of damage thirteen-year-olds can do to each other – unlike today, then you wouldn't even think that a youngster who was taunting you about your team would have a flick knife in his pocket – and damage was usually limited to a bloody nose, a split lip or a black eye. Everything was sorted out with your fists. The worst problem was getting your uniform ripped. My badge was once ripped off, and the pocket of my blazer went with it. My mum went mad. And every season I would get through about three or four pairs of grey slacks, though that was usually due to playing football in the streets after training had finished.

In the previous chapter I detailed the gross attack on me (and others) by the perverted Celtic Boys Club coach James Torbett. But I have refused to let the memory of my otherwise idyllic upbringing in football be destroyed by one evil man's actions. One fond memory I have of the boys club is the very distinct smell that existed in the air. The Barrowfield training ground was very close to a brewery, and most days the aroma of hops and yeast all being brewed up together was very prevalent. Whether or not that was a pointer later in life as to how enjoyable a part alcohol would play in my life, I have no idea. But it is a lingering boyhood memory.

The first game I played in which I regarded as a big match was an U-14s final between our club and Rangers Boys Club. It was played on the Glasgow Green, which was a large collection of red ash pitches between Bridgestone and the Gorbals. It was a sort of inner-city Scottish version of London's Romney Marsh. All other matches were off at that time, and such is the rivalry between the two Glasgow giants that there were hundreds, maybe thousands, of fans from both sides crowded around the pitch. They were so deep that I couldn't see as far as the back of the crowd. The atmosphere was so tribal that it frightened some of the young boys who were playing that day. For me, it was another step up from the ticket-line I had played in front of outside Hampden. I loved the aggression. The crowd around one half of the pitch were roaring on our every move while in the other half we were being cursed and sworn at.

I think that experience instilled in me a lifelong ability to raise my game away from home. Some of the lads that day didn't want to venture into the other half of the pitch. But I did. I was playing midfield at the time, and though I didn't realise it I was performing like Frank Lampard does today for Chelsea. I couldn't wait to surge forwards. I wanted to get into the faces of the opposition fans. 'Come on, give me all you've got!' I was thinking to myself. I ran over to take all the throw-ins. One time, as I was about to chuck the ball in, a woman behind me said, 'You're just a wee lassie with boots on.' I ignored her, but I watched carefully for the next time the ball went over to that part of the pitch. She was shouting and waving her arms around and I managed to identify the best player on the Rangers side. When the opportunity came, I went in on him with the hardest flying tackle of the day. The ball and the boy behind it went clattering up into the air. I put my hands in the air and said to the ref, 'Fair tackle, ball first.' He told me to cut out the rough stuff. Then I turned to the woman on the line and shouted, 'Your boy's been hurt by a wee lassie!' I ran off laughing.

It was just an example of the fact that we had more bottle than them. We won 7–1 that day, and from that moment onwards I was determined nobody was ever going to get the better of me physically on a football field. I vowed I would always give back what I got with a good deal of interest. That game also fully introduced me to the rivalry between Rangers and Celtic, which, if you come from where I was brought up, stays with you for ever.

I was on the receiving end of an Old Firm thumping the following year in the U-15s. Celtic Boys Club were used to winning most of the time, but on this occasion we were playing a team called Eastercraigs, a Rangers side that had drawn players from all over the city. They were dominant not only in Glasgow but all over Scotland. They won national titles, and every boy who represented them had by then been touted by a professional club. I'm sure all of them would have loved to play for Rangers in the same way that we all wanted to play for Celtic, but there were too many of them. I learnt afterwards that half of them were destined for English teams like Burnley and Leeds United. Jim Melrose was their outstanding player. He went on to pursue a long career in England. Davy Reid signed for Leeds United. They beat us 5–1. It was another great lesson in life. Again it was about rivalry, but also about how to turn negatives into positives.

I hated the feeling as I came off the pitch. It was just about the biggest gubbing I'd ever had as a footballer at any decent level. The opposition were jubilant and weren't afraid to hide it. I felt like a second-class citizen in my own city. The Bluenoses had triumphed. My feelings about Rangers became very intense on that day. I vowed I was one day going to avenge that defeat. And I was going to do it single-handedly. That schoolboy rivalry has never left me. It's still intrinsic, in a very juvenile fashion.

Many years later I was in a box at Celtic Park for a derby game. I was with a bunch of lads who ran a very successful scaffolding and pointing business called the Kilkoyne Brothers. I was sitting on the second row with Tommy Gemmell. When Celtic scored their second goal to seal the game we jumped up and down and cheered, and then we both went to the front of the box and through a huge pane of glass started waving to the Rangers fans. But it wasn't a conciliatory wave, it was a wave that said, 'Cheerio! You've been beaten, and you might as well go home now.' When I think about it, it was rather a childish thing for a European Cup winner and me, with thirteen caps for Scotland, to do. But that is the consequence of the sense of rivalry that was burnt into me at schoolboy level.

When I got into the U-16s I really started to get noticed. As I wrote in the previous chapter, that was when I made it clear I only wanted to play at centre forward, and my judgement was proved right when I scored 62 goals that season. As a consequence I started getting seriously chased up by scouts, in particular from Spurs, Everton and Ipswich. George Findlay from Ayrshire was the Ipswich scout north of the border, and he was the first to put to me the proposition of a trial. He came over to me after one of my first games in that U-16 season and asked if I wanted to go down there in the half-term holiday.

'Yes,' I said. 'Where is it?'

Not only did I not know where Ipswich was, I hadn't even heard of the place. I certainly didn't know they were a football team in the English First Division. That might sound ridiculous, but life in Glasgow in the early to mid-1970s was very insular. When I got home in a state of high excitement and told the news to my mum and dad, they too drew a blank on a place called Ipswich.

A couple of weeks later I was on the train heading south. It was easily the longest journey I had ever made. I was only fifteen but I wasn't worried at all about going out into the big wide world. In fact, I wanted it badly. Years later, somebody told me that the youth-team manager who put me on the train in Glasgow and wished me well was the father of David Moyes, the current Everton manager. David achieved something I didn't: he played for Celtic. It never quite worked out at the top for him as a player, but he has more than made up for that as a manager.

Ipswich was unlike anything I had ever seen before. In my own country I had barely even been outside Glasgow, which was a hard industrial city that sprawled across the landscape as far as you could see. You had to have your wits about you at all times. But Suffolk was very different. It was small and welcoming. The people had an oldie-worldie charm about them. There weren't gangs hanging around on street corners, and you could look people in the eye without clenching your fist at the same time. I liked just to walk the streets looking at the old squashed-up buildings, or to go down to the docks after training to watch the boats coming and going. There were plenty of docks where I came from, but they were involved in the berthing of huge cargo ships from around the world and shipbuilding in Govan.

On my first visit I stayed in the Carlton Hotel in Berners Street. These days I often use the Carlton Hotel in London's West End. Comparing the two would be like comparing a bowl of gruel to a banquet. But I didn't care about the basic accommodation plus evening meal. I was there to play football. There were dozens of young lads there all chasing a dream. One of them who was on the verge of signing on as an apprentice was Russell Osman. He later became a great team-mate of mine. He was an exceptional boy. He went to a rugby-playing school and played for England at schoolboy level in that sport before eventually winning eleven full England caps at football.

I was very nervous at the trials. It was very hard. Although I'd had some good youth footballers around me in Scotland, the ones I was mixing with in Ipswich were of a different class. They were bigger, stronger and fitter, and they wanted to win more than the lads I had been playing with up to that time. Undoubtedly that made me a better player. I noticed the same thing when I went for trials at Tottenham. Bigger and stronger. And I was quickly getting the same way with all the extra training.

In London, I was in a pub in White Hart Lane itself with another Scots lad who was down for trials at the same time when we were picked on by a group of locals because of our accents. There were six of them, and they tried to run us out of 'their' pub. But we stood our ground and took our jackets off. Neither of us was the slightest bit worried. In fact we were confident we could see them off. They were small and thin and spotty. I bared my teeth at them and invited them to come and get us. We must have given out vibrations because it was *us* who ended up chasing *them* down the road, and we were serious about trying to catch them. We had aggression in us.

I went to Everton too. I couldn't believe the size of the operation there. Goodison Park looked massive. Bellefield was the most impressive training ground I had seen, and they felt like the biggest club in the world. But when the offer of an apprenticeship came from Ipswich just before my sixteenth birthday, I took it.

CHAPTER EIGHT

IPSWICH GLORY
YEARS

*Shock and panic spread across Bobby's
face as he realised the coach was on its
way. We were all rolling about killing
ourselves laughing. And then it got even
better. Bobby suddenly pulled up sharply,
his face creased into agony. He had pulled
a calf muscle and was now hopping
around on one foot. It was too much
to bear.*

ON 5 September 2001, England played Albania in a World Cup qualifier at St James's Park. The previous evening Porky and I had held a fans' forum in a working men's club in Walker, Newcastle. That was the occasion on which my broadcasting pal nearly got lynched after telling the Newcastle fans they were not hungry enough for glory. On the night of the game Porky and I were invited to a banquet at St James's Park prior to kick-off. My old boss, and former England manager, Bobby Robson was to be the guest of honour, and I was going to be seated near to him. To this day I have great affection for the gaffer, or 'boss' as I still call him, though as I will outline below the relationship between us was not always cordial.

The transformation of Newcastle's ground since the days when I played there was quite astonishing. I remembered Gallowgate, as the locals called it, as a ramshackle old stadium that looked as though it was falling apart. But now it was a magnificent structure towering into the sky and worthy of a great team. Inside, the ballrooms were as good as anything you would find in a four-star hotel.

Before the banquet, Porky and I drifted down to the Quayside for a few heart-warmer drinks. That enclave of bars and restaurants on the bank of the River Tyne has got to be one of Britain's top fun spots. Oh, to be a young and single footballer again around here! I thought to myself as we strolled along in the breeze of a mild September evening, though that is not something I would ever admit to my wife. For me, Newcastle has a feel to it which is a bit like Glasgow. It has a very strong regional identity. The people are proud of their roots and their city, and there is a camaraderie among them that reminds me of my hometown – or, rather, half of it. I could see how Bobby Robson's character had been forged in this sort of environment.

We arrived at the ground in good spirits and made our way to our table. Within minutes somebody hit the gong. Silence, and we were all asked to stand for the entrance of the guest of honour. You could hear the muffled noise of the waiters readying the meal in the kitchens, but little else as Bobby and his entourage marched in. Bobby was not really focusing on anything as he came up the central aisle with Sir John Hall, the president of Newcastle. He had that sort of vague look about him. He had almost reached the top table when he caught sight of me out of the corner of his eye. He stopped, and everybody stopped with him. Then he walked off the main gangway, pushed past two tables to where I was standing, and peered at me.

'Where's your tie, son?' he asked me in front of 500 of the city of Newcastle's finest citizens. He spoke to me as though I was an apprentice footballer.

I was so stunned and embarrassed I just spluttered out, 'I'm sorry, boss. I was feeling the heat a bit.'

He wagged his finger at me. 'You're a guest here. Be respectful, and get yourself a tie.'

'Yes, boss,' I said. 'Right away.'

Satisfied, he went back to his position and we all gave him a round of applause.

I've probably done myself no favours over the years by challenging authority, but coming from my old boss like that it seemed perfectly natural. In a funny sort of a way I was chuffed that twenty years after I had ceased playing for him he still had enough interest in me to pull me up. When I look back, I have so much to thank him for in terms of putting his faith in me and shaping me up in those early, vital years.

However, when I first went to Ipswich I was on the youth scheme and I had little to do with Mr Robson, as us youngsters reverentially called him in those days. The youth coaches were the bane of our lives. Sometimes you could fall out with them, but they were the guys we had to please; your future was in their hands. I played on a Saturday morning on the pitch next to the stadium at Portman Road in the South-East Counties League. Sometimes, if the first team were at home that day, Bobby would be there for part of the game, and it always gave you a bit extra in the tank when you knew the boss was about. For me, it was also reassuring that he took such an interest in the youngsters. I think Sir Bobby, as I should rightly call him these days, realised what a vital period it is in a young player's life, trying to make that leap from outstanding prospect to worthy professional. Over the years, clubs have let players go who they thought would not make the grade, only for them to establish themselves as top players and return to haunt them. Graeme Souness left Spurs, and David Platt Manchester United, their first clubs, before they made their mark on the game. Ipswich had a very extensive youth policy, probably because they figured that as they weren't a big-town club they could save themselves a lot of money by developing their own talent rather than buying it in. They particularly seemed to concentrate on bringing boys down from the north of England and Scotland.

I felt at home really quickly. I settled in with a family in a lovely little village called Bramford which gave me a taste for Suffolk life at its best. After a football career which has taken me all over the world, I still live in 'Constable country'. I made instant friends with the other lads. We all earned £12 a week. We got paid on Thursdays and we were always broke on Fridays. We spent our money on flash clothes and small bets down at the bookies in the afternoons. We didn't do much boozing in those days. We were actually banned by the club from drinking because we were under age, but like all young men we challenged that rule.

The first time I got caught out it taught me that as a footballer you were constantly in the public eye and you had to behave yourself. We had all gone into a town-centre pub/disco on a Saturday night. It was packed with young people and we were letting our hair down. The landlord seemed to be constantly looking over at us, though it never occurred to us that it was because we were footballers. How would he know us? We weren't yet playing in front of crowds or having our picture in the local papers. We had only been there an hour when the door burst open and the youth coach, Charlie Woods, came rushing in. He might as well have used a bulldozer to come through the door. We were talking to a group of girls at the time. I have always prided myself on my swift reactions, and I dropped to the floor instantly and clambered under a table.

Woods rushed over and rounded up my mates. 'Where's Brazil?' I heard him shouting. 'I saw him here. Where is he?' My pals said nothing. The coach became exasperated. 'I'm sure I saw that frizzy hair as I came in. Where is he?'

One of the other apprentices with me, piped up. 'He's not here, Charlie,' he said. 'Your eyesight must be going.'

Woods warned him about his lip, then marched him and the other lads out of the bar. It was a close escape, and a valuable lesson.

In my first apprenticeship year at Ipswich, tragedy struck when I damaged a cartilage. I did in my right knee down the outside. Looking back, I am convinced it was a result of the 'doggies' we used to do in training. These were very fast shuttles that involved quick turns. Where we turned, a hole would develop in the ground, and I remember that several times I felt the strain on my knee as my foot caught in the hole. That put the mockers on that season, but I was a very determined young man and I wanted to get into the first team alongside luminaries like Paul Mariner, Clive Woods, George Burley, Paul Cooper and Brian Talbot. In fact, I think the way I came back after that early injury may have been largely responsible for me making the grade.

My second apprenticeship season, 1976/77, was a brilliant launching pad for my pro career. I scored a hatful of goals in various competitions. In one month alone I scored four in four consecutive games. One of the most memorable matches was against Portsmouth, away, in the FA Youth Cup. Ian St John, the Liverpool legend, was Portsmouth manager and was at the game. For 85 minutes I was kicked up in the air by a very robust defender called Graham Roberts. In the 86th minute I skipped out of one of his leg-breaking lunges and scored with a rocket of a shot. As I celebrated I made a very disparaging remark to him. He tried to chase me across the field, but he wasn't quick enough. Many years later we became team-mates at Spurs (I'd rather be on his side than play against him). Yes, even at that tender age I was up against players who became great friends in later life. Another player I played against, but this time in a Spurs shirt, was a young man with long hair called Glenn Hoddle.

Football is a very transient industry, and over the next decade I played with and against people, sometimes in the same week, as the carousel kept turning around. At the end of the season I was voted South-East Counties Player of the Year and was presented with a trophy by Terry Venables at the Café Royal in London. It was my first real taste of the big time, and I knew immediately that I wanted a lot more of it.

After a subsequent tour of Germany and Switzerland, our lives changed virtually overnight. On returning from the tour we were all told about our futures. To this day it remains one of the most distressing moments of my life. I assumed we were all going to be kept on because we had a very good team. What I didn't realise was that the first team was still relatively young and a lot of those top players were going to be around for many more years. Only Terry Butcher, Russell Osman and I were retained; for the others it was an envelope with a few bob and a note of thanks. It was heartbreaking. We were still only kids, yet lives were being shattered. Some of those who got the boot that day were great mates. We had bonded together and felt like brothers. There were tears, and words of consolation. Many of the lads stayed around in Ipswich. They had girlfriends there, and had put down roots. I still see some of them. They have gone into other professions and trades and made good lives for themselves.

I was given my first professional contract. I would be getting £50 a week. I was thrilled. The life of an apprentice in those days was nothing like it is today. We had to clean the dressing rooms and the older players' boots. We looked after laundry and the kit. And we were always having fights. Armed with brushes and buckets, we used to lay into each other. I supposed it was just our pent-up energy. I made sure nobody messed with me. One of the bigger guys was constantly baiting me. I knew he had this ritual of always putting his boots on last before leaving the dressing room, so on the bus to the game I found his holdall. His boots were zipped up inside a separate bag. I took them out and unscrewed all the studs from the soles. There were only five minutes to go to kick-off when he got his boots out. He went mad. He shouted and screamed and demanded we give him his studs back. We all sat there laughing at him. Apart from him, I was the last to leave the changing room. As I did I turned round and pelted him with his own studs. He never came near me again.

I made my debut for the first team against Manchester United on 14 January 1978. It was fabulous, but we lost 2–1 at home. I made only two other first-team appearances that season, but at the age of eighteen I was thrilled to have at least made the breakthrough to football at the highest level.

Ipswich had a poor season in the league, but were having a great FA Cup run. The semi-final at Highbury against West Brom was one of the classic ties of all time. Ron Atkinson, who was to figure significantly in my future career, was West Brom's manager in the days when he really was known as 'Bojangles' because of his love of glitzy jewellery. It was blood and guts; West Brom's centre half John Wile finished the game with a bloodied head bandage. We won 3–1 to book our place in the final with Arsenal, and we lifted the cup after beating the Gunners 1–0. It was a desperately sad day for centre forward Robin Turner. He had scored in every round and expected to be in the final line-up, but he was dropped for David Geddis. David was playing regularly with me in the reserves but he was much more experienced than me. He got the shout on the day, but it was Roger Osborne who scored the winning goal.

I was thrilled to be on the staff of the FA Cup-winning team, but I wasn't going to be around very long to celebrate. The following morning I was due to go to America on the adventure of a lifetime. I had been loaned out to Detroit Express in the North American Soccer League. I went to the Cup-winning celebration party at the Royal Lancaster Hotel and had a great night. But towards the end of the evening I realised I didn't have any money. Eric Gates, Ipswich Town's midfielder and resident Geordie, lent me £40, even though he was as broke as I was. I used that to get to Heathrow the following morning. I didn't need any money after landing in the US because I was being met at JFK airport in New York and being taken straight to the Giants Stadium.

I only made the game at half-time. It was a match against the New York Cosmos. We won that first game 2–1, though I didn't get off to a great start because I was feeling the effects of the transatlantic flight. Still, after the game, I struck up an immediate rapport with my team-mates. The squad was made up of a couple of Englishmen, a few Americans and some South Americans, including Brazilians. We were all young and enjoying the experience.

And what an experience. I lived in an apartment overlooking the Pontiac Silverdome, our home ground. I had a cleaning lady, and the porter in the block of flats looked after everything from my laundry to my post and ordering the groceries. My fridge was as big as my mum and dad's garage. A lot of that might sound quite normal by today's standards, but this was the late 1970s and I was still a teenager. It was like being royalty. The nightlife was good as well. There was a nightclub that we used near the ground called the Three Faces. The first time I went in there it was like walking on to the set of the film that was the great box-office hit at the time – *Saturday Night Fever*. I didn't actually buy myself a white suit, but I wouldn't have been out of place if I had. And, of course, the football was marvellous. We flew to places like Boston, San Diego, San José, Los Angeles and Portland, Oregon. Discovering those American cities was fantastic. I lined up against some of the best players in the world, including George Best. There were a host of Brazilian and German internationals, too. Trevor Francis came out and starred for us. There was a tremendous buzz because we thought we were the pioneers of a football revolution that was going to establish 'soccer' in America. That, of course, still hasn't happened. I think it's because the Americans cannot understand a game that sometimes doesn't have a winner. They like high scores, no matter what the sport. In basketball the score never stays the same for more than about 30 seconds. The Yanks would prefer that to happen in football, too. Nevertheless, a raft of good footballers have come out of the States since that era, particularly goalkeepers, some of whom have made it big in the Premiership.

This all lasted four months, and on the last night all the players got together for a farewell party. We had become great buddies, and we made the usual promises to look each other up, though I knew we'd probably never see each other again. We found a bar somewhere that belonged to the uncle of one of the boys, and he shut it for the night to allow us to party at will. In those days I was only a beer drinker, but that night I must have drunk half of Lake Michigan. And one of the South American lads got me to smoke, which I had never done before. The cigarette he gave me was a great big fat thing. I'd never seen people smoking fags like that in England. Seconds after I put it to my lips the room started spinning around. It was the weirdest feeling I have ever experienced. But it wasn't unpleasant. I felt like I was floating. I was so naive that I didn't realise it was a joint of marijuana. I remembered smelling the same sort of fumes that I could smell now in the corridors of some of the hotels I had been to. It all made sense. When I thought that the South Americans looked a bit dopey and withdrawn, they were in fact stoned.

I had no inhibitions at all when I left the party. I was laughing a lot, and I laughed even more when I got into my car, which I hadn't previously planned to be driving. Another tremendous bonus of being in America was that, as Detroit was the 'motor city', we had all been given a sponsored car called a Gremlin. I had to learn to drive before I could pick mine up. The problem was that it was the same hideous bright orange colour as our strip. I drove off on the wrong side of the road, forgetting that I was in the United States. I was still laughing when I was flagged down by a cop car. When they asked me what I thought I was doing driving on the wrong side of the road, I laughed like a drain. They made me spread myself over the bonnet of my car, *Starsky & Hutch* style. When they started waving a gun around I stopped laughing and became instantly sober. I explained as best I could that I was a footballer playing for Detroit Express. What saved me from real trouble was the fact that I had a British Airways airline ticket in my pocket to take me back to London the next day. They clearly thought their city would be better off without me, so they escorted me home (one of them drove my car) and said they would be back the next day to check I had gone.

On the flight home I had a total of $80 in my pocket. That

was just about enough to pay Gatesy the £40 I owed him when I had set off. I don't know where the rest of my money had gone. I had been earning about ten times my pay at Ipswich but I had spent it all on travelling, clothes and socialising. I was broke again.

But I came back full of optimism for the new season, which had already started. I thought about getting myself a car but I couldn't afford it on my money. I thought I had a valid driving licence because when I was in the road-tax office with a pal I had shown the bloke behind the counter my US licence. I don't know what he thought it was, but he told me it was valid. For 1978/79 I was staying at digs in a lovely little village called Capel St Mary. I needed to get to the bookies because I wanted to put a big bet on; I didn't have such a thing as a telephone account. It was raining, and the landlady said I could take her husband, Tony's, car.

As soon as I got out on the road I knew I had a problem. My car in America was automatic; this one had a clutch. I didn't know how to operate it. I kept yanking the gearstick around, making the most dreadful noises. I lost concentration on one bend, mounted the kerb, hit a lamp post and demolished somebody's garden fence. I was disappointed because I thought I was going to miss the race. Foolishly, I abandoned the car and made for the bookies on foot. I wasn't running away or anything, I hadn't had a drink, and I fully intended to go into the police station to report it. But I thought I'd better tell the landlord first, so I rang him and told him I'd written off his car. He laughed down the line, telling me that was impossible because his car was in the garage. But, as I explained to him what had happened, he went deadly quiet. What I had not considered was that I had no insurance. It also turned out that

I didn't have a valid licence either. The police were going to charge me with all sorts of things, but the club looked after Tony's car and got me a solicitor who sorted everything out. I ended up being cautioned.

I was substitute for a lot of games up to Christmas that season. Then, in the New Year, I started getting more opportunities. I was learning in every game playing alongside Paul Mariner, one of the hardest men I have ever met in the game. If I had been a defender I would have thrown a sickie rather than face Mariner.

The biggest moment of my footballing life to that date was when Bobby Robson pulled me aside while we were training in Barcelona in March 1979 for the second leg of the European Cup Winners' Cup semi-final. I thought I was along just for the ride and the experience, but I was wrong. The night before the game we went to the Camp Nou, the legendary stadium that was the biggest in Europe at the time. I had never seen anything like it. It was so huge that you could hardly see the sky unless you were lying flat on your back. It was awe-inspiring. Probably for the first time, I reflected on the privilege of being a footballer. I was sitting on a ball in the middle of the pitch with huge empty stands all around me thinking, 'Every schoolboy in the world would like to be where I am now.'

After we had finished I went back down the tunnel. The attention to detail was so impressive. Clearly the people who ran this club took tremendous pride in it as an institution. There was a picture of El Presidente in the tunnel, and even the cleaners wore uniforms in the same colours as the famous blue and claret stripes. The club's badge was embroidered on the seats in the dug-out. I had never seen that sort of thing at a club before.

I have always preferred playing under floodlights to afternoon games. For me, there is something special about a game under lights. Perhaps it's because midweek games were usually cup ties or replays, which meant they had a special edge. Or maybe it was the atmosphere of the crowd. Everybody might have had a hard day at work, but now they were here to lap up the game and voice their support. Even more so, I enjoyed floodlit games abroad. Maybe that was because of the Continental lifestyle, particularly in Mediterranean countries, where they think nothing of going out for dinner after the game until three in the morning. Barcelona was one step up from domestic floodlit games. When the floodlights are on it looks like a spaceship. Its architecture reminds me more of a cathedral than a football ground. Even way down in the dressing rooms you can hear the distinctive rumble of the vociferous crowd above you.

Barcelona were desperate for European glory because their arch rivals, Real Madrid, had by that time won six European Cups. But we had a 2–1 advantage from the first leg, when Gatesy had nabbed both our goals. We were in one of those classic situations where we had to decide whether to defend our precious one-goal lead or go for glory. The problem was that Barcelona had that vital away goal from Portman Road, so they only needed to win 1–0. That's why we decided to go at them.

As we lined up in the tunnel, the strangest thing happened. Members of their team kept disappearing and coming back. I thought they must be so nervous that they were all going off for a leak. But when I looked closer at the little room into which they were disappearing I realised it was a chapel. In this fiercely Catholic region, they were saying prayers. I wondered whether, to wind them up, I should go and say a prayer too. After all, I was of the same faith. I gave that idea up when the giant who I learnt had been given the job of marking me fixed me with a stare and pulled his finger under his throat. I bared my teeth at him and made a rude gesture with my fist.

The atmosphere was electric out on the pitch. It was very hot, but the grandeur of my surroundings inspired me. I couldn't wait to get at them. All the lads felt the same. We played our hearts out that night but went down to the 1–0 scoreline we'd dreaded. We had nothing at all to be ashamed about, though. They were a very good team, and they went on to win the final, beating Fortuna Düsseldorf 4–3.

It was a marvellous experience for me, and it kick-started a great run towards the end of the season. In our next game we lost 2–0 at Anfield to Liverpool, the champions-elect who had won the title twice in the last three seasons. Then we entertained Manchester City, and I scored in a 2–1 victory. We didn't get beaten again for the remaining ten games of the season as the team started knitting together, and in the last six games I scored seven times, including two apiece against Bolton and Chelsea – one of my best goalscoring runs for the club. Can you believe, now, that Chelsea finished bottom of the First Division that season and were relegated? The transformation at the club, which I believe was largely down to the energy and guile of Ken Bates, has been astonishing. We played there in a ground that was one-third full. Though a building programme had started, there were still parts of the ground that looked as though they should have been knocked down.

My end-of-season run could not have come at a better time. Now that the summer was upon us I was determined to get my contract and pay deal sorted out. The previous Christmas I had turned down an improved offer from Bobby Robson. He'd wanted to double my wages from £50 to £100. Players didn't have agents or anything like that in those days, but my instincts told me I was being short-changed, so I turned it down. I remember the boss saying to me, 'It's a very good offer. It might not be there at the end of the season.' I figured that was a risk I would have to take, and that if I was any good I would get a better deal in the summer. The only thing that worried me was whether or not it would affect my very solid relationship with Bobby. But it didn't. He was too much of a pro to let something off the pitch impinge upon the workings of the team. And, fortunately, I was right to wait. Before the new 1979/80 season started I was given a new deal of £300 a week with a £12,000 signing-on fee. I couldn't believe it. My dad had never earned £12,000 a year in his life.

I had, by now, got myself a proper driving licence, so I walked into a Toyota dealer and told the salesman that I wanted to buy the beautiful red Celica that was sitting in the middle of his showroom. He was at first sceptical. He asked me if I had arranged a loan. 'No, I'm paying cash,' I said. The salesman now looked suspicious. He clearly didn't follow football because I had been all over the local evening paper, the *Evening Star*, as a result of my great run of goals. At that moment one of the mechanics came into the showroom with the previous night's paper and asked me to autograph it across my picture on the back page. He explained to his colleague who I was. The salesman's attitude then changed from being slightly sniffy and unhelpful to gushing and gracious. 'What about a test drive?' I said. We went out in the car and it was the most beautiful thing I had ever experienced. I'll never forget the smell of its newness, or the fact that it had protective sheets of paper on the floor. I couldn't wait to do the deal.

I rushed off to the bank to get a cheque and went into Nusted's coffee bar in the centre of town, where the players used to meet up with each other because it was opposite the bookies. My team-mate Russell Osman was in there. I got on really well with him. We were the same age and we had come through the ranks together. I told him excitedly about my car. He seemed underwhelmed.

'Well, what have you been up to?' I asked.

'I've just bought a house,' he said.

This was unfathomable to me. How could he have bought a house? Only older people bought houses. I was quite happy in my digs. But Russell was a very canny boy. He had gone to a public school, and even before he started to impress as a footballer he had played for the English Schools rugby team. And as we got talking I could see the sense in it all. He took me up to the new estate where he'd made his purchase. A few hours earlier I'd felt I'd made it because I'd bought my first new car. Now I decided to go one better. I went into the development's sales office and bought the house next door to Russell. It cost £24,000, and I put £6,000 down. Then I rang the Toyota salesman, cancelled the car and bought a second-hand Triumph Spitfire instead.

The 1979/80 season was a breakthrough for us. That was when we put the marker down that we were going to become a power in the land. For the first four months we were pretty poor, losing games home and away. But in December we pulled ourselves together and started winning and scoring goals. In January we moved into top gear. We beat West Brom 4–0 on

New Year's Day. A month later we went to Goodison Park, my favourite ground, where the atmosphere was always fantastic, and notched up another 4–0 victory. I scored two that day, and I was on fire.

Then, on the first day of March, the mighty Manchester United came to Ipswich, managed by Dave Sexton. They were vying with the team of the decade, Liverpool, for the title. Arsenal were in third place. If we wanted to make a serious tilt at the championship and even a European place then we had to make a statement against United. Our message could not have been clearer. We walloped them 6–0 – an unbelievable result. Mariner got a hat-trick, I scored two, and Frans Thijssen got the other. Bobby Robson's signing of our two Dutchmen, Frans, and Arnold Muhren, proved a masterstroke which added real class to the side. Muhren was particularly important to me. He had the instinct to know when I was about to go, and he delivered pinpoint passes for me to run on to. Half my goals over the next two seasons came via that route.

After the first week of December we didn't lose a game until the last day of the season, when we went down 2–1 to Manchester City. Our form since the New Year had been that of champions, and as we went into the 1980/81 season it was the First Division title that we set our eyes upon. We flew through pre-season. Everybody looked strong. It was a talented team that had come to maturity. From goalkeeper Paul Cooper through defenders Butcher, Osman, Burley and Mills to midfielders Gatesy, Muhren, Thijssen and Johnny Wark, with Mariner and me up front. We believed our time had come.

Kevin Beattie had a very unlucky season. He was a hugely talented player, a rock of a defender, but he played only seven games and broke his arm with a few games to go, which effectively finished his career at Ipswich. 'Beats' was an individual. He would often do something out of the ordinary. One time when he should have got a train to Scotland to join the England U-23 squad, he diverted to his home in Carlisle to see his parents because he was feeling homesick. Apparently he forgot to inform the authorities, and panic spread as the word went out: 'Find Beattie'. But everything was fine. He was tracked down to his local pub, the Magpie, where he was supping a pint and playing dominoes with some ex-schoolmates.

We started the season on fire. We felt invincible. I got among the goals early. We realised we could take the title as early as 30 August, when we beat Everton 4–0 at home. Everton were no great team that season, but it was the quality of our performance that mattered. In the next game we beat Aston Villa 1–0. Villa had also started well and were just below us at the top of the table. Then we went to Liverpool for the real test. Nobody ever got anything at Anfield. Their home support was the most impressive in the world. In those days the Kop was a huge concrete terrace that seemed to stretch up into the sky. The fervour those 20,000 fans generated with banners and scarves was spectacular. Many times when I played there I used to see these huge surges of fans piling forwards when Liverpool got close to goal, only to drift back again as the excitement subsided. It was like watching waves on a beach. We got a 1–1 draw. All was going well.

The only thing that worried me was that I didn't seem to have the best of relationships with the Ipswich crowd. I don't know why. Nobody was more committed than me. There were other Scotsmen in the team, like my good pals Johnny Wark and George Burley, so I don't think it was that. I didn't receive as much encouragement as I thought I was due, and even when I scored goals, like the one against Everton, they seemed to be received with a muted response.

The boss was on fine form because of the team's results, but we didn't half annoy him on our away trip to Sunderland in October. He was very keen to get back to London after the match and it was going to be a tight schedule to get the coach to the station in time for the train. Before we went into the ground Bobby gave a strict deadline instruction to the driver: the coach was going at 5.15 on the dot; anybody not on board then would be left behind.

We won 2–0. Arnold Muhren and I scored the goals. He made mine, and I, in turn, supplied the ball for his. We had a great understanding. We all got back on the coach by the deadline, but Bobby was standing at the players' entrance 50 yards behind us, talking to people and signing autographs. He'd clearly lost track of the time. Just to cause mischief, we started putting pressure on the driver to get going. Club secretary David Rose tried to intervene but we shouted him down. The driver, feeling intimidated (he may not even have known that the manager was not on the coach), started up the engine. We were on the back seat hiding behind the headrests. As soon as Mr Robson heard the roar he looked up. Then the driver eased out the clutch and we were moving. Shock and panic spread across Bobby's face as he realised the coach was on its way. He sprinted after us, followed by a large group of autograph-hunting kids. We were all rolling about killing ourselves laughing as he shouted and waved his arms about, trying to get the driver to stop. And then it got even better. Bobby suddenly pulled up sharply, his face creased into agony. He had pulled a calf muscle and was now hopping around on one foot. It was just too much to bear. Tears were rolling down our faces. I was gasping for breath. The driver had stopped by now. Bobby eventually limped up the steps at the front. I'd never seen him so angry. His face was thunderous and his language was dreadful. 'Is that somebody's idea of a joke?' he said. 'I can hardly walk. Where's the physio?' Then he laid into David Rose for letting it happen. He laid into the driver, too. 'This coach goes when I say it goes, and when I am on board it!'

We lost our first game at Brighton. It was a Tuesday night game in November and it was the coldest I have ever felt on a football field in this country. There was a storm blowing in from the sea. I'm sure I could hear the waves crashing on to the front. The wind was whipping the ball around as though it was a balloon.

On Boxing Day we played Norwich City at home. I scored, and the fans' reaction defied my fears about getting a cool reception. As I was from Scotland I'd had no idea about the fierce rivalry between these two East Anglian clubs until I started playing in those matches. The tea lady could have scored against the Canaries and she would have been given the freedom of the town. We beat them 2–0, a Jock double as my Scots mucker, Johnny Wark, grabbed the other. That result would have made for a fine celebration except for the fact that the very following day we played Arsenal at Highbury and drew 1–1. There's a lot of talk in the modern game about fixture pile-ups, but that Arsenal game was our fourth in ten days. Our only defeat was away at Tottenham, 3–5.

At the halfway stage of the season our championship challenge was looking very strong. We'd progressed through the early rounds of the UEFA Cup, too, and we were ready to launch our assault on the FA Cup. I also received a huge vote of confidence from the manager. He'd been bashing on at me ever since I arrived at the club to be even tougher in my game and to work more on retaining possession. There had even been talk of him going out to buy another striker to give me competition for my place alongside Mariner. But he told a newspaper early in the New Year, 'Brazil is now much more aggressive on the ball, not a wallflower to be brushed off it. He shows composure, has electric pace, and if he keeps on progressing he can go all the way to the top. At the beginning of this season I thought I might have to buy a striker to strengthen my options up front, but Brazil's development has prevented me from having to do that. He is now truly an international-class striker.' I also heard from other sources that Bobby was talking me up big time with Scotland boss Jock Stein. I had won my first two caps the year before against Hungary and Poland, and naturally I wanted to add to that tally. But more of that in a later chapter.

In the third round of the FA Cup, the first one in which the top clubs compete, we were at home to Aston Villa, who were clearly a threat to our league championship ambitions. But we had already beaten them at home in the league and psychologically we were determined to boot them out of the cup as well. And we did just that, 1–0. We then disposed of Shrewsbury at Portman Road in a replay, and saw off Charlton Athletic at home. By mid-March we were flying and we believed ourselves to be unstoppable. We had won ten and drawn two of our previous twelve league games. In addition, by then we had also knocked the European champions Nottingham Forest out of the FA Cup after a replay. I had scored eight goals during that run, and everyone at the club felt we were heading for glory. We were also having a great season in Europe. We had got past French champions St Etienne to get to the semi-final of the UEFA Cup. That was one of the greatest achievements that season. St Etienne were a fine team and had never been beaten at home in European competition. They had some of the biggest players in the world at the time, including Johnny Rep and Michel Platini.

The first leg of that quarter-final was in France, and the day before the game a few of the lads and I went for walk. We came across a lovely little tavern, which we called Uncle Tom's Cabin, where we had some lunch. The locals were naturally all big St Etienne fans and they were telling us how badly we were going to get beaten. They had never heard of Ipswich and were convinced we were going to get hammered. Their patronising talk didn't bother us. In the previous round we had clobbered the Polish team Widzew Lodz, including their star player Boniek, and Lodz had beaten Juventus 5–0 on their way to play us. I remember that in Poland we gave dozens of bars of chocolate to loads of local kids. They treated them like they were gold.

On the night of the St Etienne game the pitch had been soaked. As we left the tunnel we got pelted with oranges and apples by the crowd. Early on Johnny Rep scored from a Platini corner. But these things didn't bother us in the slightest. When the final whistle went we had hammered them 4–1 to shatter the myth of their home ground being their fortress. The French fans even applauded us off the pitch. We weren't flying back until the next day, so that night we went back to Uncle Tom's Cabin. We were greeted like heroes, and the locals bought us cases of champagne. We added to their pain by trouncing their team 3–1 in the return leg.

In April we entertained FC Cologne in the semi-finals. We won the first leg at home, but only by the odd goal. Paul Mariner took a particular dislike to the centre half who was marking him, a giant of a man called Gerd Strack. He looked like a lumbering oaf, and Mariner said that behind the referee's back he'd been having a real dig at him throughout the game. In the return leg in Cologne we were in the tunnel and the Germans were almost celebrating victory already. They had a partisan 60,000 crowd on their side and there was no doubt that they had the advantage. Mariner went up to his marker, the dopey Strack, and put five fingers up in his face. 'That's how long you're going to last tonight, pal,' he said. 'Five minutes and you'll be off.'

I don't know whether Strack understood English or not. He probably thought Paul was trying to boast he was going to score five goals. He should have taken more notice, because after about three minutes we got an early corner. As the ball came swinging in, Mariner went up with Strack, smashed his elbow into the German's face at exactly the same time as he met the ball, and headed it just over the bar. Then, as the big German collapsed to the ground, Mariner came down on top of his opponent's ankle, twisted his studs on impact and innocently walked away. The ref had seen nothing. The Cologne defender lay writhing on the pitch. He was only semi-conscious; his nose was bleeding profusely and the stud scars were showing through his torn sock. I've never seen so many officials run on to a pitch. Two physios came on first, followed by a doctor, the coach, the trainer, the president of the club and four stretcher-bearers. All of them urged the referee to send Paul off. The crowd were going mad too, but Mariner had struck so quickly that nobody really saw the elbow, and he successfully pleaded that the landing was an accident.

It was a vital moment for us. The West Germany international Rainer Bonhof had been marking me, but now they had to reshuffle their defence. They became disorganised to the extent that our own centre half, Terry Butcher, was able to push forwards, and he scored the only goal of the game with a thumping header.

We were through to the UEFA Cup final, and it was a victory we badly needed to put our season back on track. Between the two legs of the Cologne match we had lost in the semi-final of the FA Cup, to Manchester City 1–0 at Villa Park after extra time. The game was desperately close on a shockingly heavy pitch. Near the end of the game I believed I was about to score the winner when I positioned myself to meet a cross from the left. It was falling just short of the height at which I could volley it so I moved out a yard to allow it to bounce so that I could whack it on the half-volley. It hit the ground in exactly the right place, and with the goalkeeper on the other side of the goal I knew precisely where I was going to put it when it came up off the pitch. I swung my left boot at it, but I thrashed through fresh air. The ball had hit a patch of sand and stopped dead. It was a lifeline for my marker. I was off balance, and he slid in to clear it. The dressing room afterwards was like the annexe of a mausoleum. Aston Villa and Villa Park were becoming a major factor in our season.

Our very next away game, three days later, was on the same ground against Villa. We had been on top of the league since beating Birmingham City in January, and the Midlands giants, just below us, were the biggest threat to our title ambitions. In addition to going out of the FA Cup, our league form had slumped. We had lost three successive away games to Manchester United, Leeds United and West Brom. Now the

Villa game on 14 April had become the most important of the season. I scored one of the goals as we beat them 2–1 to restore our status as favourites for the title. It was the third time we had hammered them that season.

But we were limping towards the end of the season. Injuries and exhaustion rocked us. Johnny Wark and I both suffered bouts of flu. Mariner missed games with an ankle injury. Beats played only eleven games, and George Burley was out for a long spell. The Villa victory might have been good for us, but it was negated four days later by a slip-up in our next home game, when Arsenal beat us 2–0. Just two days after that, on the Monday night, we went to arch rivals Norwich, who were desperate to stop us taking the title, and to avenge their defeat earlier in the season. We got clobbered 1–0.

The league had now become a seesaw race with Villa. We beat Manchester City at home at the end of April which set us up for the last weekend of the season. We had a game in hand over Villa, who were two points ahead of us. They had to lose at Highbury against Arsenal and we had to beat Boro to keep our championship hopes alive. It would have meant a spectacular finish for us because we could then win the title at home against Southampton in the last game of the season. At half-time in the north-east we were 1–0 up through Paul Mariner, and Villa were 1–0 down. But they went on to win and we lost. They now had a four-point advantage and we had only one game left. We had lost the title. It was another very quiet dressing room.

Bobby Robson did a magnificent job of picking us up, though. He had to. The first leg of the UEFA Cup final was scheduled for 6 May, just four days after the Boro defeat. We entertained the Dutch team AZ 67 Alkmaar at Portman Road, and we absolutely crushed them 3–0. We were of course delighted with that victory, but there was still a sense of terrible frustration that we hadn't shown that sort of form in the crucial league games of the season. Perhaps it was because we were free of the pressures of hunting three trophies that we were in such sparkling form that night. It was a full house, and after the recent disappointments it was a glorious evening. We couldn't wait for the second leg, and that sense of anticipation might have been reflected in the fact that we lost our last league game 3–2 at home to Southampton. I scored, but it was irrelevant.

Over in Holland, we played in the Olympic Stadium in Amsterdam. Despite our comfortable 3–0 lead it was a nerve-jangling night. I don't know if there were dirty tricks at work, but a very strange thing happened to us as we left the hotel. I and four of the other lads were in the lift when it ground to a halt between floors. We were stuck for an hour. It was already a hot night outside, but in that lift it reached boiling point. We had tracksuits on, but by the time they got us to the ground we had all stripped down to our underwear. It was a very unsettling experience, but we knew we had to put it behind us. Alkmaar came at us clearly believing they could still win the trophy. It was a hell of a game, and thank goodness Wark and Thijssen bagged a goal each, because the Dutch scored four. We took the trophy with an aggregate score of 5–4, so our long season ended in glory after all. It was my first major cup and medal.

What a campaign it had been. I'd played 54 games; other team-mates, like Warky, had played 64. We came home triumphant to a wonderful open-top bus parade through the town to the ground. I remember it poured down with rain that night. I was at the front of the bus and I got soaked. A young lady with a very big bust was leaning out of a window very close to us, and I asked her jokingly, 'You haven't got a spare umbrella, have you?' Within seconds she threw one in my direction, but it came at me like a javelin and I had to catch it quickly before it speared Russell Osman, who was standing next to me.

I've never seen so many fans in one place. The whole town turned out. There were people clambering up lamp posts and perilously hanging out of their office windows. I felt elated. It put the disappointments of the league and cup campaigns in the shade. I was only 21 and I just knew this was only the start, though I feared the following season would be a bit of an anticlimax in the wake of our buccaneering adventures in 1980/81.

Sure enough, 1981/82 was a real up-and-down season for me. Although Ipswich weren't fighting on as many fronts through to the end of the season, we still finished second (again), this time to a resurgent Liverpool. They beat us by four points, but we were five points clear of Manchester United. One of my favourite memories of that season is playing at United's home, Old Trafford, in early September. We had drawn our first two games and needed a win. It was 1–1 when I timed a run perfectly from a pinpoint Muhren pass. There was only Martin Buchan between me and the goal. He had no chance. I ran at him, dropped my shoulder and left him sprawling on the ground as I sprinted past. The keeper, Gary Bailey, came towards me. I drew him, then skipped around him and stroked the ball into an empty net. The ground was absolutely silent except for the cheering of a few hundred Ipswich fans who had made the long journey and the yelps of our own players. I'd scored at the die-hard Stretford End, so when I ran behind the goal to celebrate what I thought was a great strike I looked straight into the eyes of the United fans. There were some 20,000 of them on that terrace. I could see the hatred and loathing for me in their eyes. I liked that. When the opposition fans started to hate me it meant I was winning. A few years later I joined United, and I never got on with the fans from day one. Whether or not it was anything to do with the goal I scored that day I do not know. But they were hurt.

At the time I was carrying an injury, a trapped nerve between the toes in my foot. I had to have an injection before every game, and sometimes at half-time too. We went out of the UEFA Cup, the trophy we had battled so hard to win the year before, in the first round to an Aberdeen side managed by an unknown Scotsman, Alex Ferguson. It was a massive disappointment, but the boss decided that it at least presented an opportunity for me to have an operation on my foot. He described me as being like a pincushion because I had had so many jabs. It was while coming back from that operation that I had my first falling out with Ipswich.

I got back to peak fitness after being out for about three weeks, and we were due to play Leeds United in the League Cup, a night game. That October morning we did a bit of light training at the ground, and Bobby said to me, 'You're looking fantastic.' It gave me the clear impression that I would be playing. An hour before the game I was sitting with my shirt on, fastening the studs into my boots, when a group of the other lads came in. Eric Gates and Paul Cooper walked behind me, saw I was wearing my usual number 10 shirt and started laughing. I wasn't in on the joke, but I was too busy with my boots to pursue the matter. Then Bobby came in and announced the team. I was only sub.

I went mad. I started shouting, reminding the boss that I'd played through the pain barrier since the start of the season. I refused to play sub. I stripped off and went for a shower. The Ipswich coach, Bobby Ferguson, dragged me out, and I assumed the boss had relented. I put my shirt back on. But again Bobby Robson said I wasn't starting the game. I took my shirt off and threw it to the floor. I told them again that I was not prepared to be the sub, and went back in the shower. For a second time I was dragged out, and this time I was threatened with a two-week fine and a possible ban if I would not play sub. I had no choice. I put the number 12 shirt on like it was carrying cholera and spent the entire game sulking in the dug-out.

A month later we were playing at Stoke, one of the weakest teams in the division. In our previous game we had lost 3–2 at home to newcomers Swansea. We were determined to put that right, but we soon went one down to the hosts. Whenever things started going wrong Ferguson talked the boss into pulling me out left and putting Gates forward with Mariner. It reminded me of all those years as a kid when I was made to play left wing or left half because I was a rare left-footed player. I ignored the instruction and stayed well away from the left-hand side of the field. Ferguson was screaming at me, but I just cupped my hand to my ear and shook my head as though I couldn't hear him. Gatesy was summoned over to the touchline, and I saw Ferguson, red-faced and ranting, waving his arms about. Eric, who was a lovely, mild-mannered lad off the pitch, came over to me and said he'd been told to tell me to go left. 'I can't hear you, mate,' I said.

We lost the game 2–0. As I walked off the pitch Ferguson tried to confront me. I ducked down the tunnel, and, though there were about ten people between him and me, he continued to shout threats, cursing at me. I quickly stripped off and got straight into the bath, which was in a separate room. I was the only one in there when Ferguson stormed in. He was clearly furious.

'Get out of that bath!' he raged at me. 'Get out of that bath. I want to talk to you!'

I ignored him.

'Get out of that bath,' he repeated, 'or I'm coming in!'

I started laughing at the thought of him jumping in. 'You can't get in this bath, Bobby,' I baited him, 'because it's for players only.' It was a really heated moment.

He was so angry that he didn't know what he was doing. He immediately started to tear off his tracksuit, clearly intending to jump in the bath. Two of the lads who had been listening and giggling behind the wall jumped out to restrain him and dragged him away while he was still screaming threats at me. I didn't realise it at the time, but that was the beginning of the end of my life at Ipswich.

I simmered over the row in the coach on the way back to Ipswich. Over the next couple of days I didn't like some of the things I was hearing around the club. I felt I was getting the blame for our poor run of form. We hadn't won a game for a month, but to point the finger at me was very unfair. I had played for a long time with a trapped nerve. I had come back from the operation in record time, and now I felt I wasn't getting the support I deserved. Some of the other lads were also becoming unhappy. Bobby Ferguson was taking more and more responsibility for team affairs as rumours started to circulate that the boss was being lined up to become the next England manager. I simply didn't see eye to eye with Ferguson.

Back then, he didn't like me and I didn't like him. And the club was embarking on a rebuilding programme for the main stand, which meant that money was going to be tight.

In the most important decision of my football career to that date, I put in a transfer request. I didn't want anybody to think it was just a gesture so I wrote it out myself and took it to the chairman's office. I handed it to Patrick Cobbold. I regretted having to do that because I liked Mr Cobbold and his family, who controlled the club. Unlike some ruling dynasties at football clubs he did not regard the players as serfs. He valued us as professionals.

Bobby Robson was away that day, but I got a call from him that night. He told me to cool down. He said that if he had been at Portman Road that day he would have defused the situation. I remember distinctly that he added, 'I will be back at the club in the morning and we will sort this out. What you've done is on impulse. Let's lower the temperature and see the way things work out over the next couple of weeks. I wish you had spoken to me before you wrote out the transfer request. There's no way you are going anywhere. The first time I saw you play as a kid I knew you were going to be a great player. That's what you have become. There's no way I am going to let you go. I'm turning your request down flat and I want you in good spirits in the team tomorrow for Manchester City.'

They were kind words, and I have always felt a loyalty to the man I have always regarded as the boss, but I was stung and I had no intention of withdrawing my request. I didn't feel appreciated; I wanted to go somewhere where that would happen. I wasn't being impulsive. I loved Ipswich – I still do. I didn't want to leave the area. I had lots of friends there, and I had married a local girl. Jill's family were all there too, and

I was thinking of bringing my mum and dad down from Scotland.

I played in the City game on 28 November and led the line because Mariner was injured. We won, and it was the start of a run of seven consecutive victories in which I scored six goals. Liverpool then managed to put a huge dent in our season. We had reached the semi-finals of the League Cup and we had no fear of the mighty Reds as we had finished well above them the previous season and we had already beaten them 2–0 at our place earlier in the season. In the early months of 1982 they looked like they were shaping up to be our main challengers in the championship. Sandwiched between the two legs was a league game at Anfield, so we saw this first leg of the League Cup semi as a good chance to show them who was the boss.

We played them on the first Tuesday in February at Portman Road. It was a freezing cold night. I even remember wondering whether I should wear gloves – something I had never contemplated before. But then I worried that if there was a picture of me in the papers the next day wearing gloves I would never be able to show my face in Glasgow again.

A problem hit me before the match. After all the angst of the Stoke game when I made it clear I didn't like playing on the left, I was asked to do it again against Liverpool. I tried to put my heart into it but I simply didn't feel like I fitted in. Consequently, the longer the game went on, the more I felt detached and frustrated. We lost 2–0. It caused another row.

We then travelled to Merseyside to play them twice in two days on their own ground. We hoped to use the first match in the league to hit back and give us a psychological advantage for the second leg of the League Cup. I was looking forward to moving back into the middle and trying to put right the errors of the first leg, but, for the first time in my life, I was dropped. I was devastated, and at the time I felt resentful. It was altogether a disastrous night. We got hammered 4–0 – our biggest defeat of the season.

It was no fun being in that part of the world for the next three days. Aggregate score so far, Liverpool 6 – Ipswich 0. Nevertheless, there was no defeatism in us as we took the familiar trek to their ground for the second leg of the League Cup. To my great relief, I was restored to the team. We gave them a real game – I got one of the goals and Gatesy the other in a 2–2 draw – but we didn't really manage to get ourselves out of our slump.

It was about to get worse. Lowly Shrewsbury Town, who had peaked in 1979 when they won the Third Division, were our opponents in the fifth round of the FA Cup. I know you should never take anything for granted, but on the way to the game I was trying to work out who we most fancied in the quarter-finals because we were desperate to get back to a semi and go one better than the previous year. I shouldn't have been so optimistic. We got bounced out by the Division Two side.

A pall of gloom settled over the club, but I could not, in my wildest dreams, have anticipated what was coming next. Every footballer remembers the moment that was probably the peak of his career. For me it came on 16 February 1982. That night I smashed five goals past Southampton. It's a club record that stands to this day, and I can still recall the ecstasy that reverberated around Portman Road as we trooped off the pitch. Glory is usually shared around in a football team. You can go weeks without scoring, but you're still thrilled when one of your team-mates hits the back of the net. And then the lads are pleased for you when you get back on to the scoresheet. But that night I had no choice but to take all the bouquets for myself. It was a momentous night for the club, a perfect antidote to going out of the two cup competitions and an answer to the slump in form that was threatening our title challenge. I was back on form with a bang. I was in a bit of a daze after the game, but I remember saying to a reporter, 'I'm sure if I go outside now I'll see pigs flying.'

I believe that some of the impetus for my record-breaking performance was the fact that the previous day I had been called up for Scotland. It was a World Cup year, so a call-up meant a golden opportunity to go to Spain with the international squad. There was nothing more I wanted than to play for my country in the ultimate competition.

Remarkably, and perhaps to my shame I spent the afternoon before my five goal spree in a Coral bookmaker. I should have been at home having a sleep but I had received a very hot tip from Newmarket which I couldn't miss. I won £600.

Before my five-goal spree against Southampton, who were table-toppers at the time, I had never even scored a league hat-trick. For some weird reason I had told Johnny Wark in the dressing room before the Southampton match that I was going to score a hat-trick that night because he was a midfield player who had scored more goals than me so far. After just twenty minutes of the game I had scored those three goals, in the space of seventeen minutes. I honestly can't remember the other two, though I know I got one near the end because, when the whistle went a few minutes later, I grabbed hold of the ball. The problem was, I didn't realise that between my fourth in the 70th minute and the last one, the match ball had been booted out of the ground. A campaign was organised through the local paper to try to get it back. It turned up ten days later. So I have two balls in a glass cabinet at home for just one scoring spree.

To this day I wonder what happened to that first ball when it flew over the stand. Members of the groundstaff spent a couple of hours that night and more time the following morning looking for it. I have my suspicions that it was 'acquired' by a man whose son went on to play for the club and achieve international glory. The newspaper appeal to get it back put me in mind of those dreadful stories when a baby is taken from a maternity ward. Of course, as the father of three beautiful girls, I would never for one moment equate the loss of a football to the snatching of a new-born baby; it was just that the appeal used the same sorts of phrases: 'Just leave the ball at the *Star*'s office – no questions will be asked'; 'Alan Brazil badly wants to be reunited with his ball'.

The only blip in my happiness that night was that my lovely young wife Jill wasn't at the match. It was the first home game she had missed that season. She was even more fed up than me, though whether or not she would have liked all the fuss is another question. Jill has always been very down to earth from the start of our marriage. There was never any chance of me losing my perspective when she was around. Jill and I had only got married the previous December, so instead of going out on the town for a big celebration I went straight home. I honestly thought I might have concussion or something as I was driving home. Had I really scored five goals? Fortunately, it was the lead item on the local news, which confirmed things for me.

After my five-goal success I was on a high, and so were the club. I hoped that the Southampton result would re-trigger our championship bid and wipe out the pain of the previous season. Unfortunately, it didn't happen, although I scored what I consider to be my best-ever goal in our next game at Leeds United. A through-ball was delivered which was moving at just the right pace as I weighed up my options, 40 yards from goal. Out of the corner of my eye I saw that the keeper was coming off his line, so I lofted the ball like a golf-shot with a six-iron over his head. We won the match 2–0, but then we went on a run of losing away games. Despite having a good run-in, we couldn't clinch the championship, particularly after we lost at home to Nottingham Forest in the penultimate game of the season. It was very disappointing again, but at least I had the satisfaction of being one of the league's top goalscorers with 28, five more at Ipswich than Johnny Wark.

I knew that the 1982/83 season was going to be make or break for me, especially when, as was widely predicted, Bobby Robson left the club to take up the reins at England. It was a tremendous honour for Ipswich Town, particularly as the club had also provided Sir Alf Ramsey, who made England world champions in 1966. But it wasn't great news for the players Bobby left behind. We all wished him tremendous success, but England's gain was definitely our loss. His departure triggered other movements. Arnold Muhren, who had provided me with the chances for at least half of my goals, went to Manchester United. Eric Gates was also on the transfer list, as was keeper Paul Cooper. After a lot of pressure, I signed a five-year deal, which I immediately regretted. I was trying to get settled and convince myself that I had a future at the club. But the boss had recommended to the board that Bobby Ferguson take over, and personally I didn't think he was up to it.

We had a very slow start to the season. We didn't win one of our first six games. We lost twice at home and slumped to the bottom of the First Division. We went out of Europe in the first round, too. I wasn't happy, and that was reflected in my form. I wanted out. I could not see Ipswich achieving the heights we had enjoyed under Robson. I re-filed the transfer request I had put in earlier in the year. When Ferguson realised I was determined to leave, I was granted my request.

As soon as it became public knowledge the speculation started as to where I might go. Ron Atkinson at Old Trafford was known to be a big fan, and Spurs started to show some interest, as did West Brom. I was naturally interested in United because that was where Muhren had gone, and I wanted to link up with him again. Ipswich said they wanted £800,000 for me, which would work out at over £10 million today. I was flattered by the valuation but wondered whether they were putting such a high price on me to frustrate the transfer process. They were also asking for cash rather than player exchange – a huge outlay for any club.

Inevitably, my relationship with Ipswich became strained. I didn't like the way Ferguson was handling things. I have never been accused of not trying, but he started to make those sorts of suggestions. That is anathema to a professional footballer. Every time I pulled on my boots I was prepared to use up every ounce of energy I possessed for my club. The manager went public to say that if I didn't continue to score goals then I would be tossed into the reserves. I didn't need telling that. I wondered if he understood footballers. I was the shop window. In addition to my own pride and principles, I had to impress a prospective buying club.

When you are in dispute with your club, situations often take on a very different perspective to reality. Such a thing happened to me with pretty hilarious results in January as we started our FA Cup campaign after a miserable Christmas (on Boxing Day we got beaten at home by arch rivals Norwich). We had been drawn against Charlton away. Whenever we played away and our destination was London or the south coast, I didn't have to go to the ground to board the coach; because I lived in a little village called Stratford-St-Mary, I had an arrangement that I would be picked up on the main A12 road into London. Jill would run me to the main road and I would hide in the bus shelter until the coach arrived.

It was very cold that day, and I was stamping my feet waiting for the lads. The rendezvous time came and went. Half an hour after that I still hadn't been picked up. By this time I was anxiously pacing the grass verges, and fans on their way to Charlton were waving and hooting their horns at me. One driver coming from the direction of London stopped to tell me that he had seen the coach powering towards the capital twenty minutes earlier. I couldn't figure out how I could have missed it. After all, it had to motor along the A12. But, for the time being, I had to figure out what to do to catch up with it.

There were no mobile phones in those days, but very luckily Jill, who had dropped me off an hour earlier, came driving past on her way home from the shops. I jumped in the car and told her to put her foot down because we had to catch the coach at Brentwood Services, where I knew the team would be stopping for tea and toast. I was shouting at her to go faster and faster, anxiously looking at my watch. We hurtled into the services car park, but there was no coach. I dashed inside to be told that they had only stopped briefly and had left twenty minutes ago.

The problem now was that I had no idea which way the coach would go into London. I didn't have a clue whether

Charlton was in west London or north London. It is in fact in south London – I had to stop at a garage to find that out. I was panicking like mad. We just followed the signs for London, headed south, and went through a tunnel. But, frankly, I may as well have been on the moon. We were driving blind.

Then I spotted a car with a red and white scarf in it. I flagged them down. I could see the startled look in the eyes of the driver and his mate as they saw me rushing towards their car. I'd been in the paper a lot over the last few weeks because of my transfer saga, and they recognised me immediately. I tried to explain and told them I needed an urgent lift to the ground. I jumped in and waved to Jill, briefly worrying that it might take her about three days to find her way home. I was running out of time so I urged the driver to put his foot down.

He jumped a red light, I heard the dreaded sound of a police siren, and we were pulled over. I jumped out immediately and explained to the policeman what had happened. The young cop was more interested in talking football and asked me if I was going to go to the club he supported, Spurs. 'I don't know,' I said. 'But I've got to get to the ground as a matter of urgency. And please don't book this guy who was driving me. It was my fault.' The cop was brilliant. He told me to get back in the car and he would give us a police escort. It was just what I needed.

Ten minutes later, after cutting through the traffic as though the Red Sea had parted, I arrived at the ground in a blaze of blue lights and wailing sirens. I gave the boys in the car £20 and dashed into the dressing room.

A furious row ensued with Ferguson. He said that the coach had turned up outside my house but I wasn't there. I pointed out that I was always picked up in the lay-by. I thought I'd done really well to get myself to Charlton anyway. I learnt later that the suggestion had been put to the manager that I had deliberately avoided travelling so that I would not be cup-tied when I went to my new club. There was plenty of speculation around at the time that I was going to Manchester United. Ron Atkinson had said plenty of nice things about me to intermediaries, and I was well aware of his interest. One assistant coach on the bus even said he thought he saw the curtain twitching in the bedroom at my house. What rubbish. I gave everything for Ipswich up until the very last minute I represented them.

Despite the all-round anger, I played, and we won 3–2. Nevertheless, it was an indication that relations were becoming very strained. I had another row with Ferguson before the next round of the cup, Grimsby at home. I had been told to play with the reserves in midweek at Spurs. Ferguson had accused me of having the wrong attitude. I was staggered because it wasn't true. I didn't deserve to be plonked into the second team. By coincidence we had lost 1–0 at Stoke the previous Saturday – the venue for my last great row with the manager. It was horrible playing at an empty White Hart Lane. It did nothing to make me reconsider my transfer request. Just the opposite, in fact. I really hoped now that a club would come in for me. And it was obvious to me now that while Ipswich had made great play of saying that, they wanted to keep me, in fact the money for my sale was needed to pay for the new stand. Muhren and Mick Mills had already gone, and Johnny Wark, Paul Mariner, Eric Gates and Russell Osman were to follow. The great team I had played in was breaking up.

On the Friday before the Grimsby game Ferguson told me that I was in my regular slot for the cup tie and that my role

Above: The
victorious UEFA
Cup winning
squad of 1980-81.
(© Popperfoto)

Right:
Celebrating
wildly with Paul
Mariner and
Johnny Wark
after our UEFA
Cup victory in
'81. Johnny still
lives near me
in Ipswich.
(© Popperfoto)

Above: Arriving at Malaga airport with Alan Hansen in our official Scotland blazer for the 1982 World Cup campaign.

Below: A boyhood dream that came true. Playing for my country at Hampden Park against Holland. My childhood home was just up the road from the stadium.

Above: World Cup '82. Living with the legends. A Scotland line-up with such luminaries as Kenny Dalglish. I am standing next to Jock Stein, the manager who later fell out with me over a bet on a horse.

Below: In the opening game of the '82 World Cup campaign, we walloped New Zealand 5-2. Here I am tussling with NZ keeper Frank van Hattam.

Left: It was always a strange feeling for me to play *against* Ipswich. Here I am after I moved to United, turning out against old team-mates.

Below: My first appearance for Tottenham following my transfer from Ipswich. I never really settled at the club.

Above: On the gantry. For five years I was the co-commentator for Sky TV's Nationwide matches.

Below: Porky and me in our studios at 'talkSPORT Towers'. Mike probably came up with another mad idea – like suggesting that jockeys should have wing mirrors on their helmets.

Right: Porky and me broadcasting from the beach in Marbella the week that Celtic lost the UEFA Cup Final in Seville in 2003.

Left: Meeting Rod Stewart outside his Spanish villa during the '82 World Cup campaign. With me are team mates Asa Hartford, Alex McLeish and John Robertson.

Below: Porky and me on Capitol Hill in Washington DC after leading the charge across the Atlantic following the terror attacks in New York.

Above: Porky and me accepting an award for our show from the Heritage Society. It was presented by the *Are You Being Served?* actor John Inman.

Above: Porky and me at Birmingham City F.C. where we spoke after dinner at the club's end-of-season banquet.

Above: Here I am with my other broadcast partner, Graham Beecroft, at Brighton races proudly stroking my winning horse, Sands of Barra.

Below: Porky and me at York races presenting the trophy to a winning owner.

with the first team wasn't in question. But later that day I learnt that the manager had told a reporter I was only in the team because Eric Gates was injured. I wasn't told that to my face, and it disgusted me.

We disposed of Grimsby 2–0 but then went out of the competition when we were beaten 1–0 by Norwich. That was horrendous. Our league form picked up, though, and things got better with two home victories against Luton Town and Birmingham City. When I scored against Birmingham, early in March 1983, I didn't realise that was the last time I would hit the net in an Ipswich Town shirt.

The following week we got battered 4–1 at West Bromwich Albion. As I got off the coach when we arrived back Ferguson took me to one side and said that Ipswich had accepted a bid from a big club for me. I immediately assumed it was United. But it was Spurs.

I was asked to meet Keith Burkinshaw, their manager, at the White Hart Hotel in Braintree the next day. There were no agents in those days so I drove there on my own. Burkinshaw was with just one other club official, and we shook on the deal in less than an hour. I set off for home with a four-year contract in my pocket paying me better money than Ipswich.

I stopped at the first phone box I came across and rang Jill. The conversation was short and to the point.

'Hi, darling,' I said. 'All done. Ring the estate agents. We're going to London.'

CHAPTER NINE

SPURNED AND DISUNITED

The fans were still hostile towards me, to the extent that I couldn't even warm up on the touchline when I was a sub because of the abuse. One bloke even spat at me. I very nearly pre-empted Eric Cantona's kung fu attack by about ten years.

THE 'doctor', or whatever you could describe him as, came into the room bent over double. If he had had a cigar in his mouth he could have been Groucho Marx. Considering I was here to see him about my own back I was not immediately filled with confidence that this guy was going to provide the miracle cure I needed to get my career back on track. I was lying face down on the consulting table with just my shorts on, but my immediate instinct was to get up and flee because the last time I saw anybody as strange-looking as this guy was in an Alfred Hitchcock movie. Had it not been for the fact that I was so desperate for somebody to put me right and banish the pain that now permanently shot up and down my spine, I would have run. But I had no choice except to grit my teeth and hope that, despite appearances, this Faustian figure, who looked about 109, was going to trigger my recovery.

I wondered why he had his hands behind his back. For a moment I genuinely believed he was trying to impersonate Groucho Marx. If you'd seen him you'd probably have said to him something like, 'You, man, make me a crocodile sandwich, and make it snappy.' He started rubbing the base of my back, concentrating on the two discs at the bottom of my spine. I winced with the pain and my head shot up. I could now see what he was doing in the reflection of a glass cabinet in front of me. To my horror, I saw him bring his right hand from behind his back to reveal an enormous syringe full of dark fluid.

Now I was going to flee. I tried to remove my legs from the table but he was holding me down with such force that I couldn't move. Even when I tried to look round I was struck with terrible pain though my pelvis and down my legs. This guy could have been about to paralyse me and there was absolutely nothing I could do about it. I started effing and blinding. Normally I would try to get into a reasoned and rational argument, but this wasn't the time for such a measured approach.

'Mr Brazil,' he said, 'do not be alarmed. This method of treatment has proved to be very successful for many different species.'

Species? What on earth was he talking about? Did he think he was treating a horse or something?

'Now, please, lie still,' he went on. 'I am going to give you just a small injection and then you will have to rest while the treatment circulates around your system. There is absolutely no reason to be alarmed.'

I told him that if he stuck that needle in me I would knock his block off.

'No, you won't,' he replied. 'I don't think you'll be able to move for some time after the treatment.'

I started to sweat. I genuinely started to wonder whether I was in the clutches of a madman. As a kid I had watched the classic film *10 Rillington Place* in which Richard Attenborough played the role of the woman-killer Christie. The victims' bodies were bricked up in the cavities of the walls in the house, and there was one nightmare scene where you could see the eyes of a dead woman peering out at you before the last brick went into place.

I screamed out my defiance. 'Leave me alone, you mad old geriatric! Plenty of people know I am here!'

'Be quiet, and don't excite yourself,' said Groucho.

Then he stuck the needle in me. The initial prick was like any injection, and I had had plenty of those over the years. It was just a short scratch-like feeling followed by a cold sensation around my spine as whatever fluid he was pumping into me took hold. If there was anything sinister about it, it was already too late.

But then it did actually turn into the stuff of nightmares. Normally an injection lasts as long as it takes to squeeze the fluid out of a small phial. But here, three minutes later the mad professor was still standing over me and the needle was still sticking into my back.

'Just brace yourself for a minute,' he said. 'I am going to make some small adjustments.'

He shifted his hand upwards and the needle moved inside my flesh. I screamed and let out a new tirade of obscenities. Perhaps he was deaf, because all he said to me was, 'Calm down, Mr Brazil, try not to move. This can be very delicate.'

I couldn't physically move, but the manoeuvre he had just made was so painful I wanted to hit the ceiling.

I was actually now praying that he would finish and remove the needle. But seconds later he moved it again. He seemed to be moving it around in a circle in my back, and it got so painful that I couldn't even scream. I just opened my mouth and thought I was going to retch. What was this nutter doing to me? I felt sure I was going to be paralysed.

At last, he removed the needle. I gasped with relief.

'Everything will be all right, Mr Brazil. Please don't move for twenty minutes. The treatment needs to travel to hit the vital spots. You should have come to see me some time ago.'

With that, Groucho shuffled out of the room and I never saw him again. I can't remember his name or if I ever paid his bill.

I thought I had better lie still as he had told me. I had no idea what fluid he had pumped inside me, and I had learnt from experience that when so-called 'specialists' tell you to do things it is better to do them because if you don't and the treatment turns out to be useless or worse, they can always turn round and accuse you of messing it all up by not following their instructions.

As I lay there, I reflected on what had brought me to these consulting rooms near Regent's Park in London at the age of only 27. It was over three years now since I had left Ipswich, supposedly to move to bigger clubs and greater glory. I was thinking that I should now be at the peak of my career. My good pal and fellow Glaswegian Johnny Wark had left Portman Road, like me, and gone on to greater glory at Liverpool, but my career had never really moved forwards from the time I left Ipswich. This was the third time I had visited a 'specialist' in the last eighteen months to try to sort out the injury that was destroying my career. To be truthful, even thinking about it in those terms meant I was fooling myself. Maybe I didn't want to face up to the stark truth: unless I could get my back sorted out very quickly I had very little of a career left. I knew I would probably never play at the highest level again, because once you come out of that loop you rarely get back in. And that was frightening because I was still so relatively young. I had a wife and two little girls, and because of my age I had never really given any thought to how I would earn a living when I got out of the game.

By this stage I was playing for Queen's Park Rangers in the then Second Division. The glory days seemed decades ago, but in fact just over two years earlier I had picked up my second UEFA Cup medal, this time with Spurs. My back wasn't bothering me in those days, or at least not consciously. But when I considered over and over again my career after Ipswich, I wondered whether I had always had my back complaint. Maybe it had always been there, hiding away at the bottom of my spine, and as I went through my twenties it started to take hold. I had certainly had trouble establishing myself at both Tottenham and Manchester United. I never hit the form for those teams that I had shown consistently at Ipswich. It always mystified me why I didn't seem to be able to find the bursts of speed that were so much part of my game.

I wasn't conscious of having a back or a disc problem until after I left Manchester United, my third top club. It was shortly after I moved from Old Trafford to Coventry that my disc problem started to materialise. I began to feel unsteady on my feet after a game. After sitting down for dinner at home on a Saturday night, it was hard to get up. On Sunday mornings I had to roll out of bed, and simple things like cleaning my teeth became an endurance test. I had to hang on to the washbasin with one hand while using the brush with the other, standing up straight. Sometimes I would just lie on the floor in the lounge because it was too uncomfortable to put my body in any other position. I remember once trying to explain to my eldest girl, Michelle, who was then three, that Daddy had a back problem. As I stretched out on the floor, she grabbed my leg and tried to pull it to help me. She had seen Jill doing the same thing the night before in order to try to alleviate my pain. At least I could comfort myself that I had my family around me.

There is no other way I can explain how my form as a footballer petered out as it did. I was one of the stars of that very successful Ipswich side that twice finished second in the First Division, won the UEFA Cup, and was widely regarded as one of the top three teams in the land. When it became clear that I was going to leave Ipswich I was rated in some circles as a million-pound player. That's the equivalent of about £12 million today, which is double what Everton paid Southampton for English international James Beattie. I never really wanted to leave Ipswich, as I documented earlier, but it was inevitable. The minute Bobby Robson took over the England job in the summer of 1982 everything changed at Portman Road. But I was full of confidence about the future. I had utter self-belief in myself as a footballer. Even though I had a new long-term contract at Ipswich I still felt it was better to go because I wanted to meet a new challenge.

When I arrived at White Hart Lane in the spring of 1983 I had absolutely no doubt that I was going to make as big a mark there as I had done at Ipswich. I loved the scale of the Tottenham ground compared to the relatively smaller Portman Road. I was greeted warmly, and I had a feeling that this was my next launch pad. Every footballer knows he has a 'honeymoon period' at a new club, but I was determined I wouldn't need one. I was going to cement my relationship with the supporters from my first appearance.

It was an exciting time, but also very challenging. Jill and I had only been married just over a year and we had barely settled into our new home together. My wife was an Ipswich girl. She had a lovely local accent and all her family around her. It was going to be daunting for her to move to London. But she never hesitated. Her job was to sort out the move and find us a house in the suburbs of north London while I got on with the job of establishing myself at my new club.

I needed to integrate myself into the new set-up, get to know all my team-mates and how they played together, and find out precisely what my new manager wanted from me.

But I was hit by a very early and unexpected blow by the boss which I believe was critical to the miserable time I went on to have at Tottenham. In just my fourth game, towards the end of April 1983, I was substituted. We were playing away at West Brom and we had taken the lead in the 29th minute through my Scottish international team-mate Steve Archibald. Next to scoring myself, that was the best thing that could have happened. I'd established a striking spearhead with Steve when I made my first full international appearance against Hungary in Budapest nearly three years earlier. We had done well that night, and I was determined that we would carry it on at Spurs. Steve put away a perfectly measured cross from Glenn Hoddle to grab us the points. I thought I had drawn defenders away from him to me, so the partnership, it seemed, was coming together.

So when my number came up in the dug-out halfway through the second half my stomach turned over. I had never been substituted before. To me it was a public declaration that you were no good. I had always felt sorry for the lads who were taken off at Ipswich and grateful that it was never me. I doubted at first that they meant me. I had to think hard about what number I was playing in because I didn't want to believe it. And when the penny dropped, I didn't really know what to do. Do you smile, put a brave face on it and try to pretend that this is some sort of brilliant tactical ploy by the manager, or do you curse and shout about the injustice of it? I was stunned and very disconsolate, but I trooped off with good grace, shaking hands with my replacement. I felt unable, however, to look any of the coaching staff in the eye.

On the bench the proceedings on the field passed me by as I went through a process of self-examination. I was annoyed that I had not had a better game. I was trying to fathom out what had gone wrong. I had to reluctantly admit to myself that I had had a very average game. For some reason – and this now harks back to whether or not I was already suffering from my back problem – I simply hadn't been able to get going. I felt sluggish and short of pace. Still, I thought the manager should have been more considerate about the fact that I had only just arrived at the club and given me more games before replacing me. After all, we were leading, and well on top of the Baggies. Some managers would give their new signings up to ten games to establish themselves, and that wouldn't have been unreasonable in my case. I came to the club with a very good track record behind me and I felt it was only natural that there should be a settling-in period.

Also, I had been overwhelmed by reaction from within the football industry to my move. I know for certain that Ron Atkinson had been trying to put a spanner in Tottenham's spokes. Loads of people who I admired as great footballers themselves had spoken up and said that I was a great acquisition for Spurs, and that if necessary my new club might have to buy again to provide me with the sort of midfield support and service I'd enjoyed at Ipswich, mostly in the form of Arnold Muhren, who, of course, had moved to Old Trafford. One such tribute came from one of the men whose goalscoring feats I was determined to try to emulate. Malcolm Macdonald, the former Newcastle and Arsenal striker who once scored five in one game for England, said that my signing had given Spurs the kiss of life. He went on to add this:

Brazil will put Spurs back in business. It is easily the best piece of transfer business this season. Spurs were in danger of dying without him. The fans at White Hart Lane can now expect some lucrative years. Brazil stands alongside Kenny Dalglish, and Ian Rush. That's how highly I rate him.

He's a marvellous buy for a club that was going nowhere. In fact they could well have been going backwards because some of their top players have been murmuring about wanting to move on. Players like Glenn Hoddle will now see this as a fresh impetus. They'll start to believe in the management. If I was Hoddle I would now have no hesitation whatsoever in signing a new contract. I would do it just for the opportunity to play with Brazil.

You couldn't find two players better able to complement each other. Brazil has vast reserves of ability, particularly when it comes to collecting the ball, knocking it back and then running into space. I can see Glenn feeding him continuously.

Brazil is definitely his own man, and his style is similar to what mine was. I watch him and sense that same hungry anticipation I had when seeing the whites of the posts.

The transfer is also a message of sanity to the game. A less astute coach than Keith Burkinshaw might have paid a great deal more than the bargain half a million pounds that he shelled out to settle the deal.

That could be one of the transfer bargains of all time. Brazil can be a top player for another seven or eight years and pay his new club back ten times over.

With an endorsement like that from one of the era's top marksmen, I felt I had a justifiable right to say to my manager and the fans, 'Don't panic. I've come here to succeed.'

Arriving at a new club in the last couple of months of a season is not easy. It's as though you have been brought in as a miracle worker so that the manager can tell the fans the team finished with a flourish and things are looking great for the new campaign in August. In a way, I think that is what happened with me. And I came up with the goods. I scored six goals in the twelve games of the season that were left when I got there, and we got into Europe for 1983/84.

That meant that despite the initial turmoil at Spurs I went into the summer break in good heart. I was still worried, though, that Jill might not have been able to settle in Hertfordshire, where we chose our new home. She was, and still is, very much a country girl. Her roots are all around Suffolk. Her family had been there for generations. But she actually settled in much more easily than me. Right from the start she was a great organiser, which is essential if your partner is in the football business, always away from home, sometimes for weeks at a time. Her family were very supportive, not only of her but of me as well. Her late father was a real character, a true football fan. He was delighted that his daughter had married a footballer when so often in those days it was the opposite.

I used to constantly ask myself, with all the wisdom of a 24-year-old, 'Is football the most important thing in life?' Well, I was about to be put to the test, because Jill was expecting our first child during that close season. Michelle, the first of our three girls, arrived in early August, and I don't think I could have felt happier.

An old journalist friend, Steve Stammers, came round to my new house in Digswell, a lovely little village in Hertfordshire just off the A1, to do a piece on me. He was only a couple of years older than me, and I talked to him about my aspirations for the new season. Footballers take so much for granted in their lives because wealth and fame creeps up on them slowly but relentlessly, from being a kid in the streets to being fêted by people who want to give you money and make you famous. Big houses, nice cars and good-looking girls inevitably follow. When you are very young you don't realise that the people who are being nice to you are like that because they have a vested interest. If you succeed as a footballer, they win as a manager or an agent. It's a fair deal, but right from the very start it means you are treated differently to most other people. And the longer it goes on, the more you expect it, not because you are trying to be a big shot but because it has always been that way.

As Steve and I were chatting over a cup of coffee after he had finished writing down all his notes, he said to me, 'You've cracked it here, Alan. Lovely new house, new club, new wife, new baby. In the space of about twelve months you've cracked what it takes most men to do over a big part of their lifetime.' I had simply never thought about it like that. When he left, I stood out on the driveway for a few minutes and realised that he was right. Everything was in place.

All I had to do now was play to my full potential, which I was certain would see me winning things for Spurs, not to mention a load more international caps.

Pre-season training was the usual slog. It was a time of year I dreaded. I didn't put much weight on in those days whether I was playing or not, but it was at least four weeks of physical torture no matter what shape you were in when you returned. There was one particular exercise at all my clubs which I, in particular, found very hard – 'doggies', the series of shuttle runs which often involved bending to pick something up and then twisting and turning to run back. It was very uncomfortable for me. Not exactly painful, just a bit like putting your foot flat down on the accelerator in your car: the engine never sounds as though it's about to blow up, but you fear you may be doing it a bit of damage anyway. I had a psychological problem with that exercise, and once again, thinking about the back problem that ended my career, was I exacerbating a problem lurking at the bottom of my spine?

Still, I could not have been more fired up for the opening day of the new season, which I remember distinctly. I was particularly pleased because Glenn Hoddle, as urged by Malcolm Macdonald, had signed a new contract. The longer I'd trained and played at Spurs with Glenn the more I had come to appreciate his skills. The things he could do with a ball were quite unbelievable. His control and passing were simply immaculate. I could set off on a run and be 95 per cent certain that the ball would drop perfectly for me. Glenn was a quiet boy but he had such a shrewd football brain. His vision and his ability to size up a situation in a split second, and then to react to it, were quite phenomenal. I have played with and against some of the greatest players in the world and each has had his individual strengths. But I have never come across a player who could actually predict what was about to come – and that is something Glenn seemed to be able to do. Years later it was said of him that as a manager he used to get frustrated with his players because they couldn't always do the things he asked them to do. I'm not surprised. Nobody could do what Glenn used to do. It came so naturally to him that he failed to realise it was a unique talent.

A few weeks earlier we had played at Parkhead in a pre-season friendly. It was a magical moment for me, even though I wished I was wearing a hooped shirt rather than one adorned by a cockerel. It would have been nice to have been the star of the show, just to show the Scottish crowd what one of their own could do, but with Glenn on the field there was absolutely no chance. He was magical. Some of the things he did were greeted with silence, and on Clydeside that is the highest compliment the fans can deliver. They are the noisiest bunch of supporters in the world, but they can be struck dumb by genius, particularly if it's the opposition dishing it out.

So with Glenn on board I was optimistic about the season ahead. I knew he could provide me with the ammunition and I was determined that I was going to improve on my already impressive goal rate of one every two games. And, as fate would have it, Spurs were to travel to Ipswich on the opening day. I had tremendously warm feelings about my years at Ipswich, but every player likes to go back to his previous hunting ground with the intention of reminding the fans of what they are missing. But it wasn't to be. We lost 3–1, and that defeat triggered a crisis of confidence.

Six games into the season I still hadn't scored a league goal. It was frustrating and debilitating. It's hard to look people in the eye when you are paid to hit the net and win games and you are not producing the goods. That was the time when I needed, more than ever, the support of the manager to get me through. As long as he didn't lose his bottle, I knew I wasn't going to lose mine. And I knew the goals would come. I had no doubt about my ability, it was simply a matter of finding the right formula and the right pattern to make it work.

In early October we played Nottingham Forest at home, and to my despair I was substituted. It was a live televised game on a Sunday afternoon with a big audience that included many of my friends and family. I felt sick about it. But despite my disappointment I bottled up all my feelings, consoling myself with the belief that I didn't think I had had such a bad game, and we won 2–1, so I was part of a winning team. I prayed it was only a temporary blip. Surely the manager wasn't going to mess around with a team that was now getting results?

Our next game was just three days later, a Milk Cup tie against Lincoln City. I am not one to attack soft targets, but in my head I was saying to myself, 'These guys are not up to your standard. This is an opportunity to get about them. And when you have done so you will have rediscovered that magic art of goalscoring.' I was in the squad that travelled up there. We had a lead from the first leg anyway and to play in that game would have lifted any psychological barrier in my mind and helped me to get on with my season. But when we got there I was given a ticket to sit in the stands. I felt humiliated. I wasn't even first choice for the subs' bench. To have to sit among the fans was ridiculous. The following day I was ordered to play for the reserves against Swansea.

If there was one thing I really hated as a footballer it was playing for the reserves. You play in empty grounds where you can hear the echo of your own voice coming back off the roof of the stand. You are often playing against a bunch of kids, and the infrastructure of a proper match just isn't there. How motivated can you be as a First Division and international footballer when you have to climb over a hoarding to recover a ball because there are no groundstaff? I never minded it if it was part of a fitness programme on the way back from injury, but to be banished there when you were fully fit and eligible for the first team was like a punishment, and I didn't think I deserved punishing. Even if I was playing badly, it's not as if I was doing it deliberately. I was trying very, very hard to make things work. Significantly, the manager, Burkinshaw, said I looked edgy and lacking in confidence. But players who are new to a team often look like that. Time and again new players at a club are a disappointment. The only way to get the best out of them is to show belief. Strong managers do that, but weak ones bottle it. There was a section of the crowd getting on my back, and that is something you have to expect. But, once your manager starts to give out the message that he's losing faith in you, you become a marked man for the boo-boys.

The best modern example of a manager who put his personal reputation on the line and showed faith in a player in whom he believed was that of Rafael Benitez and Peter Crouch at Liverpool. Crouch was a surprise acquisition during the summer of 2005 after Liverpool had won the European Cup for the fifth time. Despite that enormous success the manager wanted to beef up his forward line. People in football were scratching their heads when he signed the six-foot-seven-inch striker who was regarded as a journeyman from Southampton. But Benitez, who had won honours in Spain and in Europe with Valencia, bought him for a purpose. He had a clear plan as to how he was going to utilise Crouch in the Liverpool set-up. And he clearly decided that, to make him feel like an important member of the squad, the boy needed a run in the first team. That would probably mean about four or five games during which he would hopefully score a couple of goals. He might be dropped back to the bench after that, but he would be safe in the knowledge that he had become a useful component, and that he formed part of the manager's plans. However, things didn't quite work out like that. Crouch went fourteen games without scoring. After each game the pressure increased upon him, but he got relatively little stick because the manager was always publicly behind him. And Benitez kept him in the team until he did score. Since then Crouch has become a vastly improved player, a very important player to the club and a vital part of the England set-up.

Burkinshaw wasn't bright or steely enough to be able to act like that. As a result I suffered at club and international level. Needless to say, I began to doubt myself. All my life I'd had enormous belief in my ability as a footballer. One of the reasons I had been so successful was because I had so much confidence. But now, no matter how hard I tried, it was starting to drain away. I was beginning to suspect that it was becoming a personal issue between me and Burkinshaw. I can't remember doing anything to upset him, but communication was obviously breaking down, and in my experience that's the way in which a bad situation gets worse.

What was galling was that I had chosen Spurs over Manchester United because of the desire he had shown to sign me, and an assurance that I would become an immediate first-team choice. When I met Burkinshaw at the White Hart Hotel in Braintree everything had been so positive. I explained that I needed a midfielder who could thread balls through the defence for me. Spurs at the time played a closer, short-ball game, but I was told that wouldn't be a problem. The team would be fashioned around me as I was going to get all the goals. Steve Archibald and Garth Crooks were, until then, the regular strikers, but I was going to be first choice. When I drove home that afternoon with the details of a good four-year contract in my pocket, I was a very happy man. A new and exciting life lay ahead of me. But now, having lost my place in the team, the dream was turning into a bit of a journey to hell.

I kept having to repeat to myself in my head: 'You're a good footballer, you'll get back with a bang.' And that belief was reinforced when I bought the London *Evening Standard* after training one day and read that Ron Atkinson was making a new attempt to take me to Old Trafford. It could have been newspaper talk, but I knew how keen the United boss had been to get me in the first place. A week later I received information that Howard Kendall of Everton was also pursuing me. How could I be a poor player if two of the biggest clubs in the country were after me? It steeled my resolve to get my career back on track.

In fact, it was after I read the Everton report that I first started thinking about moving clubs again. I had only been at Spurs for six playing months, but a footballer's career is very short and I did not want to waste any more of it in the reserves. Without breaking any rules, I did not discourage approaches from other clubs. It would have been very easy to sit it out with the security of my four-year contract, particularly as I had just moved house and had a growing family, but I would have no respect for myself if I did that. I did not want to put Jill under any extra pressure, coping as she was with the baby in a strange environment and putting the house together, but I could feel it in my bones that Spurs was not going to work.

I was incensed when I learnt that Burkinshaw had turned down flat the approaches from United and Everton. Here I was being sidelined at Spurs, yet he was issuing statements saying that I was going nowhere because I was such a valuable member of the squad. He'd never given me an assurance like that, but I hoped that in being forced to go public on me he would now realise that I was still highly regarded, and he would reconsider giving me a regular place in the first team.

A big row blew up between United and Spurs, with Burkinshaw accusing Big Ron of being out of order. He told the world that even if Spurs did ever sell me they would not do business with Manchester United. This made me even more frustrated and angry. Not only were Tottenham not giving me first-team football, they were trying to block clubs where I could go to pursue my career. I started having sleepless nights. I would lie staring into the dark until four o'clock in the morning, trying to figure out what to do. Then I would get just a couple of hours' sleep, and the next day, not unnaturally, I would appear sluggish in training.

The disappointments continued to come thick and fast. We had UEFA Cup games against Feyenoord in October and November, and I genuinely believed the manager would want to draw on my European experience. I had, after all, won the UEFA Cup with Ipswich two years earlier. But I was overlooked. I thought it was the very sort of thing Spurs had bought me for in the first place. I was shattered.

By December I had reached boiling point. I was so out of favour that the manager wouldn't even acknowledge my request to try me in other positions. I had always been a traditional centre forward, but I could play on the left side or behind the attack. I was told that square pegs don't go into round holes. My whole life felt blighted. I was a misery around the house and I didn't want to go out. I played in just one game over Christmas, to make it a measly four since the start of the season. But in that one match even I have to admit I was very poor. I couldn't summon up the form that had made my reputation. I was very disappointed, and now convinced that I was caught in a vicious circle of loss of place followed by loss of form followed by loss of place again.

Several weeks into the New Year the manager sat down with me and gave me some assurances about my role and the value he felt I gave to the club. It was good to hear that sort of thing, but it was only really putting off the inevitable. Either I played first-team football or I was going. In a run of six reserve-team games I'd scored eleven goals. That was the best return of my career, but in the wrong arena. I didn't need to prove myself at that level. I decided I was not going to play any more for the reserves and posted a transfer request.

Jill went mad. She stopped talking to me for a week. She urged me to be patient, but I thought I had been patient enough. I was travelling back to Ipswich on a regular basis to see old friends, and that was making me even more determined to rid myself of the misery of White Hart Lane.

Two days after I announced I wanted to go, I was put in the team for a trip to Notts County. I found a bit of my old form in that match, and even Burkinshaw gave me rave reviews. But I was badly wounded by now and needed a consistent run. I stayed in the team long enough to renew my acquaintance with European football, scoring a vital goal in the quarter-final victory over FK Austria Vienna. But then, inexplicably, I was booted out of the team that played the semi-final against Hajduk Split. Again I found myself feeling disappointed and angry. I'd proved my European pedigree, and it meant nothing.

My career at Spurs effectively came to an end three weeks before the end of the season in the dug-out at Queen's Park Rangers. We went one down and were playing really badly. We hadn't had a single shot on goal. As substitute I expected to be put straight on, but the manager just ignored me, even though I made a show of warming up. We went another goal down and he turned to me, almost as an afterthought, and said, 'I suppose you'd better go on now.' He said it as though circumstances were forcing him to use me but he didn't really want to. Months of total frustration suddenly exploded in me. I stood up and spat my chewing gum at him. I was at boiling point. I felt bad enough to go for him. He tried to be conciliatory by saying something like 'Don't you want to go on?' I answered him by saying, 'Not for you, Burkinshaw. There's no way I want to play for you any more. You're not a real football manager, you're a pen-pusher, and you don't know how to handle good players.'

I refused to go on. It was unprofessional, but I couldn't help myself. It was all I could do to restrain myself from thumping my own manager. The daft thing was that Burkinshaw had already announced he was leaving the club at the end of the season, and if I had just bitten my lip for a few more minutes then maybe I could have looked forward to the 1984/85 campaign under a new manager. As it was, I was now adrift because of the bust-up. Needless to say, I wasn't even in the squad of eighteen players that went to Brussels for the UEFA Cup final against Anderlecht. I watched the game from my lounge at home. Luckily, though, my contribution to the campaign was sufficient for the club to give me a winner's medal – my second one in that competition.

I had by now had a very firm approach from Manchester United. When I finally signed in June 1984, I was delighted. I was relieved to be getting away from Spurs after the most nightmarish year of my life, and I was particularly pleased at the size of the fee. Ron Atkinson shelled out £700,000 – £200,000 more than Spurs had paid for me. To me, that was vindication that I was a worthy footballer who had been playing for a manager who did not recognise my strengths and who had continually messed me around. I felt I was never given a fair crack of the whip at Spurs.

The United chairman, Martin Edwards, personally handled the deal. After we had sorted out the paperwork he poured me a glass of champagne. I immediately felt at home. I was very enthusiastic about being at Britain's biggest club. After initial reluctance, Jill too accepted that it was a good move. She did the usual great job of sorting out a move, to a new house built in stockbroker-belt Cheshire. Everything felt right.

Unfortunately, that feeling didn't last for long. United was to turn out as badly as Spurs did. I have never looked back in my life because I'm positive and I move forwards. A footballer's career is short, and when an opportunity comes along you have to take it. Nevertheless, I couldn't help but yearn for the Ipswich days. I trained very hard all summer but I knew I was not reaching that peak of fitness I'd enjoyed three years earlier. My legs ached. I have to keep reminding myself these days that I had a back condition then that was deteriorating but which had not been picked up in the medicals when I joined both Spurs and Manchester United.

United's first game of the 1984/85 season was at home to Watford. They had been turned into an exciting young club by Graham Taylor and were then the FA Cup runners-up on the march to glory. I was very nervous before the game, which was unusual for me. Sure, this was Old Trafford, and I had scored one classic goal for Ipswich here in the past and really baited the crowd, but I was a United player now. Part of the problem seemed to be that I had taken the place of young whizz-kid

Norman Whiteside. He was a crowd favourite, a boy who had been brought up through the ranks. And, again, I have to admit I had a poor game. It was a real blow when after 73 minutes I was hauled off. The crowd cheered Whiteside wildly. To be shown that the crowd think a lot more of the man replacing you than they do of you does nothing for a player's confidence. I have never cried as a professional footballer, but I came close to it that day.

I tried very hard, but I failed to recover from that poor start. A section of the crowd took to giving me tremendous stick. I was told it would go away, that it had happened to great names like Ray Wilkins. Just a month into the season a 'boo-boy' brigade had been established full-time at each match, but I was determined not to fail. I battled through it all and started to put a run together when I scored five goals in seven games. But just as I thought I was winning the crowd over, I turned my ankle and I was suddenly out of contention. By the time I was fit again I had lost my first-team place.

I played again on New Year's Day 1985, and then slipped into the reserves. Talk about *déjà vu*. It was the Tottenham horror happening all over again. The other problem was that I was slipping out of contention for my country. What a frustration it is to be unable to show your national team manager what you can do. My record so far was quite acceptable. I had scored seven goals in fifteen appearances, which is a pretty good average. But with the fans and the injuries I just hadn't been able to settle. I was losing Atkinson's support as early as the spring of 1985. He actually accused me of not trying after a cup tie at Norwich. I was flabbergasted. I thought my biggest problem was that I was trying too hard. I was competing for my place by then with Frank Stapleton and Mark Hughes. Two great players, but I thought I could match either. There were many heated discussions in Ron's office. I didn't feel I was being given a chance.

One of my worst moments came on the morning of the 1985 FA Cup final. I knew I had no chance of making the starting line-up, but I really hoped I would get the substitute's shirt. United were playing Everton, who had already won the league championship and the European Cup Winners' Cup. They were the best club in the country, if not in Europe. I was waiting for the word, one way or another, in my room at the Royal Lancaster Hotel in London with my room-mate and club captain Bryan Robson. The manager hadn't even told him who was going to be used as sub. It was generally known that it was going to be me or Mike Duxbury. I had scored twice for the first team the previous week against Queen's Park Rangers so I was full of hope that I would get the nod.

We watched the build-up to the game on television. You can imagine how I felt when ITV's Dickie Davies suddenly announced that Duxbury had been named as sub. 'Well, thanks a lot,' I said in exasperation. I wasn't directing the comment at Bryan, who remains a great pal. I was just at the end of my tether. Needless to say, the whole game was a bit of a blur to me. I didn't even enjoy the celebrations on the train on the way home.

That summer was miserable, and it didn't get any better when the new season started. I seemed to have fallen out of the loop altogether. I was playing reserve-team football in empty stadiums, and my relationship with Atkinson had become almost non-existent. One of the worst things to endure was the training. You know you've become cannon fodder at a club when you are called over especially to act as a defender in a wall for set pieces. It happened to me so often that I would whistle one of my favourite tunes, Pink Floyd's 'Another Brick in the Wall'. I don't think I got enough support from the management. The players, though, were marvellous. I think there is a bond between footballers, and some of my team-mates at United, Arthur Albiston and Gordon McQueen as well as Bryan Robson, are great pals to this day.

The fans were still hostile towards me, to the extent that near the end of my time at Old Trafford I couldn't even warm up on the touchline when I was sub because of the abuse. One bloke even spat at me. I very nearly pre-empted Eric Cantona's now legendary kung fu attack by about ten years. I was disgusted by the lout's behaviour, and it made me wonder what I had done to draw such venom out of people. I wasn't a murderer or a rapist. I was just a footballer trying to find his form.

There were a few bright spots. I scored twice in a 5–1 win at West Bromwich Albion in September 1985, for example, but no matter what I did I couldn't retain my place. Atkinson clearly wanted to get rid of me. It is an irony of my life that he chased me for two years with a big contract and, twelve months after he got me, he wanted me to give it up. He tried the humiliation tactic. He ordered me to play for the 'A' team one Saturday morning against a college team in Stoke. He said it was a great opportunity to rediscover my goalscoring touch. But it was horrible. I travelled on a minibus with a group of kids. I scored two goals, but I didn't want to be there. I think there were about 30 spectators, and when they realised who I was they gave me unbelievable stick. Tall poppies and all that.

In January 1986 I was down to play in the reserves at Barnsley, but I was pulled out at the last minute. Ron arrived on the scene. He was clearly agitated. 'You are finished,' he said. 'As far as I am concerned you can rot in the reserves.' As I was wondering what had prompted this outburst, he went on, 'I've done a deal with Coventry. I want you to go.' I protested that despite everything I wasn't ready to leave. I wanted to get my place back and play for Manchester United. 'You've had your chance at this club,' he barked. 'I know you are on a big contract with two-and-a-half years left, but if you don't go you are in the stiffs for ever. I'll make sure of that. I've had enough of you.' I didn't really have an option. Coventry manager Don Mackay appeared on the scene. We travelled back to my home together and I signed that night.

I reflected on Ron's behaviour. He had become almost irrational. I didn't believe it was a personal grudge he had against me. I think he was under pressure because he had spent a lot of money on me and the transfer hadn't worked. We both knew that. But every transfer is a gamble. I feel strongly he could have handled the situation better, but I hold no grudges. If I saw Ron in an airport departure lounge today we'd have a drink, as we have done a couple of times already.

Coventry gave me only brief respite. I saw the move as yet another chance to re-establish myself at the highest level. I intended it to be permanent and Jill and I moved house once again. But again things didn't work out. It was as if I had become cursed. Injuries plagued me again, and with great disappointment I moved on at the end of the season to join QPR.

Clearly managers still had a regard for me because clubs in the top flight were prepared to buy me, but by now I had become convinced there was something seriously wrong with my back. After every game I was in agony. It wasn't just a strain; I had reached the stage where, after a game, I was hanging on to work surfaces in the kitchen just to stand up. I'd told doctors about it, but backs are notoriously difficult to diagnose or treat. That is why it has always been the favourite choice of illness for malingerers who need a sick note from their doctor.

At the beginning of the 1986/87 season it was flaring up in training on a regular basis. The club, and in particular the manager, Jim Smith, were first class about it. Their own doctors could not diagnose what was wrong but they had no hesitation at all in paying to send me on intensive therapy courses and to see specialists. I also did my own research about alternative forms of treatment. I was desperate. I was determined to try anything, including going to see the sort of crank I described at the start of this chapter. But none of it worked.

In the second week of December I saw a top specialist in a clinic in London. He told me that he thought it would be foolhardy for me to continue playing. He warned of permanent damage. That was hard to accept. I wanted a second and third opinion, and so did the club. There was little joy in our house over Christmas because I knew that in January a decision was going to have to be made about my football career. I had started only two games for QPR and scored one goal. It couldn't go on.

On 16 January 1987, in the company of club officials, I listened to yet another specialist's verdict. Again, he warned of the dangers of carrying on, so very reluctantly I agreed to let QPR issue a statement on my behalf. It began, 'Alan Brazil has decided to give up playing because of a back injury ...'

So that was it. My football career was over.

CHAPTER TEN

SCOTLAND THE BRAVE

I have never been so inspired by a stadium full of fans. I have always loved my country. I was brought up on a hill overlooking Hampden Park, and to be playing in front of my countrymen was something I had dreamt of all my life.

I'M SURE I was hallucinating, because what was left of the sun had become like a Belisha beacon on top of the main stand. One second it was there, the next it wasn't. Although we were playing with a white ball, it also turned orange, as did the grass. I was waiting desperately for the half-time whistle. There was a thumping noise in my ears that wasn't just the sound of 35,000 ecstatic Scottish fans cheering our 3–0 lead.

This was the opening game of our 1982 World Cup campaign, against New Zealand. The game hadn't kicked off until nine p.m., but it felt like it was midday. We were playing in Malaga, and everything was going to plan except for the fact that it was even hotter than we had expected. The temperature inside the ground was over 100 degrees. We had spent weeks preparing ourselves before the tournament by training in neighbouring Portugal, but we could not have anticipated the hottest summer in the Mediterranean for a quarter of a century. The sun was so strong it felt like somebody was holding an iron about an inch away from my skin. Despite being fair-skinned I usually like the warmth, but this was like being in an oven.

The whistle finally went, and I trooped off. We were all looking limp, and as I entered the darkness of the tunnel everything turned orange again. I got into the dressing room, and as my eyes adjusted I realised I had double vision. Jock Stein was standing there asking us if we were all right. I could see two of him, and each of them was swaying from side to side. I nodded my head because I couldn't speak. My mouth was so dry that my tongue had stuck to my palate. I grabbed a bottle of water and poured it all over my head, neck and back, and down my throat. My shorts were slipping off and my boots felt too big. That was because I had already lost ten pounds in body-weight, though I didn't know it at the time. I tried to look positive, but my face must have told a story.

'Are you sure you're all right, son?' the manager said over and over again.

I kept nodding. There was no way I was being taken off in this game. I had had a good first half. I hadn't scored yet, but I had come close on two occasions and set up my Ipswich team-mate Johnny Wark for the second goal. Johnny also got the third. Kenny Dalglish, my striking partner, had bagged the other. There was a hatful more goals in this game and I was determined to be among the scorers.

As I left the tunnel for the second half I hoped that the temperature might have dropped, but it felt even fiercer. Nevertheless, I sprinted straight across the pitch and back, determined to kick-start my body. I'm not sure that was the wisest thing to do, though, because I was immediately gasping for breath.

One huge motivating factor was the fanatical support we had in the stadium. The capacity was 36,000, and we were told that there were only 800 fans from New Zealand. I have never been so inspired by a stadium full of fans. I have always loved my country. I was brought up on a hill overlooking Hampden Park, and to be playing in front of my countrymen was something I had dreamt of all my life. There was no way I was going to let these people down. Most of them were bare-chested, but they had smuggled bagpipes and drums into the ground and the atmosphere was intoxicating. We had labelled the fans the 'San Miguellians', because every time we saw one of them they had a can of the local beer in their hand. It was also a nice variation on the Tartan Army.

Jock had told us we had done the hard work and gained a three-goal lead so we should try to conserve some energy without letting New Zealand back into the game. The extreme heat had taken him by surprise as well as the players. In three days' time we were taking on the mighty Brazilians, and the manager could see that at this rate he was in danger of losing players through exhaustion for the big fixture.

Ten minutes after the re-start I had treble vision and had started walking like one of those people I have seen in newsreels who run the whole of the marathon course but then collapse with rubber legs just a few yards from the line. I didn't even understand the instruction to come off; one of the coaches had to run on to the pitch and guide me to the dug-out. I got such a fantastic ovation from the fans that I thought we had scored again. We hadn't. In fact, seconds after I lay down on a bench covered by a blanket, New Zealand scored. And ten minutes later they scored again. In my confused state I rolled off my bench and started mumbling, 'Let me back on, let me back on.' Somebody bundled me away to the dressing room. I was in a daze. The next thing I remember was Gordon Strachan limping in. I hope I didn't look as bad as him. He seemed to have halved in weight since I last saw him.

We soon had the match sewn up. John Robertson, twice a European Cup winner with Nottingham Forest, whipped in a free-kick, and Steve Archibald, who I went on to join at Tottenham, completed the tally.

I couldn't even move to get into the shower. Some officials

came into the dressing room and pointed at me. I thought they were doctors, but they turned out to be dope testers. I had been picked at random to give a sample. All I had to do was urinate into a glass bottle. I couldn't. The lads drifted in and changed as best as they could. Some were as debilitated as me and just put a tracksuit on before limping aboard the coach to get back to the hotel. A half-an-hour wait turned into an hour, but still I couldn't pass any water, even though since being taken off I had been drinking by the pint. One of the physios made me go steady. He said I might flood my brain. I thought I was hallucinating again, but I wasn't. Apparently, if you drink gallons of water when you are dehydrated you can do yourself terrible harm and make your brain swell. I tried a couple of beers to see if that would go through me, and loads of orange juice, but nothing worked. When the body is as dehydrated as mine was, it has to replenish all its stores in the bones and muscles first. I couldn't take diuretics to try to speed the process up for fear of violating the rules on banned substances, so I just had to wait. It was five hours later when I was finally able to produce enough fluid to satisfy the drug testers.

My biggest fear now was that I was not going to be fit for the Brazil game. I had been looking forward to that match so much from the minute the draw was made the previous December. Of course I didn't know then that I was going to be in the squad, but once I was selected I couldn't stop thinking about playing the three-time world champions. I had this image in my head of the scoreline: Brazil 0 Scotland 1 (Brazil). That wouldn't half confuse the world of football.

Naturally I was overjoyed when the final squad was named a month before the start of the tournament. I hadn't booked any holidays, and I'm sure I would have become a lifelong manic depressive if I had not been included. My only consolation would have been that I might still be in contention for World Cup 86 in Mexico. But, of course, by that time my back injury had become so bad that I had virtually retired.

I believe I have an Englishman to thank for sealing my place with Scotland for the 1982 World Cup. The peak of my club career, as I've mentioned, was scoring five goals in one match for Ipswich against Southampton in February 1982. Southampton were top of the table at the time and full of internationals, including Alan Ball, Kevin Keegan, Mick Channon and goalkeeper Peter Shilton, who was not playing that night. We comprehensively flattened them, and not unnaturally I grabbed all the headlines with my five goals, three of them coming in a seventeen-minute hat-trick. Their manager was Lawrie McMenemy. He has long been regarded as one of the straightest guys in the game. A former Guardsman who played football at a very low level, he battled through to become a top manager, taking the south-coast club to FA Cup glory at Wembley in 1976. The story goes that after my five-goal spree he met Jock Stein at some football function and bent his ear all night about my performance. It's not often that somebody gives you a leg-up like that in football, so to this day I owe him a big thank you.

Getting together with the lads prior to the competition was one of the best experiences of my playing days. We went to a training camp in Portugal to try to acclimatise to the Mediterranean heat. We sometimes trained twice a day, but we were also encouraged to keep active with other sports like tennis and golf. One day we were at Penina, an exclusive championship golf course. It was an immaculate setting, and

I was going around with, among others, Alan Hansen and Kenny Dalglish. On the eleventh tee we were approached by an old chap who asked us if he could join in. He was a very charming Englishman who looked as though he might have just stepped off the eighteenth at St Andrews. We didn't want to be rude to him but we weren't sure he was going to be able to keep up with us, so we passed up his offer. When we got back to the clubhouse the old chap was there. We felt a little bit uncomfortable, but he came over and introduced himself. It was Henry Cotton, the legendary pre-war golfer who had won the Open three times. I was kicking myself. I loved my golf, and to have passed up the opportunity to play with a man who had won the Claret Jug was a major error. Ever since, I have tried not to take people at face value.

During the same round of golf, and during many others we had while we were away, we were constantly in danger of being ambushed by fans. The San Miguellians were everywhere. Most of the fans heading for Spain had come to Portugal first just to watch us training. Whenever we left our hotel complex they would follow us. There was no malicious intent at all; they were just very happy and enthusiastic about the team and their country. But turning up at exclusive golf clubs with carloads of crazy jocks in tow didn't always please our hosts. Once, as we were going round, we heard the unmistakable sound of a Scotsman wailing. We followed the noise and found one of our countrymen barely conscious deep in the rough singing a line from the Paul McCartney song 'Mull of Kintyre'. He thrashed at the bracken to his own strains of 'Deep is the heather, right here in the glen, carry me back to the days I knew then ...' We left him to it.

I have read lots of stories over the years about footballers going mad in training camps, but that never happened to me. In the run-up to the World Cup we were so normal it was boring. We played cards for very small amounts of money compared to today's footballers. And I don't think I saw one player take an alcoholic drink until it was all over. The only player who got carpeted for a breach of discipline was Graeme Souness. Graeme loved the sun and sunbathing. He liked his skin to be tanned at all times, and this was before the era of the walk-in-spray-on tan parlours. Because of the fierce heat, the boss had banned us all from lying on loungers to mop up the sun's rays. But Graeme ignored it twice, and Jock went mad.

After Portugal we moved to our base camp in Spain, which was in Sotogrande. By the time we got there thousands of Scottish fans had arrived ahead of us. We loved to have them there and needed their support, but we didn't realise they were going to turn up in such numbers. Malaga, which was the location of two of our three group games, was undoubtedly going to be the centre of the world for tens of thousands of Scots. We all assumed they would take over nearby Torremolinos for a long, and what we all hoped would be an extended, summer holiday. God help the rather posher resorts of Marbella and Puerto Banus if my countrymen decided to set up home there, I thought. But, for the 72 hours after the New Zealand game, my main concern was not the San Miguellians but whether or not I could get myself fit for what would be the biggest match of my life.

When the doctor examined me back at the hotel his forecast was gloomy. He told me that dehydration can make you weak for days. My salt levels were all over the place, and the sudden and dramatic drop in weight was further punishment to the body. I knew I wasn't going to make it the day before the game.

I was just too weak. I hadn't been able to train, and against the Brazilians, who would be playing in what for them were perfect conditions, I would be short of pace.

It was agony sitting behind the dug-out and watching us get beaten 4–1 in Seville. I wanted to be on the same pitch as legends of the game like Zico and Socrates. There were two consolations, though. The first was that I had the opportunity to study the Brazilian girls at close quarters. That was certainly good for morale. There were hundreds of them in the stadium, and they all looked like beauty queens, with copper-coloured skin, dark hair and flashing green eyes. And they were wearing what appeared to be the national costume of their country – skimpy bikini tops and wrap-around skirts in blue, yellow and green. The second saving grace was that I had been told I would probably be fit for the third group game, against the USSR. That had become a vital match for us now because of the way the group games had gone. To go through to the knockout stages we had to beat the Soviets, who had drawn with Brazil.

I was desperate to get back into the firing line, but when Jock Stein read out the team in the dressing room in the same stadium where I had suffered dehydration against New Zealand, I was named as sub. I could understand some of his thinking. I had only been training for the last three days, though I felt strong and sharp. But the weather conditions were similar to the first game and there had to be a question mark over my staying power. Perhaps, as a sub, he would bring me on for the second half if we needed goals.

We were on course for a victory when one of those bizarre accidents happened that change a game. Alan Hansen and Willie Miller both went for the same ball but crashed into each other, leaving a Soviet forward free to level the game. It was an injustice because our boys had been battering their goal. With twenty minutes to go I was brought on.

'Score, son, that's all I and your country ask of you,' said Jock. 'Just score.'

I was cursing him as I sprinted on to the field to a terrific reception from the fans. I would have had a better chance of scoring if I had been on from the start.

You couldn't see a single Soviet flag in the whole of the stadium. Not surprising really, considering that the Iron Curtain was still drawn and the Soviet people weren't allowed out of their own country. It was also reputed to be a brutal regime, and our lads were taunting their players with things like, 'It's back to the salt mines for you tonight, pal, after we've wellied you, you Commie tosser.' This sort of thing elicited only smiles; presumably our opponents could not speak or understand a word of English.

We battered their goal. I struck two on target and it took a terrific save from the Soviet goalie to keep the second one out. But we ran out of time. The final whistle went and the lads were on their knees. Heat and disappointment combined to make us feel collectively wretched.

You could not have blamed the fans if they had turned on us. Some of them had given up everything to be there. Summer holidays, jobs and even marriages went as a result of the devotion of the San Miguellians. And, not unnaturally, we felt we had let them down. But, even as we shuffled off the pitch, some of us in tears, the fans were chanting louder than ever. Every footballer will tell you that their fans are the best in the world, but that title has to be bestowed on the travelling Scotsmen. As a congregation they were adulatory, and as we got to the tunnel individuals were leaping over the wall and wrapping scarves around our necks. Many of them were crying, but these were not tears of despair. One old guy wrapped his arm around me and said, 'You poor wee boy. All that effort, all that fight. And nothing. But your mamma will be very proud of you.' I reflected on the folks back home. There were no mobile phones in those days and I didn't know when I'd be able to talk to Jill or my parents. If they felt like the fans did here in the stadium then we had not let the nation down.

Still, the dressing room was as bad as any I have been in after defeat. I thought losing to Manchester City in the semi-final of the 1981 FA Cup at Villa Park was the worst I had experienced, but this was just as bad. We were all silent. We just went through the motions, hardly speaking to each other. Every player was going over the game in his head. Could I have blocked that ball? Should I have left that cross? Should I have passed to Johnny? Should I have taken on the defender on my own? A thousand questions, but it was too late for answers now.

Disconsolately, we filed out of the players' entrance to the bus. By the sound of it not a single fan had gone home. In fact there seemed to be even more fans now than there were during the game. And there probably were, because we learnt later that there might have been as many as 10,000 Scotsmen who couldn't get in that day. It took an hour to get the bus out of the ground. The police had a hell of a job keeping the fans back, but these were happy fans, celebrating our campaign rather than focusing on the result against the USSR. They cheered us up.

Once we were on the open road we started planning what we were going to do next. We still felt pretty low and none of us had had an alcoholic drink for three weeks. We weren't even sure we wanted to go out. Initially I voted to go straight back to the hotel. I was weary rather than tired. I wasn't in the mood for partying. But soon we saw signs for Marbella, and then Puerto Banus. I hadn't been there but had heard it was a very lively nightspot. One or two of the lads said they were going to go for a 'quick' drink, but first it had to be cleared with the boss. We delegated Archie Gemmell, the captain, to go to the front of the bus and talk to the manager.

A few minutes later Jock came down the aisle and gave a Stonewall Jackson type speech. 'You should all be proud of yourselves,' he said. 'You have served your country magnificently. To all the people back home you are heroes. As a manager I could not have asked more of you. One of these days you will look back and you will remember this campaign.'

We were all thinking the same thing: 'Great speech, boss, but what about the request to stop in Puerto Banus?'

'So, in conclusion,' Jock continued, 'let me say that if one or two of you want to slip off the bus for a beer or two I'll ask the driver to drop you in Puerto Banus. But remember, you are still ambassadors for your country. Act with the dignity you have shown throughout this competition.'

I was suddenly in party mood. A few minutes later the coach pulled off the main drag and made its way down a narrow lane to the sea. There were Scottish fans everywhere. As we turned the corner on to the strip I was struck by two contrasting images. One was the biggest army yet of San Miguellians. It was like landing on another planet where every inhabitant was dressed in tartan. The other was a fleet of boats and yachts that were stunning in their magnificence. You couldn't tell if it was day or night, it was just very bright.

The moment the first fan saw the coach a cry went up. Within seconds we were swallowed up by a street carnival. The fans swarmed around the coach. It was just like being on the bus that took us on a victory parade through Ipswich after we won the UEFA Cup. This wasn't supposed to be a victory parade, but there seemed to be about ten times more people here and they were squashed into the tiny roads of this Mediterranean hotspot. The San Miguellians were going berserk. The bus had soon ground to a halt – right outside the resort's top bar, Sinatra's. There was another bar next door called Salduba that had also been taken over completely by Jocks. In fact, that corner of the square in Puerto Banus that night looked like an outpost of the Scottish Empire. The fans were waving their Scotland shirts and their scarves. They were right up against the coach windows, banging so hard that I thought they were going to shatter. Then there was one tremendous bang. I thought we had been hit by another vehicle. But a fan had fallen off a lamp post on to the roof and he was now peering at us through the skylight.

'OK, boys, anybody who wants to get off better do so here,' said the driver. 'We're not going any further. We'll have to get the police to escort us out backwards.'

We were now all moving towards the front of the bus. As the pneumatic release was activated, the door hissed open. It was like watching water go down a plughole as every player siphoned quickly off the coach. I reckon it took about ten seconds flat. It was as if we were being sucked out by the frantic crowd. A few bouncers had come out of the bar, and they formed a human wall to ferry us through the masses and into Sinatra's. Despite that, we were mobbed. Not in a threatening manner, though. These boys just wanted to share the glory of our country with us. The trouble was, their enthusiasm knew no bounds.

We were only dressed in tracksuits after coming directly from the ground. By the time I got into the bar – after the bouncers had pulled us into the club and then roped off an area on the far side to try to give us just a foot or two of space – my tracksuit top had gone and somebody had to give me a vest. During the course of a very wild night, my tracksuit bottoms also disappeared. Don't ask me how. Again, to preserve my modesty I had to borrow a pair of shorts. All the lads had the same problem. Not one of us who went out that night returned home with our tracksuits. Some of the players had put a clean playing shirt on after leaving the ground, and that was an even bigger draw for the souvenir hunters. More than once I saw two fans arguing over the same shirt, in danger of tearing it in half in their desperation to take it home from the World Cup. (Many years later I was playing golf in Portugal when a man I had never seen before in my life came up to me and claimed he had my Scotland shirt from that night.)

The champagne started flowing from the moment we got into Sinatra's. Within minutes, I felt unsteady on my feet. A combination of alcoholic abstinence for a month, the hot and heady night, and the adrenalin rush of the welcome from the fans made us instantly light-headed. I wish I could have bottled the formula that night and brought it home with me; it would have saved me tens of thousands of pounds in bottles of champagne ever since. I'd love to see again the first few minutes after our arrival because we were literally falling about after a glass or two of champagne. John Wark and I were leaning on each other to stop ourselves falling over. With us was Alex McLeish. If you had told somebody then that Alex

THERE'S AN AWFUL LOT OF BUBBLY IN BRAZIL

would one day become the manager of Rangers (and then
Scotland) and win them a bag full of titles and cups, nobody
would have believed you. We also needed gallons and gallons
of water because of the dehydration problem.

It wasn't long before we told the bouncers to take the ropes
away from the VIP area and we joined the fans. It was the
party of all parties. Music, dancing, all crushed together. It was
like being at Hampden Park at an England v. Scotland game.
If for a moment we had feared a backlash for going out of the
competition, we could not have been more wrong. Obviously
we were never going to win it, but we had come so close to at
least buying ourselves another week in the tournament. But
these wonderful supporters were treating us like heroes for
qualifying for the finals in the first place and giving them a
fantastic two-week crusade. So many of them told me through
the night that this was the greatest moment of their lives.

I don't know how long I had been there when another huge
roar went up as somebody else walked in. I hoped it wasn't
Jock Stein, the manager. I feared he had come to spy on us,
and he was going to drag us all back to the hotel in disgrace.
As I turned round, I wondered whether this was the end of
my international career. Where had all the other lads gone?
Had they had a tip-off and fled from the madness of the bar
before Jock had spotted them? But it wasn't the boss who was
beaming at me and gripping my shoulders. It was somebody
considerably younger and less bear-like. It was Rod Stewart,
world famous singer and fanatical Scotland fan. He grabbed
my head as he started singing 'Flower of Scotland'.

This had now become surreal. Rod Stewart usually played
to crowds of thousands of people who paid good money to
watch him perform live. But tonight he was here with me and

the boys in Sinatra's and, amazingly, for that evening alone we were a bigger draw than Rod.

We had met the rocker earlier in the trip. On our way back from training one day before the competition started we took an excursion down a dusty road and saw a magnificent villa in the distance. What made it particularly interesting to us was the gigantic St Andrew's flag flapping above the main gate. We didn't have a clue who lived there until somebody rang the bell. Rod Stewart came trotting out of the front door. He was as enthusiastic to talk football with us as a schoolboy would have been in the company of his football heroes. He was a chart-topper all around the world. There are some people who are so famous that until you see them in the flesh it's hard to believe they actually exist, other than on television and in the pages of newspapers and magazines. Rod Stewart was like that for me. I felt exactly the same many years later when I met Tiger Woods for the first time.

I looked at Rod's face and his wiry body and honestly wondered if he was made of the same sort of bones and blood that we were. I remembered just before we had left Britain that a few of the lads at Ipswich had had a bit of an end-of-season thrash. We'd got together at a hotel in Ipswich and danced into the early hours to the strains of 'Maggie May'. The song was now playing over and over in my head: 'I know I keep you amused, but I feel I'm being used, oh Maggie I wish I'd never seen your faaaaace ...'

Throughout my life I have met many of the great and the good, but the picture that takes pride of place on my grand piano at home is the one of Rod, me and a group of my Scotland team-mates outside that villa. Asa Hartford, John Robertson, Alex McLeish, Rod and I are crammed into the stairwell of the team bus, all wrapped in his St Andrew's flag. And now, here in Sinatra's bar, I was celebrating the World Cup campaign with the rocker himself. My most vivid memory of that night is that at one stage Rod, Alan Hansen and I were all dancing on the bar.

Dawn was almost breaking when we poured ourselves into a taxi and made our way back to the hotel. We knew we were going to have to be alert because even at this early hour there was a possibility the manager would be out prowling around the grounds looking for the night's 'casualties'. We were also certain that the boss would know what we had been up to the night before. I don't know how he used to do it, but nothing happened to a group of Scottish players without Jock Stein finding out.

I went to bed and woke up at lunchtime. I have never felt so ill in my life. I don't think I had ever had a night like that one. I was barely 23, and for all of my adult life I had been a professional athlete. Footballers may have got a reputation over the years for being excessive boozers, but that was not the case with my team-mates at Ipswich or with the Scotland squad. We were certainly not experienced drinkers, and the volumes of alcohol some of us had consumed over the previous 24 hours were alien to us and having a devastating effect.

I had a shower and wandered around the hotel in a daze looking for signs of life. I discovered only two other people. Alex McLeish, who felt as bad as me, was trying to drink black coffee, and Davie Provan was asleep by the pool. Davie was a lovely, mild-mannered boy, but I did wonder why I so often found him asleep. It was revealed later that he actually had some sort of illness that involved falling asleep a lot. I made sure he was in the shade so that the sun wouldn't get him.

I was starting to get nervous that everybody might have gone home without us. Then I went to the reception and found an invitation to go for lunch aboard somebody's yacht berthed out at sea. It seemed to be some sort of trip organised by Kenny Dalglish, and I hoped I hadn't let anybody down.

Playing with Kenny was one of the greatest things that happened to me in my career, but also one of the most difficult. He was my boyhood hero. When I used to look out of my bedroom window down the hill to Hampden below, I used to dream that one day I would play there. I had to believe it was attainable because that was what drove me through my childhood and teenage years to become a professional footballer. But I never ever dreamt I would play in the same team as Kenny. As a kid in the playground his name rolled off our tongues as if it was the mantra of a spiritual religion – 'Dalgleeeeesh'. He was a god. I felt the same way about Kenny as I did about Rod Stewart. He was awe-inspiring. As far as I was concerned he was the best footballer in the world.

When I went to Ipswich, Dalglish was still a hoop. So, with my own Celtic dream gone, not only did I believe I would never play with him, I thought it was highly unlikely I would ever play against him. Then, in 1977, after Liverpool had won the European Cup, Kevin Keegan surprisingly decided to leave Anfield to seek further fame and fortune in West Germany with SV Hamburg. To plug the enormous gap left in the Liverpool side by the disappearance of Keegan, Liverpool turned to the man they believed was the only player in the game who could take his place – Dalglish. Kenny was Mr Celtic at Parkhead. He had latterly been part of a tremendous run of success in the wake of the 'Lions of Lisbon' era during which Celtic won nine consecutive titles. And in 1977 they had won it back again after it had escaped to Ibrox for two years. Nobody had even considered him leaving. But the lure of joining the European champions and the club that was threatening to dominate English football for years to come was too big a draw for a man who relished bigger and bigger challenges.

That meant that I would soon be facing him out on the football fields of the English First Division. The first time I ran out against him I didn't know how I would react. It wasn't just that he was such a great player, he also played in such a fabulous team. Fortunately my professional instincts took over the minute the whistle went. He scored against us over the next few seasons, using the chip technique that was one of his trademarks, but in return I scored against them too.

I never really got to know Kenny until I joined up with the Scotland squad for my debut in May 1980. Over the period of a week, as we travelled behind what was then the Iron Curtain to Hungary and Poland, I discovered that his private image was totally different to the one people saw in public. To the outside world he appears to be a dour Scotsman of few words with no sense of humour, but he is actually the complete opposite. He never stopped talking throughout the trip, and in all the time I have known him he has been exactly the same.

As a young recruit to the squad I was naturally concerned about whether I would be accepted by the older brigade. Kenny knew that people like me would be nervous around him and he put me at ease by taking the mickey. But it was always good-natured. And it wasn't just me: he was always winding up the whole squad, gently, in a way that brought us all together. The Scottish lads were a good bunch. I have been witness to deep changing-room rivalries, but none of that existed whenever I played for Scotland. They were all intelligent men. Training was a joy because we could spend hours talking things through. We understood each other and how we wanted to play.

Another member of the squad who was great to me on my first trip was Graeme Souness. What a player he was. As tough as a plank of teak. You wouldn't want to get in his way on a football field. The first time I met Graeme he wanted to know all about my career and my aspirations. We went for a stroll, and he instilled into me the virtues he valued in life. Respect for yourself, for your body, for the people around you, and for the great institutions in life – like the Scottish football team. He reminded me how lucky I was as a young man to be earning my living by playing football. I've had enormous respect for Graeme ever since.

Fortunately, by the time we got to the World Cup in Spain I had come to terms with playing alongside my boyhood hero Dalglish. One of the proudest moments of my life remains seeing the team sheet for the opening game of the tournament: Dalglish and Brazil in attack.

All these thoughts were going through my mind as I wondered what to do in the hotel on the morning after the night before. I got in the shower, and by the time I got out I had decided to go back to Puerto Banus. Dressed in just shorts and T-shirt, I headed back to Sinatra's. I had to steel myself for the first beer, but once that had gone down I reckoned I had beaten my own system and the drinks started flowing. It's impossible to remember how many bars with how many people I went to that afternoon. Needless to say, after two days of partying, the place resembled a battlefield from *Braveheart*.

As night approached, the party moved on to the beach. All of a sudden it was like being in a hippy colony. Bonfires were lit and all sorts of strange people appeared playing guitars. In a beachside bar I started to wilt as if somebody had stuck a tube in me and was sucking out my energy. It must have shown in my eyes because a fan came up to me and told me I looked like I had hit a cliff. I nodded, while trying to figure out the way off the beach so that I could hail a cab and get back to the hotel. But then the fan said, 'Och, you dinna wanna be going just yet. Here, these will help.' He handed me two white tablets, which I took to be aspirins.

I swallowed them, and within minutes I felt like I had been reborn. I felt so energetic that I wanted to swing from the ceiling. And I had a renewed thirst and capacity for drink. I've no idea what was in those tablets, but as the years have gone on I've often reflected on whether or not I was given speed that night.

The next thing I knew I was waking up on the beach. It was all quiet, and the bonfires of the night before were smoking pyres. I literally didn't know what day it was. I felt detached from, rather than frightened of, my surroundings. How come there were none of my team-mates around? There were plenty of people flaked out on the sand, but none of them looked like Scottish footballers. Come to that, I would probably have had a difficult time convincing anybody that I was a footballer at that moment. What was I still doing on a beach in Spain? We'd gone out of the World Cup. Surely I should be back in Ipswich by now?

I staggered off to the road to try to find a taxi. There were plenty of cabs about but none that would take me back to the hotel in Sotogrande. The main problem was that I didn't have any money. In fact, I couldn't remember having any money for the last two days. I certainly didn't have any when I hit

Sinatra's on the first night, and I couldn't imagine where I would have got any since then. To complicate matters I didn't speak Spanish, and the drivers didn't speak English. My third problem was that apart from a general location I didn't have a clue where the hotel was.

Panic started to set in because I had a fairly good idea that the squad were supposed to be going home that day. I wandered off up a side street to try to find some of the San Miguellians. I needed some money and somebody to speak Spanish to the cab drivers. I came across a sports bar where the cleaners were mopping out the patio. It wasn't open, but I went in. It was very dark, but I could make out a chap sitting at a table near the bar counting money.

'Sorry, not open yet,' he said.

'It's not a drink I'm after,' I replied. 'Do you speak Spanish?'

With that, he got up, put his hand on my shoulder and moved us into the daylight.

'Crikey, you're Alan Brazil, aren't you?' he said in a strong Birmingham accent.

Seizing on this opportunity for assistance, I nodded affirmatively and he shook my hand enthusiastically.

'What are you doing in my bar at breakfast time?' he asked.

I half explained the circumstances and told him I needed some help.

'What you need first,' he said, 'is a coffee and a liqueur.'

The coffee was good, the liqueur was better. As I drank them I explained my dilemma fully to the man I can only remember now as Birmingham Bill. He was a huge football fan and had nothing but praise for the Scotland fans who had made his bar their home during the World Cup. 'They'll all be here soon,' he said. 'Wait until they see who's in today!' But I pointed out that I had to get going for fear of missing the team's departure. I needed money and I needed help. He did even better than that. He got one of his lads to take a picture of us supping ale at his bar, and then bundled me into his car.

As we tore over to Sotogrande he told me the fascinating story of how he had set up his business in Spain. He'd given up a job at British Leyland in Birmingham to try his luck on the Costas. After working as a barman for a year he had saved up just about enough money to get a short lease on a run-down café. He wanted to turn it into an olde-worlde English pub, but he had no money to do that, so he went to a local building site where a new hotel was being built and tried to do a deal with the foreman to take away a pile of cut-off wood and timber remnants for a few pesetas. The foreman didn't want to know. He called him an English pig, poured petrol over the wood in front of him, and set fire to it. They had a terrible row.

To get his revenge, he went back to the building site after dark that night and stole 30 long wooden beams which he and his mate carried away on their shoulders. Then, knowing that the foreman would single him out as the thief the next day, Bill and his mate worked through the night with drills to attach the beams to the wall and ceilings. They also painted them black and white. By the time the Guardia and the foreman arrived the next morning the café had been transformed into a medieval-style English pub. The cops hunted around in every room, in the cellar and in the backyard, but they could not find the timber. It never occurred to any of them that the wood was actually on the walls all around them. Bill never got caught, and he opened his pub a week later.

As we pulled into the driveway of the hotel the team bus was standing there with its engine idling. A lot of the players were already in their seats. I told Bill to swerve around the back. I couldn't turn up at the front door looking dishevelled like this. I thanked him heartily and scampered up to my room. As I burst in, Johnny Wark screamed at me, 'Where the hell have you been?'

'Too long a story,' I said.

Johnny had packed all my gear into my bags and suitcases and had even left my Scotland blazer on a hanger on the back of the door. What a pal. After a quick shave I was ready.

As I got on the bus, Jock boomed at me, 'Where were you this morning, Brazil?'

'Out running,' I said.

We set off for the airport, and I started to feel as bad as I had done the day before. When we got off the coach I felt remarkably strange. My heart seemed to be beating at about three times the normal rate. I could feel it bouncing around in my chest. I started to panic and sought out the team doctor. When I found him I told him I thought I was having a heart attack. 'Highly unlikely, I should think,' he said. But he got his stethoscope out and his eyes widened as he listened to my chest. I told him about the white tablets I had taken. Amazingly he seemed quite relaxed about it, and told me I had probably been given amphetamines. Things soon calmed down, and I tried to relax. I remember looking out of a window on the plane, seeing the Pyrenees below me, and realising I was completely done in. Home couldn't come quickly enough.

I must have done OK in the World Cup because I remained a part of Jock Stein's plans for the following season, but we fell out big time during the home internationals in May and June 1983, by which time I had joined Spurs. I had been searching desperately for my first goal for my country. In my last full season for Ipswich I had scored 28 goals, but I hadn't hit the net for Scotland in seven games. Whenever I joined up with the squad I always seemed to be on goalscoring form for my club. Jock was always seated in the reception of our hotel whenever we got together, and he always said to me, 'You're scoring lots of goals. Now score some for me.' And it was very frustrating as every game went by and I drew a blank.

The squad met up in a hotel just outside Cardiff for the game against Wales. I scored my first goal for my country in that match, past the Everton keeper Neville Southall. Everton weren't all that hot at the time but they went on to sweep the board through the eighties and big Nev was adjudged to be the best goalkeeper in the world. It was the perfect time to score because the next match was against England at Wembley, which was my ultimate dream game. The previous season I had played against England at Hampden and we had lost 1–0; now I was about to go to what some believed was the world citadel of football to try again.

We stayed at a hotel in Harpenden in Hertfordshire. Two nights before the game a few of us sneaked out of the hotel and went off to a pub two miles away. We had no intention of drinking anything except Cokes or lemonades. We just wanted to get out of the confines of the squad headquarters. The barman wouldn't serve us. He told us he was under strict instructions not to serve us even soft drinks. We went to another pub a further mile out and got the same response there. It was uncanny. Jock had his spies everywhere, but we couldn't believe he had sent his coaching staff to every pub within a radius of five miles from Harpenden to issue the instruction that Scottish footballers must not be served drinks.

On the Monday night before the game, Jock came up to me and said, 'I hear you've had a bit of luck with a horse, son. I was thinking, would you like to be giving me a bit of it?' Right away I knew what he was referring to. I mentally kicked myself for having told my team-mates. The Epsom Derby, the greatest Flat race in the world, was taking place on the same day as our game against England. Through my connections at Newmarket I had been put on to a horse months earlier that I was told had a great chance of winning. The horse was called Teenoso, and I had £100 each way on it at 33/1. But now that it was known that the legendary Lester Piggott would be riding it, it had become the favourite. I had told one or two of the lads, and clearly Jock's antennae had picked up the information. He asked me for 'a bit of your bet at twenty-fives'. I genuinely thought he was joking. I couldn't believe he was seriously trying to muscle in on one of his player's bets. I just laughed, shook my head and said, 'No chance.'

The following day the manager pulled me at training. Looking very stern, he said, 'Have you had a chance to think about what I said? Maybe we could agree on sixteens?'

I started to realise that he was serious about this. But more on a point of principle than anything else I was determined not to give anything away. I tried to laugh it off. 'No, you wouldn't want it,' I said. 'Supposing it didn't win? You might drop me.'

On the day of the game, and the race, we just did some light training, a few set pieces, and had a bit of lunch. Again, Jock pulled me aside. 'Twelves is my last offer, Brazil,' he said, 'and if you don't take that it's because you are being too greedy.'

I shook my head.

To watch the race, we all gathered in Jim Steele's room. 'Steeley', as he was known to all, was the masseur at Celtic and a permanent member of the international set-up. In addition to working on the players he was also a close confidant of the boss while being a big pal to all the players. Steeley had set up his room like a betting parlour. He had the *Sporting Life* pages spread out everywhere and he was able to handle bets through his account with one of the bookmakers. Nobody was gambling the sort of amazing figures that you read about in football circles today, though. Steeley wouldn't have allowed anybody to go mad anyway, but most of us were having a punt on the big race. My bet, of course, was already sorted.

As the horses were about to go into the stalls, Jock said to me, 'This is your last chance. Have you ever played at Wembley, son?'

That question hit me right between the eyes. I couldn't believe what he had just said. Surely he couldn't be serious? I ignored him. Minutes later, Lester Piggott was in the winner's enclosure. I was over four grand better off, and Jock's face was as black as thunder.

In my delight at the big win I'd forgotten about the manager's harsh words. Our team bus received a police escort to Wembley that night and there was not a happier player on board. As we approached the stadium I started thinking about the World Cup a year earlier. I think there were more Scotsmen at Wembley than there were in Spain. This was supposed to be an England home game but all you could see were oceans of Scotsmen.

I was in awe as we crawled the last few hundred yards up to the stadium. Wembley! I could hardly believe it. It looked magnificent. White, sitting on a hill, huge and sturdy. One minute we were surrounded by clapping, banging and cheering fans, the next there was almost total silence. We had driven inside the stadium itself and were parked right outside the dressing rooms.

I took a walk up the tunnel to the pitch and thought of all the great players over the years who had played there. In particular I remembered the Scottish team of 1967 who had beaten world champions England 3–2. Back in Glasgow we claimed that we were the rightful world champs that day.

Back in the dressing room, we sat down to listen to the manager's game plan. He read out the team. I thought I must have misheard. I wasn't in it. I had scored in my last game but I had been dropped. It was the only change. Charlie Nicholas of Celtic was taking my place. I couldn't understand that. There was one thing Jock had always been adamant about: he didn't believe that players who were unsettled at their clubs could give their full attention to an international game. Charlie, a great player who I admired a lot, was at the time subject to building transfer speculation. He eventually went south to Arsenal. Yet he was picked, and I was substitute.

The magic of Wembley seemed a bit watered down from the bench. The atmosphere was fantastic, though, and eventually I got on the pitch. I will never know for certain why I was dropped that night. I just hope that in the eyes of the manager it was down to merit, not the fact that I had refused to share my bet with him.

Whatever the case, I never played for Scotland again.

CHAPTER ELEVEN

WORLD CUP BRAZIL

When England's tournament was over,
Sven made the plea to England fans and
supporters not to judge Rooney harshly
for the sending-off. But when he said
'You must look after Rooney, he is the
best you've got', I thought it was rather
pathetic. Sven had the major duty of care
to his best player, and he failed to fulfil
that duty.

I HAVE nothing but sympathy for my many English friends over the performance of their country in the 2006 World Cup. England were very, very disappointing. A team that was going to mount a realistic challenge to become the best in the world turned out to be average. And the only person you can blame for that is Sven-Goran Eriksson.

Hindsight is a great thing, and it's easy for me now to look back and criticise. But two weeks before the World Cup started in Germany I tipped Italy to win it in my newspaper column. And I didn't put England in the top three. Italy, of course, duly won it and England got nowhere near the trophy, so I feel entitled to tell you where I think it all went wrong.

Any manager who has Wayne Rooney in his squad has been sent a gift from God. He is England's best player. Why, then, did Sven ask Rooney to try to fit into a system in which he was always going to feel uncomfortable? Surely it would have been better to start with Rooney and then construct a formation that worked *for* him, not against him? Peter Crouch should have played in that up-front role. He might not be the most able player but he wreaks havoc in penalty areas with his gangling presence. He can be useful with his head and will always draw players across the box. Rooney would have benefited enormously from his presence. He would have picked up everything that spilt out from the rough and tumble involving Crouch and probably two defenders. It would also have given the youngster a very clear idea in his head of his role and how he could best use his enormous skills.

Sven took the easy option. For some reason he felt he had to accommodate other players in the team. Why do that at Rooney's expense? I have to assume it was because Sven did not want to make the toughest decisions – that is, to drop established internationals, maybe even David Beckham. The price that was paid for that weakness was Rooney's sending-off. I know the United striker swore blind that he did not deliberately trample on the Portuguese player Carvalho, and I'm sure he believes that but, nevertheless, frustration led him into that situation – frustration about playing alone up front. Apparently he agreed to take on the role, but when your national team manager puts that proposition to you, you're not going to say no, are you? Your greatest fear if you do that is that he may not play you at all, and may go for an entirely different formation.

Rooney shouldn't have to be chasing backwards and forwards in search of the ball. Just before he was sent off against Portugal he created a chance for himself. Twice Portuguese defenders tried to chop him down, but to his eternal credit he stayed on his feet, though he was again frustrated. When the offending foot came down on Carvalho I think it was a split-second misjudgement. I think he could have withdrawn his foot but wasn't particularly inclined to do so, without any malicious intent to injure another player.

When England's tournament was over, Sven made the plea to England fans and supporters not to judge Rooney harshly for the sending-off. But when he said 'You must look after Rooney, he is the best you've got', I thought that was rather pathetic. Sven had the major duty of care to his best player, and he failed to fulfil that duty.

Maybe some of the England manager's 'tactical' measures were his last throw of the dice. Clearly he felt that, as this was his last tournament with England, he could make some bold decisions. But the main bold decision he made was a disastrous one. I am referring to his squad selection and the inclusion of Theo Walcott. Now, I don't have a problem with youngsters being promoted early. It worked with Rooney, and with Lionel Messi of Argentina. In the past it has worked with Pelé and Maradona. But look at the calibre of the footballers I've just listed. Where does Walcott sit with them? Maybe one day he will deserve to be spoken of in the same breath as those people, but on the eve of the World Cup he was a Premiership reserve. Sven admitted he had never actually seen him play.

But even that is not as important as meeting the boy and talking to him at length over a number of weeks to assess his character. In short, to find out if he has the heart to be pitched into battle with the world's greatest players. Rooney was schooled in friendly internationals and European qualifiers. Walcott was expected to morph from non-Premiership footballer to the biggest stage, the World Cup finals, in one move. By the time England fielded Wayne Rooney in the European Championship in Portugal in 2004 he had proved his strength, physically and mentally, his resilience and his extraordinary talent.

Walcott had gone through no such procedure. It is my bet that, when Sven really got to know the boy and assessed his characteristics, he suddenly discovered he did not have a Rooney or a Messi on his hands. I base this assertion on the fact that when Michael Owen was sadly crocked there was never, for one moment, a discussion about using Walcott.

Therefore, England, who didn't take enough forwards to

start with, were suddenly another *two* short. Walcott effectively became a non-playing member of the squad.

I hope that in years to come the England boss will explain why he took Walcott and not a tried and tested player, which, for me, would have been Jermain Defoe. My theory is that as Sven was on his way out, he decided to do something he had not done for the previous five years in charge: he would take a chance, try to amaze the world by doing something quite extraordinary.

A few months before England went off to the World Cup, Porky and I were speaking at a lunch at the Café Royal in Regent Street, London as guests of the National Sporting Club. Porky is a terrible groveller to the football authorities and there was a table full of executives from the Football Association right in front of the stage. Sven was the guest of honour. My broadcasting pal couldn't help but combine his desire to suck up to the FA bosses with his demonic admiration for Wayne Rooney. As he was about to sit down after we had been (hopefully) entertaining the room for about an hour, Porky suddenly went into a long diatribe about how Sven had been a genius to show such enormous faith in Rooney. He got the whole room to stand up and applaud the England coach. Afterwards, Sven thanked Porky for his tribute.

I wonder whether that triggered something in Eriksson's head. Did he start to believe that he was the man who had made Wayne Rooney at Euro 2004 in Portugal, and, if so, could he discover another new, very young star at the World Cup? If it wasn't for some reason like that then it was just gross incompetence, for the decision completely unbalanced the squad. He should be roundly condemned for that.

The other issue that became very clear to me as the

competition progressed was the respective fitness levels of the teams. The Germany v. Italy semi-final was played at a tremendous tempo. It took my breath away. I know what it is like to play in the sort of tropical conditions Germany was experiencing at the time, as you will have read earlier.

Going on what I'd seen from their earlier performances, I don't believe England could have lived with either of them if they had played them in the final. Both Germany and Italy were fitter than England. Maybe they worked harder on the fitness regime once they realised what the conditions were going to be like. Maybe a long season for players like Steven Gerrard, whose campaign had started twelve months earlier in the ridiculous saga of Liverpool having to pre-qualify for the Champions League, had its effect. Brazil also looked like a team short of the pace. It's not very instructive to say that Ronaldinho was a massive disappointment, but maybe the Champions League victory had taken it out of him and the other Brazilian players who competed in the final in Paris.

When Brazil don't perform at a World Cup, it takes a big chunk away from the competition. Brazil are not just another country playing in the finals, they are a footballing culture. As well as sublime skill and entertainment, they bring with them to the tournament the whole Copacabana carnival experience. And that includes armies of beautiful girls and swathes of musicians and colour. When they don't tick, the competition slows down. The only one of their players who impressed me was Kaka of AC Milan. He was tremendous in an average team. He's only 24 and we will soon be talking about him in Europe in the same terms we currently reserve for Messi and Ballack.

Italy were worthy winners, even though they were not an outstanding team. They had the best three players in the tournament. Fabio Cannavaro was fabulous. You could tell he had played nearly a hundred times for his country. I can't remember the last time I saw a player who could read a game so well. To have somebody so dependable at the back who's always there to bring finality to a situation spreads tremendous confidence through a team.

Gennaro Gattuso is a master of breaking up the opposition's attacking moves and he never stopped running and creating on the counter-punch. And Alessandro Del Piero was majestic in front of goal.

I watched the World Cup from my television at home, and from the talkSPORT studios. Some may wonder why I did not travel to Germany. Well, I'm not the only ex-footballer who finds it hard to sit through live football matches. Some of my contemporaries have never been to watch a match since the day they retired. Ask anybody who moves into management, even if they are very successful, and they will always tell you that nothing can replace the playing days. And maybe that loss, for some, is too hard to bear. I don't come into that category, but I only really enjoy going to a match these days in which I have an emotional attachment, and for me that is either watching Ipswich, where I easily had the best years of my club career, or Scotland, my country, for whom I played thirteen times. I am a very patriotic Scotsman and I don't really have any interest in watching another country.

By way of further explanation, I would put this question to the millions of English listeners (as well as the Scots, the Welsh and the Irish) I have on talkSPORT: 'Would you go to watch Scotland play with any great enthusiasm?' I'm pretty sure that for the vast majority of England fans the answer would be no. Why should it be any different for me? And that is why it was decided that I should anchor my breakfast show from London during the World Cup in Germany.

I am not anti-English in any respect, and particularly when it comes to football. Some of my longest-standing friends in the game have served England with rare distinction. In fact, I can think of at least four former England captains who are among my best mates: 1966 World Cup winner Alan Ball, my former Ipswich skipper Micky Mills, my Manchester United team-mate Bryan Robson and racing supremo Mick Channon. At talkSPORT we have a clutch of England internationals including Rodney Marsh, Gary Stevens and Alvin Martin. Gary and Alvin played for England in the 1986 campaign in Mexico, the competition that threw up the infamous 'Hand of God' goal. It was a clear handball by Maradona against the colossus, Shilton, and it was obvious to anybody with one glass eye that the little Argentinian had handled it. But the referee missed it. Anyway, history has largely consigned the incident to the back of the cupboard because the Argentinian ace went on to score a second goal, now regarded as one of the greatest of all time. That is what his name will be remembered for.

The point is, it made clear sense that ex-players with that sort of experience should represent us in Germany. It's fair to say that if Scotland had been in the competition I would have been there, but emotionally I don't really have what it takes to empathise with Englishmen, even though, whenever anybody wants me to go out and cover a tournament in which England are playing, of course I go.

Even though I say it myself, talkSPORT did a brilliant job in covering the finals for our millions of listeners. We had a very large team in Germany. We were represented in all the major cities – Frankfurt, Munich and Berlin – and criss-crossed the country to the venues where England were playing – Nuremberg, Cologne and Stuttgart – as well as taking in the other world powers like Brazil and Italy. We had a base in Baden-Baden where the England team were staying, and set up four other broadcasting studios across the country. It was a real thrill to anchor such a big operation from talkSPORT's HQ. Each of the lads on the ground brought a flavour of the competition wafting over the airwaves. Porky, naturally, who brought his own brand of debate to the show, regularly described Portuguese manager Phil Scolari as 'a bum'.

I watched the England games in casinos and wine bars in London and Suffolk.

I had some tremendous banter with the English fans. I was continually put on the spot by being asked, 'Do you want England to do well?' Of course I wanted England to do well, in every game they played. Quite apart from everything else, it made commercial sense for talkSPORT to want England to be in the competition right to the end. It fired the enthusiasm of our audience and of our investors. But, if I was then asked, 'Do you want England to win the World Cup?', I have to say I had to answer that one through gritted teeth.

Many people in Scotland over the last 40 years have resented the arrogance of the English parading around their 1966 World Cup victory. Of course it was a magnificent achievement, but for how much longer does the rest of the world have to suffer having that fact rammed down their throats? Italy have just won their fourth World Cup. Germany have won three and lost in four other finals. France, who are not even supposed to be a major footballing nation, have won the World Cup and lost in a final in the last eight years. Holland, a tiny nation, appeared in two successive World Cup finals. Apart from winning the trophy on home territory, what have England ever done in the competition? My old boss Bobby Robson took them closest to fresh glory in Italy in 1990, when they were thwarted by the Germans in the semi-final. But the real answer is, nothing.

OK, so Scotland have not appeared in the World Cup finals as often as England. But what do you expect? We only have five million people. And, when you think about it, the contribution Scottish players have made to the tapestry of British football has never been properly recognised. All the English clubs that reaped great European success in the seventies and eighties were full of Scotsmen.

However, despite this, I can still claim to have done my bit as a broadcaster to support England in their campaigns. For instance, what would the English have done without me in Turkey in October 2003? Porky and I took our breakfast show out there to cover England's final game in their European Championship qualifying campaign.

England had to make sure they did not lose in order to guarantee a place in the tournament in Portugal the following year, and to try to win their group. We were flying out to Istanbul. I had not been there before and was quite intrigued by the prospect of visiting this city that everybody told me was the bridge between East and West. Nevertheless, I did not think I was going to like it. I am a South of France or Caribbean type of person. From what I had been told of Turkey it was dusty and struggling to achieve economic prosperity.

We landed in Istanbul and took a taxi to our hotel. I didn't like what I saw. It was very hot, very dusty, and there did not appear to be a beach within a hundred miles. Worse still, on the 30-minute trip into town I didn't spot the sort of 'Mayfair' area of the city that is my natural habitat. It didn't look as modern as London or the nicer parts of Paris, and I wasn't at all sure if I was going to enjoy this four-day trip. Porky, on the other hand, was like a little kid on a school trip. His new god, the boy Wayne Rooney, was probably going to lead England's attack, and as usual my broadcasting pal was loudly predicting a 3–0 England victory.

In the build-up to the game, Porky, as usually happens, started going native. Whenever we went anywhere he never liked the country (except America) when we first got there, but after a few days he would start expressing great admiration for the place and its people. Turkey, which according to Porky had only been good for making kebabs a few days earlier, was suddenly the cultural centre of the world. Wonderful people, wonderful culture, wonderful architecture. He became so enamoured that he decided to go out and interview some 'local' people about the big game. I went with him and sat at the table of a little tavern sipping a glass of wine while Porky was in a park across the road organising a group of Turkish people to talk about their wonderful country.

'Great people, these, Al,' he shouted to me across the road.

'They love you, Porky,' I said with mock admiration.

They were crowding around him with tremendous enthusiasm. Too much enthusiasm. Alarm bells started going off in my head. Then I saw it, out of the corner of my eye. Two young kids had moved in at the back of the crowd and they snatched our satellite dish and transmission machine. They were away like the wind.

Instinct took over. I leapt out of my seat and sprinted down the road after them.

I was shouting and swearing, and waving my arms. I had literally never moved so fast for years, but these kids were trying to pinch thousands of pounds' worth of valuable equipment that we needed to be able to broadcast every day. If we lost it we would go off-air. As soon as they saw a very red-faced, very angry Scotsman bearing down on them like a bulldozer, the thieves dropped their booty and fled. The crowd of people around Porky disappeared just as quickly. We got our equipment back, and the broadcasting of the England game to London went ahead uninterrupted.

England drew their game and a place in the finals in Portugal was assured. Next stop Lisbon ... but that is another story.

CHAPTER TWELVE

SIGN HERE PLEASE

Whenever one of the customers asked where Porky was there was this muffled cry from behind the bookcase and an arm appeared waving a pen around.

EVEN THOUGH he was a fellow Scot, the man driving our 'taxi' was one of the most miserable human beings I had ever come across.

It was midnight in the wilds of Suffolk. Porky and I were making our way home from a book signing in the quaint little market town of Bury St Edmunds. It had been a nightmare for me getting out there from London and now it was proving just as difficult to get home.

Our driver was from Tayside, with an accent so strong that even I could not understand him. All I know was that most of the noise coming out of his mouth was a moan about just about everything in his life.

The vehicle in which he was transporting us was supposed to be a people carrier but it was more like a cattle truck. Two of the seats had been ripped out and there was clear evidence that animals had been in the vehicle, with straw all over the floor and mud splattered on the seats.

Nevertheless 'laughing-boy' was complaining that we were spilling wine on his floor.

He was right. Porky and I were sharing a well-earned bottle of Chardonnay in the back, but this vehicle didn't appear to have any springs or shock absorbers. If we went over a pebble the floor reared up towards the roof and good wine splattered across the windows.

On pot holed rural roads in the dead of night this was more like being on a horse than in a car.

More than once I saw Porky concentrating intensely to get a glassful of wine into his mouth, trying desperately to anticipate the next bump. But, bang, he got it wrong again and splashed even more white wine over his bearded face.

Porky and I burst into laughter simultaneously when the Scots whinger announced: 'Ah'll be charging ye a cleaning bill for the car with all that drink yer spilling.'

I responded with: 'If you learnt how to drive, you weren't half-blind and this old wreck had any springs we could have a drink in peace, you daft old get.'

He replied with a string of expletives in his extreme Scottish guttural. Best to ignore him.

We had to settle for 'laughing-boy' to bring us home because we were in such a remote spot we had no other choice.

Earlier that evening we had been to our twenty-fifth book signing, an event at Waterstone's bookshop in Bury St Edmunds and we had made plans for an orderly return to London.

But, as usual, we had not factored into the equation our propensity for the hospitality extended to us as we made it around the country.

A mate of mine called Jim turned up. He runs a publishing operation and he bought twelve signed books to dish out to some of his staff. It would have been rude not to have bought him a drink afterwards so we hooked up at a hotel around the corner after the signing.

Porky was on one of his health-kicks and protested that he didn't want a drink and that he had to get back to London on the last train. But he's very predictable and as soon as the first glass of wine went down his throat it was clear that he had settled in for the night.

A couple of years ago my broadcasting and writing buddy had a very serious health scare. Following the 2004 European Championships in Portugal he was rushed into hospital suffering from acute heart failure.

At first I made a joke of it but all the joking stopped when, halfway through the breakfast show about two weeks later, I received a message that Mike was being transferred to Harefield Hospital in Middlesex to be assessed for a heart transplant.

A few days later I went up there to see him and I was shocked at his condition. He was strapped to a respirator with wires attached to all parts of his body. He looked as though he had lost about four stone overnight.

I'd noticed that Porky had been getting bigger and bigger over the previous year but I just assumed that he was drinking too much and getting fatter.

In fact he was suffering from what the doctors believe is a genetic illness and his heart was closing down on him. It was getting weak and flabby and not pumping fluids around his body properly. Hence he was retaining water and blowing up like a balloon.

In the event Mike never had his transplant, though he was in hospital for nearly five months. The doctors somehow managed to keep his heart going and he now exists on a diet of about twenty tablets a day and a vastly different lifestyle.

But one consequence of that is he's almost given up drinking entirely, and when he does have a glass now it has the same effect on him that a bottle used to have. He starts trying to chat women up, and when their boyfriends object he starts getting lippy. I have to move quickly to keep him out of trouble.

On this particular night, however, he was just happy that

the signing had eventually worked out and he was behaving himself. Merry, but very good-natured with it.

The night had started disastrously for me. I had been late leaving a business meeting in London and missed the train that would have linked me up with Porky in Ipswich from where we would have gone on to Bury St Edmunds.

Instead I travelled to Stowmarket, hoping that there would be a cab there to get me across Suffolk for the signing which was due to start at 6.30pm. There was no cab at Stowmarket, another small market town, but fortunately there were a couple of talkSPORT fans.

They saw me flapping about and immediately agreed to give me a lift to Bury. I'd have been lost without them and, though they didn't want to be paid, I bunged them £25 and made sure they got a signed book.

I thought I was going to walk into Waterstone's to see a fuming Porkmeister ready to give me a hard time. But it was the opposite. My pal was enjoying his moment in the limelight. There was a queue of people snaking out into the street and there was Porky sitting at the desk signing copies of the book like he was the star of the show.

The shout went up: 'Brazil's here'. Fortunately there was more cheering than booing. Though I was really sorry to have kept people waiting, I had endured the journey from hell. Overcrowded trains stopping and starting all the way up from London, no cabs, rush-hour traffic queues.

What happened next was really funny to me but not so amusing for my pal. The manager of the shop was a big tall guy who sported a very loud Nottingham Forest tie. He was clearly an avid football fan and he came bounding over to me, hand outstretched.

'Alan, thank goodness you're here,' he said. 'Mike's trying his best but it's you that my customers have come to see.'

With that he moved over to the table and hauled Porky out of the chair just as Mike was rising to greet me. For the signing they only had one chair at the table, and it was such a tight space that there was no room for another.

Just as Porky was about to protest, the manager pushed him out of the way and my pal disappeared behind a bookcase full of military books. There was a narrow gap where three or four books had been taken out, and all we could see of Porky were his eyes through the gap.

Whenever one of the customers asked where he was, there was this muffled cry from behind the bookcase and an arm appeared waving a pen around between a biography of Lord Nelson and a concise history of the American Civil War.

I was laughing my head off. The shop manager didn't seem to appreciate that we had written the book together and that for five years we had created one of Britain's most popular radio breakfast shows. He had never heard of Mike Parry.

Eventually we made a space to get my co-author back into the fold. We signed everybody's book and then the whole of the stock left in the shop. But by then it was after 9.30pm. I had a breakfast show to do the next morning and Mike had to get back to London. Needless to say, once we had had a glass or two in the hotel neither of us felt like battling it back to the capital.

That is how we ended up in the miserable Taysider's battered blue van. It was the only thing we could find on four wheels in Suffolk at nearly midnight.

I was now taking Porky back to my place in Constable country and we would travel into London together in the morning.

Right from the start I knew we would have a problem with the grisly Scotsman. Upon being asked how much the fare would be, he snapped: 'Forty-five pounds and not a penny less.'

My writing pal produced three £20 notes. He always got foolishly generous when he had had a drink and he was going to give the guy a £15 tip. He proferred the money towards the driver and said to him: 'Look, the deal is ...' but before he got any further the Scotsman raised his hand and barked out, very loudly: 'There is no deal. It's £45, not a penny less.' He went to slam his door.

'Whoa,' I said. 'What's your problem?'

'I have no problem. Now do you have £45 or shall I go home?'

Mike duly gave him £45.

The only contact we had with our driver during the journey was the swapping of insults. We couldn't understand him and I doubt if he could understand us.

As we got close to my place there was, by now, a sea of white wine floating around on the floor, and if any of the discs were still in place in my spine I would have been amazed.

I was envisaging getting into the house and settling into my favourite chair, and then putting a glass of cold bubbly to my mouth without it first having to do a loop-the-loop. But there were more fun and games to come from laughing-boy.

My home is in a fairly remote location down a winding country road so I tried to give the driver the benefit of my local knowledge, particularly as, by now, he didn't appear to know where he was going.

I shouted a few instructions to him. He then immediately slammed on the brakes, catapulting what was left of our wine all over himself and his windscreen.

'What the bloody-hell do you think you're doing?' I shouted in exasperation.

He had lost control of himself. He had turned around in his seat and was shouting wildly.

'I know what you two are up to. I've heard you plotting in the back there. You're going to try to get me to take you all the way back to London along these lanes. Well, I'm not having it. I have never been to London in my life and I'm not going now. You're not going to cheat me. And, if you think you are, you can get out of the vehicle now and I'll fight you for it.'

With that he flipped open his door and leapt on to the road. In the glare of the headlights he was parading around with his fists raised.

If Porky and I hadn't been so anxious to get home it would have been hilarious. But now I had visions of being stranded in the coal-black countryside until well after my breakfast show started in the morning.

Porky slid back the door and jumped out. He saw himself as the peacemaker between two warring Scotsmen. He calmed the mad Jock down and convinced him we were just a mile or two from home. He produced the £15 tip, which this time was accepted, and eventually our journey resumed – in total silence.

Minutes later we were on the gravel approach down to my house. I wanted revenge on this nutter who had made our journey such a misery but I pretended to be reasonable about it.

'Come on, mate, shake hands,' I said.

He did so reluctantly. Then I went on: 'Now, the best way to get yourself back is to do this.' I gave him a set of directions which were completely wrong. If he stuck to my route he would end up going down a one-track lane that got narrower and narrower as it progressed to a point where a van his size could go no further. In pitch-blackness he would be wedged between trees and bramble bushes without any chance of going any further forwards or turning around. I hoped he might get stuck there all night.

That was the most troublesome ending to a book signing. Others had been much more fun.

I suppose the most poignant one for me was going to Glasgow. It is after all my home town. It's very hard to gauge what sort of response the public will have to a book until you get out there with them.

One of the signings I did in Glasgow was on a Saturday lunchtime in Sauchiehall Street, probably the city's most famous thoroughfare. It was one of the early signings and I hadn't really been able by then to judge the popularity of our book. When I arrived in the street I wondered what was going on. There was a huge crowd of people spilling off the pavement into the road and a police officer was trying to control things and direct traffic. I was in the back of a car and I thought we were going to drive past as I didn't know where the shop was, but once again I was tight for time and I didn't want to be late.

'What's going on here?' I asked the driver.

'They've come here to see you,' he said.

At that moment people started banging on the windows and it started to dawn on me that we had arrived at the shop.

I hadn't expected this. The car was now surrounded and someone from the store fought his way through the throng to allow me to force open the door. A huge cheer went up.

This was amazing. I had never even played for Celtic at senior level and I'd played maybe half-a-dozen times at Hampden but here I was receiving a hero's welcome. I'd forgotten that a couple of weeks earlier the book had been serialised in the *Daily Record* and it must have been popular because it gave the newspaper's circulation a real lift.

But I thought that there would be maybe only a dozen or so people who would want to come out and buy a book to be signed. There was an awful lot more than that and I was humbled. The returning son and all that.

That was the longest signing I did. I stayed for over three hours and the people could not have been nicer. I posed for pictures, patted babies on the head and spoke to friends and relatives on mobile phones.

I was also asked to endorse a book in the most unusual way. A young girl said that her boyfriend was an avid talkSPORT fan and his dad had been a big fan of mine when I was playing for Scotland.

She asked me to take off my shoe and sock on my left foot and to tread on the inside cover of the book. It just fitted. Then she drew around my foot with a felt-tipped pen and I signed my autograph in the middle of the footprint. Whatever keeps the fans happy.

After such a marathon signing session I really did need a drink.

I'd had an invitation to go to The Sports Café. To my delight two of my oldest school-friends had been in the shop to see me and we got together over the bubbly. Arthur Gordon had become a tremendously successful financier in the City of London and Neil Casey had pursued a career as a bookie and built himself a great business.

It was one of those great impromptu sessions that always turn out to be the best. When we had first met about 35 years earlier, we were just three anonymous kids full of dreams and ambitions, which for most people probably never come true. But we had been the lucky ones. Lucky in the sense that we had each been given a talent – whether it was a skill or just the drive to work hard – and none of us had wasted it.

It would have been perfect if at that moment Jim Kerr, the lead singer of Simple Minds, and another class-mate, had walked through the door.

I went on to do signings all over the country. I did three in Ipswich which were very well received. Thank goodness for that – it has, after all, been my home patch for most of the last 30 years. For some reason I also seem to be well-liked in Chelmsford in Essex where, again, loads of people turned up.

Although I really enjoy signing books and meeting people, the actual physical act of writing your name can take it out of you. I went down to the publisher's warehouse, near Worthing on the south coast, to sign a pallet of a thousand books. I didn't think it would be much of a problem but it was quite daunting to see a mountain of books in front of me. By the time I was getting towards the end I had lost the strength in my right hand. Although I am left-footed as a footballer, I am right-handed in everything else. I had to use my left hand to support my right hand because it got so weak.

But any dismay that I suffered was dispelled on the way home. After I came off the M23 and onto the M25 I saw a sign for Epsom and realised I was in Porky territory. Mike constantly brags that he lives in stockbroker-belt Surrey. You're more likely to see stock cars than stockbrokers in his neighbourhood. If I was running Surrey I'd throw him out.

I punched his number out on the phone and we arranged a rendezvous at a country pub nearby. It took me about a quarter of an hour but as I got within half-a-mile there was a cyclist on the road in front of me who looked very unsteady on his bike.

I was on a narrow country road and I didn't fancy overtaking this bloke in case he weaved into my car. So I crawled along at about six miles an hour behind him. He didn't look like much of a cyclist to me. He was clearly overweight, and huffing and puffing as though his bike was too heavy for him. I didn't hoot him because I thought he might fall off into the road.

The entrance to the pub appeared a few hundred yards up the road. Thankfully, I'd soon be rid of the menace on the bike. But then the cyclist turned into the pub car park. My suspicions started to stir. No, surely, it couldn't be.

But it was. It was Porky. As he stopped he failed to get his foot down quickly enough and he came tumbling off his bike on to the gravel of the car park. His hands and knees were cut but he just turned over and lay on his back, completely exhausted.

I couldn't get out of my car for laughing. He had developed this mad fitness kick. But being stretched out on a pub car park, writhing in pain, didn't look like a great way of getting fit to me. I hauled him off the floor and we went into the pub.He couldn't drink beer because he felt too ill. He had a Coke and I had a pint of lager and decided it was best to get him home. He couldn't possibly cycle back, it was about three miles.

I was driving a Mercedes at the time so I thought we could probably get the bike across the back seat. But it wouldn't go in. I left him as a forlorn figure trudging home pushing his bike.

A week later Porky told me that his bike, for which he had paid more than £400, had been pinched from his garage. Remembering the state he was in on the floor of that pub car park, I reckoned that it was a good thing it had been stolen; it had probably given him another twenty years of life.

One of the signings we did, which I thought was going to spell trouble, was in Enfield, in north London. It was a Saturday lunchtime event and Porky and I met at Liverpool Street station.

What I hadn't allowed for was the fact that Spurs, one of my old clubs, was playing at home that day and the train to Enfield was also the one carrying the Spurs fans up to White Hart lane.

I didn't have a great time at The Lane so I feared a bit of grief off the fans. But they were fabulous. We went into one of the station bars while waiting for the train and I was surrounded by supporters wanting autographs and taking photos on their mobile phones. It was the same on the train. I told a few stories about my days at the club and there was a good feeling of bonhomie.

I think it proves that over the years – and particularly since I have been working in television and then in radio – my relationship with football fans has changed. I don't believe I am regarded any more as an ex-footballer. I think I am a current voice on their radio when they switch on in the mornings.

And realising that, I am even more grateful for the life that I have had. Most people don't reach particularly great heights in their first and, usually, only career. I have been lucky enough to make my mark in both football and broadcasting.

There has, indeed, been an awful lot of bubbly in Brazil.

INDEX